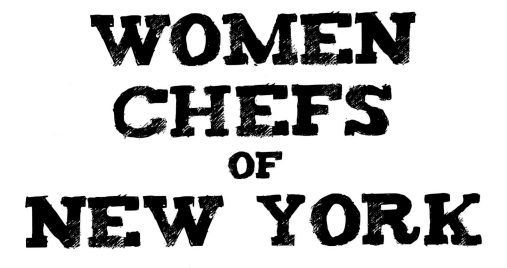

WOMEN CHEFS OF NEW YORK

Nadia Arumugam

Absolute Press
An imprint of Bloomsbury Publishing Plc

1385 Broadway
New York
NY 10018
USA

50 Bedford Square
London
WC1B 3DP
UK

www.bloomsbury.com

ABSOLUTE PRESS and the A. logo are trademarks of Bloomsbury Publishing Plc

First published 2015

ISBN: HB: 978-1-63286-076-7
ePub: 978-1-63286-077-4

Library of Congress Cataloging-in-Publication Data
has been applied for.

2 4 6 8 10 9 7 5 3 1

Printed and bound in China by C&C Offset

To find out more about our authors and books visit www.bloomsbury.com. Here you will find extracts, author interviews, details of forthcoming events, and the option to sign up for our newsletters.

Bloomsbury books may be purchased for business or promotional use. For information on bulk purchases please contact Macmillan Corporate and Premium Sales Department at specialmarkets@macmillan.com.

Dedicated to Lynn Akka and Meera,
in celebration of sisterhood!

WOMEN CHEFS OF NEW YORK

Nadia Arumugam

CONTENTS

INTRODUCTION

hen I was interviewing the chefs in this book, there would come a point—after we discussed their career trajectory, whether they were raised enlightened gourmands or fed on a diet of mac and cheese, and what inspired them that morning as they deliberated their daily specials—when I would have to apologize. I had followed up with the question "What has it been like to be a woman in a professional kitchen?"

Why the apology? Precisely because I already knew what the answer would be. Even when I reached out to the chefs when researching the very idea of the book, it was clear that not one of them would participate in anything that hinted at "affirmative action." These are successful entrepreneurs, razor-sharp businesswomen; and above all, these are chefs at the top of their game. They don't feel hard done by or let down by the system, because, for the most part, they are otherwise occupied focusing all their physical energy and mental strength on being the best damn cook they can be, and then aspiring to be an even better one tomorrow. The fact of the matter is that being a chef, whether you're the executive chef or scaling the ladder, whether you're a man or a woman, is unspeakably hard work. It requires

persistence, stamina, endurance, humility, affability, ingenuity, and an inquiring mind. And all these qualities the chefs in this book have in spades.

Of course, I'm not trying to sell you the unlikely notion that these chefs have not encountered any gender bias. Prejudice and partiality exist, but more outside the kitchen than within. Nowadays, at any rate. Many of the conversations I had touched on the scarcity of media attention devoted to female restaurant chefs. The legendary Alice Waters and Lidia Bastianich aside, household names like Martha Stewart, Rachael Ray, Giada De Laurentiis, Ina Garten, and, of course, Julia Child gained renown primarily as TV chefs and cookbook authors. In published compilations of best chefs and best restaurants women chefs and establishments helmed by them have been conspicuous for their absence. Mainstream food magazines prefer featuring portraits of men in their chef's whites, with sleeves rolled up and arms sporting burns, barely healed cuts, and tattoos rather than showing their female counterparts in the same stark light. (This in itself inspired the biannual *Cherry Bombe*, a publication centered on women in the food industry.) Then there is the question of money. The complaint of a "boys' club," buttressed by investors who pass up noteworthy women chefs in favor of financing restaurants where men run the kitchens, was an oft-recounted one.

Still, as it turns out, the woman chef is a persevering breed, and her successes are prolific. Over the course of the 15 months that this book was in the making, six of the featured chefs unveiled new restaurants in New York City. Jody Williams opened Via Carota in the West Village; the trio behind Brooklyn-based Pies 'n' Thighs brought their second-to-none fried chicken to the Lower East Side; Amanda Cohen closed the pint-size original Dirt Candy, only to resurrect it a few months later in a larger, swankier space on the cusp of Chinatown; doughnut aficionado Fany Gerson, of Dough, debuted a Manhattan store in the Flatiron; Einat Admony expanded her mini-empire with her modern Israeli eatery Bar Bolanat; and Amanda Freitag introduced her unique brand of elevated diner fare to Chelsea with Empire Diner.

If the impetus behind this book isn't already abundantly clear, let me spell it out: to celebrate great culinary talents, to pay tribute to their achievements, and, yes, to help redress the imbalance of shelf space and printed pages allotted to the notable female presence leading professional kitchens.

Then there was my more private motivation: to get to know the people behind some of my favorite meals. And I really did get to know them. Intelligent, funny, generous, and warm, these women are all as delightful as the food they artfully craft. Aside from recipe testing Ghaya Oliveira's intricate dessert plates, perhaps the most trying element of working on this compilation was deciding on which chefs to include. As a New Yorker—I think I can call myself one, having now lived in Manhattan's West Village since 2008—I decided that confining the selection within the city's boundaries was an obvious first step. Then I drew up my wish list and followed this with the arduous phase of refining and regrouping. Top priority was to feature chefs that are superlative in their field. It was also important to represent a wide swath of New York City, geographically speaking, as well as a wealth of cuisines. Check. Check. The women that grace the following pages are an exciting mix of established masters and up-and-coming stars; and the diversity of food they cook, a pertinent depiction of the wondrous cultural medley of the city they cook in.

Nadia Arumugam

AMERICAN
AND MODERN
AMERICAN

JEAN ADAMSON 11

Heirloom Tomato and Watermelon Salad · Lamb Carpaccio ·
Roasted Char with Smashed Beets and Soubise Sauce ·
Rabbit Stroganoff with Spaetzle

CAROLYN BANE, SARAH SANNEH, AND ERIKA WILLIAMS 21

Brussels Sprout and Squash Salad with Curry Aioli
and Candied Pepitas · Pies 'n' Thighs Fried Chicken Box ·
Corned Beef · Lemon Blackberry Pie

APRIL BLOOMFIELD 31

Warm Bacon-and-Egg Salad · Chickpea and Lentil Salad with Feta,
Cilantro, and Onions · Roasted Pork Shoulder with Chianti ·
Balsamic-glazed Duck

AMANDA COHEN 41

Portobello Mousse with Truffled Toast and Grilled Portobellos ·
Chard Gnocchi with Goat Cheese Sauce and Grilled Chard ·
Smoked Cauliflower with Buttermilk Waffles and Horseradish Cream ·
Potato Noodle Salad

AMANDA FREITAG 51

Buttermilk Pancakes · Charred Octopus Salad, "Greek Style" ·
Empire Diner Patty Melt · Orzo "Mac 'n' Cheese" with Asparagus
and Black Truffle Butter

GABRIELLE HAMILTON 61

Canned Sardines with Triscuits, Dijon Mustard, and Cornichons ·
Celery Hearts Victor · Cod in Saffron Broth with Leeks, Potatoes,
and Savoy Cabbage · Roasted Capon on Garlic Crouton

JEAN ADAMSON

Jean Adamson wants to be clear: she's a chef, but she isn't *the* chef. Her food businesses are varied and numerous. In 2008, just north of Dumbo (Down Under the Manhattan Bridge Overpass), in Brooklyn, Adamson and her boyfriend, Sam Buffa, opened the snug Vinegar Hill House restaurant, named after the historic, quaint neighborhood it inhabits. Next door, she runs an event space that hosts a dinner series with visiting chefs, as well as parties, weddings, and even a regular Sunday and Monday football-watching gathering during the season. Somewhat farther afield, on the Rockaway Beach Boardwalk, Adamson cofounded, with chef Lindsay Robinson, a fry-shack and frozen banana stand, quirkily named Motorboat & the Big Banana. (Adamson is responsible for the devilishly tasty fried fish and shrimp po' boy sandwiches.) The pair is also in charge of renting out space on the boardwalk to other vendors.

It's understandable, then, why she is not at Vinegar Hill House prepping her famous cast-iron skillet roast chicken or cooking her Red Wattle country chop to juicy, buttery perfection. At least not anymore. For the first eight months of the eatery's existence she was doing exactly that, and more. She was in the kitchen every day from 8:00 a.m. until 2:00 a.m. With a scant crew, consisting of a bartender friend who knew nothing of cooking and her mother, who made dessert in the basement, Adamson was constantly fielding (metaphorical) fires inside the kitchen and out. "We didn't have a floor manager, so I would be screaming at people across the pass." Over time, she took on more help, eventually stepping back from the pass altogether to hand the reins over to an executive chef.

Less time in the kitchen means more time to address the restaurant's other needs. Adamson lives upstairs with her boyfriend and baby. She consults on new additions to the menu, defined by an elegant, comfort-food sensibility that revolves mostly around a wood-burning oven. She often dines in the restaurant, amid the vintage curios and salvaged wood décor, to ensure that her exacting standards are upheld.

Her favorite thing is to cook the "family meal" for her staff, like some heaven-sent lunch lady. When this happens, they're in for a treat. Adamson's cheffing credentials are impressive. She moved to New York from Utah in 1997, age 22. While taking night classes at the French Culinary Institute three days a week, she worked at Tribeca Grill. After graduation, she started work at the heaving SoHo bistro Balthazar, relishing the high-precision atmosphere of a kitchen that feeds 1,500 diners a day. A quick learner, she was on the fast track and after two years Adamson had progressed from *garde-manger* to sous-chef.

Burnt out from expediting 200 orders of *steak frites* daily, Adamson then traveled to London and worked a three-month stint at the River Café. Back in New York, she returned to Balthazar, this time working the bakery. Her energy recouped, Adamson took on a sous-chef position at the fashionable Pastis in the Meatpacking District to run the gauntlet once again. "Being creative is only 10 percent of being a chef. The rest of it is having everything run like clockwork."

Her next stop, at Freemans, on the Lower East Side, was notable not only because she turned its lackadaisical kitchen crew into a well-oiled machine, but also because she met Sam Buffa there when he was helping with the construction of Freemans' expansion. Lucky for her and us, really, since when it came to building out Vinegar Hill House in the ramshackle spot near the Navy Yard, he made it fit for her to cook in, and for us to eat in.

What's your earliest memory of cooking?
I remember putting up fruit and tomatoes with my mom every September for our larder. We lived in a small town outside of Salt Lake City, and my mom cooked on a wood-burning stove and made our own granola and yogurt and fruit leathers.
What is your favorite condiment, and with what do you eat it?
Branston Pickle. I pretty much keep it classic and enjoy it with sharp Cheddar cheese on pullman bread.
What's your most prized possession in the kitchen?
My Microplane.
What naughty food-related habit would you never admit to (except to us!)?
I love powdered cheese.
Can you offer one restaurant tip/technique to home cooks that will improve their cooking?
Use sharp knives and learn how to keep them sharp.
What's the best piece of advice you can give to an aspiring cook?
Get some sleep and ask a ton of questions.

HEIRLOOM TOMATO AND WATERMELON SALAD

SERVES 4

This recipe evokes the height of summer, when tomatoes are at their best and need only some good salt and olive oil. I wanted to stick with those basics but add just a few more ingredients to play with that simplicity and create a fun version of the classic Greek salad.

2 large heirloom tomatoes, halved or quartered and cut into ¼-inch-thick slices
¼ medium seedless watermelon, cut into slices about the same size as for the tomatoes
½ cup Pickled Onions (see recipe below)
¼ cup strained pickling liquid from the Pickled Onions
3 tablespoons pistachio oil
3 tablespoons olive oil
¼ pound soft feta cheese
¼ cup pistachios, toasted and chopped
4 sprigs of fresh mint, leaves picked off and roughly torn
Maldon sea salt

Layer the tomatoes, watermelon, and onions on a large platter, overlapping the slices a little. Drizzle the pickling liquid, pistachio oil, and olive oil over them. Crumble the feta cheese evenly on top, then sprinkle the pistachios over this, followed by the torn mint leaves and the Maldon salt, to taste. Serve immediately.

Pickled Onions (makes ¾ quart)
1 large white onion, sliced into ¼-inch-thick rounds
1-inch piece fresh ginger, peeled and cut into thin matchsticks
1 teaspoon cracked black pepper
¾ cup red wine vinegar
¾ cup water
5 tablespoons granulated sugar
1 tablespoon kosher salt
4 bay leaves

Equipment
A glass quart jar with a lid

Place the onion, ginger, and pepper in the glass jar, and set aside.

In a small saucepan, combine the vinegar, water, sugar, salt, and bay leaves and bring to a boil over medium-high heat. Using a funnel, pour the hot pickling liquid into the jar over the onion mixture. Place the jar in the refrigerator, uncovered; when cool, screw on the lid. The onions are now ready to use.

The pickled onions are delicious in sandwiches, as a garnish for soups, and in other salads. They will keep refrigerated for at least a month.

LAMB CARPACCIO

SERVES 4

This dish was born out of my obsession with Cara Cara oranges a couple of winters ago and a hankering for meat that developed after I had my baby in the middle of that season. I found myself raiding the citrus aisle at the Fairway Market grocery store in Red Hook, digging for oranges with the "black label"—having been told that this particular producer was the best. Sure enough, it turned out to be true. Paired with lamb and another favorite ingredient of mine, za'atar, this fruit really shines.

8 ounces deboned leg of lamb, trimmed of fat
¼ cup Greek yogurt
2 tablespoons whole milk
½ garlic clove, very finely grated
salt, as needed
¼ baguette loaf, cut into ⅛-inch slices
4 tablespoons extra-virgin olive oil
freshly ground black pepper, as needed
2 large oranges, peeled and segmented (preferably Cara Cara or other navel variety)
½–1 tablespoon za'atar spice mix
juice of ½ lemon

To finish
Maldon sea salt

Preheat the oven to 350°F. Place the lamb in a freezer-proof dish and place in the freezer for 45 minutes to 1½ hours (depending on the thickness of the meat) until almost frozen.

Meanwhile, in a small bowl combine the yogurt with the milk and the garlic and season with salt to taste. Whisk thoroughly, then set aside.

Next arrange the baguette slices on a sheet tray, drizzle with 2½ tablespoons of the olive oil, and season with a little salt and pepper. Bake until golden brown and dry, about 15–20 minutes. Remove from the oven and allow the bread to cool completely.

Slice the near-frozen lamb as close to paper thin as possible using a very sharp knife. Lay the slices side by side on a large platter and arrange the orange segments over them. Stir the yogurt mixture and spoon it evenly over the lamb and oranges. Sprinkle generously with the za'atar, then drizzle the lemon juice and the remaining olive oil on top, to taste.

Break up the baguette slices into bite-size croutons and scatter over the dish. Finish with a sprinkling of Maldon salt. Serve immediately.

ROASTED CHAR WITH SMASHED BEETS AND SOUBISE SAUCE

SERVES 4

The story behind this recipe is quite simply that I wanted to create a dish that would evoke the flavors of the "everything bagel" with cream cheese and lox that you get at the iconic Russ & Daughters Jewish eatery in New York City.

For the beets
10 medium beets, scrubbed cleaned and trimmed
2 tablespoons olive oil
salt and freshly ground black pepper, as needed

For the soubise sauce
½ stick unsalted butter
1 large onion, halved and sliced
⅓ cup heavy cream
2 tablespoons sherry vinegar
salt, as needed

For the fish
2 tablespoons olive oil
4 (¼-pound) Arctic char steaks, skin on (or substitute salmon)
¼ stick unsalted butter, sliced
salt and freshly ground black pepper, as needed

To garnish
2 tablespoons poppy seeds
4 sprigs of fresh dill

Preheat the oven to 350°F.

First roast the beets. Place the whole beets in a large bowl, add the olive oil, and season well with salt and pepper. Toss until the beets are thoroughly coated, then transfer to a sheet tray. Roast for 50 minutes to 1 hour until tender, so that a knife inserted into the center of the largest beet slides in and out easily. Remove from the oven and set aside.

Meanwhile make the soubise sauce. Heat the butter in a small saucepan over low heat. When the butter is melted, add the onion and cook, stirring occasionally, until the onion is very soft but not colored, about 15 minutes. Remove from the heat and leave to cool slightly. Transfer to a blender along with the heavy cream and sherry vinegar, and purée until the mixture is completely smooth; season with salt to taste. Keep warm.

To cook the fish, heat a large cast-iron skillet or heavy-bottomed sauté pan over medium-high heat. Once the pan is hot, add the olive oil. Season the fish steaks with salt and pepper on both sides, then carefully place in the hot pan skin-side down. Do not move the fish but gently press down on the flesh side of each steak with a spatula to ensure that the entire surface of the skin is in contact with the heat.

Reduce the heat to medium and continue to cook the fish skin-side down for about 3–4 minutes, depending on the thickness of the steaks. Flip the fish over and add the butter to the pan, swirling it around as it melts. Cook for 1–2 more minutes, then transfer the fish to a plate or sheet tray and keep warm.

Finish the beets by placing them on a cutting board and smashing down on each one with the flat side of the blade of a large knife.

To serve, spoon about 3 tablespoons of the soubise sauce onto each plate (or shallow bowl). Arrange a few beets to the side and place a piece of fish, skin-side up, on top of the sauce. Garnish with the poppy seeds and picked dill. Serve immediately.

RABBIT STROGANOFF WITH SPAETZLE

SERVES 4

I was moved to create this dish while reminiscing about the days, back in the late 1990s, when I would eat spaetzle as a quick pick-me-up while sweating away as a line cook at Balthazar. Incidentally, this was also the first place I had eaten rabbit outside of culinary school.

For the stroganoff

6 rabbit legs, skinned (about 2½–3 pounds)
3 tablespoons olive oil
1 large onion, cut into large dice
2 medium carrots, peeled and cut into 1-inch pieces
2 cloves garlic, halved
3 bay leaves
4 fresh sprigs of sage
2 tablespoons unsalted butter
2 tablespoons all-purpose flour
2 cups white wine
4 dried shiitake mushrooms, rehydrated in 2 cups of just-boiled water
3 cups chicken stock
3 tablespoons Dijon mustard
⅓ cup crème fraîche
salt and freshly ground black pepper, as needed

For the spaetzle

1½ cups all-purpose flour
1½ teaspoons salt
¼ teaspoon ground nutmeg
¼ teaspoon freshly ground black pepper
¾ cup milk
2 large eggs, plus 1 egg yolk
olive oil, as needed
2 tablespoons unsalted butter

For the parsley oil garnish

1 bunch of flat-leaf parsley (about 2–3 ounces), rinsed thoroughly
½ teaspoon salt
3 ice cubes
½ cup olive oil

For the onion and mushroom garnish

16 red pearl onions, peeled and kept whole
3 tablespoons red wine vinegar
3 tablespoons granulated sugar
½ stick unsalted butter
6 tablespoons olive oil
8 ounces maitake mushrooms (or substitute any other mushroom), torn into large pieces
salt and freshly ground black pepper, as needed

Equipment

A spaetzle press (optional)

Prepare the stroganoff. Preheat the oven to 325°F. Liberally season the rabbit with salt and pepper.

Place a cast-iron braising pan or Dutch oven over medium-high heat and add the olive oil. Once the oil is hot, add the rabbit to the pan and sear until well browned on all sides. Transfer to a plate. Add the onions, carrots, garlic, and herbs to the pan, and cook until the vegetables are browned. Next, add the butter; once it is melted, stir in the flour. Cook for about 5 minutes, stirring occasionally. Pour in the white wine to deglaze the pan, scraping the bottom of the pan to loosen any stuck-on bits. Bring to a boil, and reduce the liquid by at least one half. Next add the softened, rehydrated

dried mushrooms, with their soaking liquid, and the chicken stock. Bring the liquid up to a simmer and return the rabbit legs and any accumulated meat juices to the pan. Cover and cook in the oven for 1½ hours or until the rabbit is fork tender.

While the rabbit is cooking make the spaetzle. In a large bowl, combine the flour, salt, nutmeg, and pepper. Place the milk and eggs in a separate small bowl or pitcher, and whisk until combined. Make a well in the flour mixture and pour in the wet ingredients. Using a fork, draw in the flour from the sides of the well and mix until you have a smooth batter. Cover with plastic wrap and let the batter rest, refrigerated, for at least 1 hour or up to 1 day.

Once the rabbit is ready, remove the legs from the braising liquid using tongs and transfer to a plate. Strain the braising liquid (discarding the solids) then return the strained sauce to a clean saucepan. Bring to a boil over medium-high heat and reduce the liquid by one half. To finish the stroganoff sauce, reduce the heat to medium-low, then whisk in the mustard and crème fraîche. Taste and adjust the seasoning as needed. Pick the rabbit meat off the bones and tear into bite-size pieces, then return the meat to the pan. Stir to coat it thoroughly in the sauce. Cover and set aside.

When ready to cook the spaetzle, bring a large pot of salted water to a boil. Push the batter through a spaetzle press, letting the thick ribbons fall into a boiling water. ➤

Alternatively, use a spatula to push the batter though the holes of a colander. The spaetzle will sink when they first enter the water. Once they float back to the top, let them cook for 2 more minutes, then remove using a slotted spoon and transfer to a sheet tray. Drizzle over a little olive oil and toss the spaetzle so they don't stick. Leave to cool.

Make the parsley oil. Roughly chop the parsley and place in a blender. Add the salt and ice cubes, and run the motor while slowly drizzling in the olive oil. Blend until the mixture is smooth and emulsified. Transfer to a small bowl and set aside.

Prepare the mushroom garnish. Bring a small saucepan of salted water to a boil, add the pearl onions, and cook until tender, about 5 minutes. Drain the onions, transfer them to a dish, then rinse out and dry the saucepan. Return the onions to the pan and add the vinegar and sugar. Bring to a simmer over medium heat and cook, stirring occasionally, until a glaze is formed and the onions are coated. Remove from the heat.

Place a skillet over medium heat, and add the butter and the oil. When the butter has melted and the oil is hot, add the mushrooms and sauté until browned and tender; try to move the mushrooms only once or twice to ensure an even browning. Season with salt and pepper, remove from the heat, and keep warm.

To assemble the dish, gently reheat the stroganoff over medium-low heat. Meanwhile, brown the spaetzle. Place a skillet over medium heat and add the 2 tablespoons of butter. When melted, toss in the spaetzle and cook, stirring occasionally, until browned in places. Remove from the heat.

Spoon some rabbit, together with some of the sauce, onto each plate. Add a few onions and some mushrooms on top, followed by the spaetzle. Finally, drizzle the parsley oil over the stroganoff, and serve.

CAROLYN BANE, SARAH SANNEH, AND ERIKA WILLIAMS

Top-rated contenders in the New York City fried chicken wars, Sarah Sanneh, Erika Williams, and Carolyn Bane opened the second of their hugely popular southern-style eateries, Pies 'n' Thighs, on Manhattan's Lower East Side in January 2015. The first, in Brooklyn, is still going strong. Their flourishing catering service has been the highlight of many a hipster wedding, and their takeout-only "Bucket System" offers stiff competition to Colonel Sanders and the like. They have been featured in every food magazine that counts. They have made so many TV appearances that media requests are now generally met with a tired groan. In short, they seemingly have it all, including busy, fulfilling family lives.

Incredibly, this success sprouted from a cramped, unsuitable spot beneath the Williamsburg Bridge. It all began in 2006 when Sanneh, who hailed from California, and Georgia-born Steven Tanner hatched the plan while working at the nearby Brooklyn culinary institution Diner. Sanneh, an inveterate baker and a graduate of the French Culinary Institute's pastry program, made the pies, cookies, giant, pillowy doughnuts, and biscuits. A month in, and Bane jumped on board to help with the fried chicken and BBQ; Williams followed by the end of the year (both had also been at Diner) when Tanner sold off his interest in the business.

For Bane, the unorthodox eatery was right up her alley. ("I have a wild streak!") The Boston-raised art history major had graduated from Harvard and was working in public relations when she decided to pursue an interest in cooking. After much beseeching, the management at Diner took her on as a barista and eventually allowed her to cook. Williams, who grew up in New Jersey rolling matzoh balls and filling knishes in her father's kosher butcher shop, similarly transitioned with ease from employee to entrepreneur. Following art school and a few stints in restaurants in San Francisco, she had moved to New York City to attend the Natural Gourmet Institute. After graduating, she cooked northern Italian fare at the Park Slope favorite Al Di La before her spell at Diner.

The crew of three under the bridge quickly amassed a cult following for their no-frills comfort food—fried chicken and biscuits, fried catfish sandwiches, pulled pork, collard greens, and hush puppies—served to diners in a concrete yard. But in 2008, they closed down. The Department of Health had taken away their smoker, and the women conceded that the hot-as-hell, barely there kitchen wasn't going to cut it if they were going to run a business like grown-ups. "The old place felt to me like a bunch of kids playing restaurant," says Bane.

The neighborhood was disconsolate. Fortunately, two years on, Pies 'n' Thighs reopened in a more civilized but still somewhat higgledy-piggledy space on 4th Street. With the rustic charm of the original premises but *sans* the health code violations, the new restaurant boasted a diner-style front room that looked into an open kitchen, an outdoor seating area, and a large, airy back room with exposed brick walls and wooden beams across the ceiling. The biggest treat, however, was the expanded menu, which riffed off their southern staples, as well as the more eclectic flavor profiles of some of Sanneh's desserts, such as her guava cheesecake. Working with Christina Tosi at Momofuku's production kitchen while the new location was under construction had clearly rubbed off on Sanneh.

The transformed Brooklyn Pies 'n' Thighs, with its now 30-strong team of staff, took Sanneh, Williams, and Bane into grown-up restaurant territory with a steep learning curve. Now, with their shiny and spanking-new outpost across the East River, they are undisputed veterans.

What are your favorite family meals to enjoy before service starts?
S.S. Messed-up doughnuts left in the hallway or one of Erika's layered hippie casseroles.

What has been your most memorable moment professionally?
C.B. The pure joy and relief of reopening in 2010 followed by the chaotic, sleep-deprived first few weeks that followed.

What's the most underused/underrated seasoning/spice/pantry ingredient?
E.W. I can't get enough cinnamon, paprika, cumin combo on ground meat. Especially with lots of fresh cilantro and mint ... not exactly in the Pies 'n' Thighs flavor profile.

If disaster struck and your restaurant no longer existed, which item(s) would you be most aggrieved about losing?
S.S. A painting my friend Andrew Kuo made of me, Carolyn, and Erika that he gave us for our opening.

BRUSSELS SPROUT AND SQUASH SALAD WITH CURRY AIOLI AND CANDIED PEPITAS

SERVES 4

When the cold weather approaches, this salad is a real crowd pleaser. It combines classic fall flavors with fresh herbs and creamy, comforting aioli. The aioli can be made in advance and stored in the fridge, but the gremolata is best used as soon as it's prepared.

For the candied pepitas
1⅓ cups granulated sugar
1 cup water
⅓ cup hulled pepitas
canola oil, for frying
salt, as needed

For the curry aioli
6 egg yolks (about ½ cup when
    lightly beaten)
1½ teaspoons lemon juice
1 large clove of garlic, roughly
    chopped
1 teaspoon curry powder
1 cup olive oil
½ teaspoon salt
pinch of freshly ground black pepper

For the gremolata
½ cup roughly chopped fresh flat-
    leaf parsley leaves
¼ cup olive oil
finely grated zest of 1 lemon,
    plus juice of ¼ lemon (about 1
    tablespoon)
1 large garlic clove, roughly
    chopped
½ teaspoon salt

For the vegetables
canola oil, for frying
1 pound peeled and deseeded
    winter squash, such as butternut
    or acorn squash, cut into ⅜-inch
    cubes
1 pound Brussels sprouts, stem ends
    trimmed and quartered
2 tablespoons cornstarch

Equipment
A deep fryer (optional)

Start by candying the pepitas. Place the sugar in a small saucepan and add the water. Place the pan over low heat and heat until the sugar dissolves completely. Increase the heat and bring the syrup to a boil. Cook for 3 minutes then add the pepitas and simmer for 5 minutes. Strain, shaking off any excess syrup from the pepitas, then transfer them to a bowl.

Preheat the canola oil to 325°F in a deep fryer; or fill a heavy-based pot with about 2–3 inches of oil and preheat to 325°F, measuring with a candy or deep-frying thermometer clipped to the side of the pot. Fry the pepitas for 2 minutes—use a timer so they don't burn! Shake off any excess oil, drain well, and transfer to a clean bowl. Sprinkle generously with salt and toss well. Set aside.

Make the curry aioli. In a blender or food processor combine the egg yolks, lemon juice, garlic, and curry powder and blend until the mixture is fluffy and lightened in color. Slowly drizzle in the oil while the motor is running, and continue to

process until the mixture thickens and emulsifies. Season with the salt and pepper, transfer to a bowl, and set aside.

Precook the squash for the salad. Heat the canola oil in a deep fryer to 325°F, or fill a heavy-based pot with 2 quarts of canola oil and heat to 325°F, using a candy or deep-frying thermometer clipped to the side of the pot. Immerse the diced squash for about 2–3 minutes in the hot oil, until just tender. Shake off any excess oil, then transfer to a platter or baking sheet lined with paper towels and leave to drain.

Alternatively, spread out the diced squash in a single layer on a lightly oiled baking sheet and cook in a preheated 350°F oven for 15–20 minutes. Set aside and leave to cool.

Make the gremolata. Combine all the ingredients in a blender or the mini bowl of a food processor, and blitz until finely processed. Transfer to a small bowl and set aside.

In a large bowl combine the precooked squash and the Brussels sprouts. Sprinkle the cornstarch over and toss well. Increase the heat in the deep fryer, or the pot of oil, to 350°F. Shake off the excess cornstarch from the vegetable mixture and fry, in 2 or 3 batches, for about 3 minutes, until the sprouts are golden brown and slightly curled at the edges. (Be careful, the oil will spit vigorously when the vegetables are added.) Drain off any excess oil and transfer the vegetables to a clean large bowl.

Add the gremolata and toss the warm vegetables to coat evenly and completely.

To serve, spoon a generous amount of the aioli onto a platter, arrange the squash and Brussels sprouts salad over this and sprinkle the pepitas on top. (Leftover aioli will keep for 2–3 days in the fridge in an airtight container.)

PIES 'N' THIGHS FRIED CHICKEN BOX

SERVES 3–4

One of the most popular offerings at Pies 'n' Thighs is the Fried Chicken Box, a feast of crisp fried chicken accompanied by a buttermilk biscuit and the diners' choice of one of the eatery's delicious sides. Here we present it with our favorite, the spicy black-eyed peas.

Fried Chicken (serves 3–4)

Not all fried chicken is created equal. We use an assertive brine to flavor our air-chilled, free-range, hormone- and antibiotic-free birds. We opt for air-chilled poultry because it has a clean, savory taste, having retained all its natural juices. This means that it doesn't need much dressing up to make delicious fried chicken, so our batter is as simple as can be.

For the brine
¾ cup kosher salt
½ cup granulated sugar
1 tablespoon ground paprika
2 teaspoons cayenne pepper
1 teaspoon freshly ground black
    pepper

1 (3-pound) organic chicken, cut
    into 10 pieces
3 cups all-purpose flour
canola oil, for frying
salt, as needed

Equipment
An instant-read thermometer

To make the brine, fill a large, lidded pot with 4½ quarts of water and add the salt and sugar. Bring to a boil over high heat, then whisk until the salt and sugar have fully dissolved. Add the paprika, cayenne pepper, and black pepper, and stir. Remove the mixture from the heat and allow the brine to cool completely before using.

Add the chicken pieces to the prepared, cold brine, submerging them completely. Cover the pot with the lid and refrigerate for 18–20 hours.

When you're ready to cook the chicken, fill a large, heavy-based skillet with canola oil to a depth of 2 inches and place over high heat until a deep-frying or candy thermometer reaches 350°F (be sure not to let the thermometer touch the bottom of the skillet).

Put the flour into a shallow dish or bowl. Drain the chicken, discarding the brine, and rinse very well under cold running water. Dredge the chicken pieces in the flour, being sure to coat them completely. Shake off any excess flour, then add the dredged chicken to the hot oil. Using tongs, place half the chicken pieces in the skillet; turn as necessary until the chicken is golden brown and crisp all over and an instant-read thermometer reaches 165°F when inserted into the thickest portion of each piece, about 15–16 minutes in total. Transfer the cooked chicken to a paper towel-lined platter to drain. Season with salt to taste and keep warm in a low oven while you cook the rest of the chicken. Serve immediately.

Buttermilk Biscuits (makes 9–10 biscuits)

Our bakers mix, roll, and bake biscuits all day, every day. A couple of tricks give the biscuits the look and texture we like. Cold butter and quick hands yield flat, soft layers that peel off like Post-it Notes. Flipping the patted-out dough over to cut the biscuits and then flipping the biscuits back before baking makes for neat, sharp top edges. Still there's no question: any way you cut them, they're delicious!

5½ cups all-purpose flour, plus
    more as needed
1 tablespoon baking powder
2½ teaspoons kosher salt
1 teaspoon granulated sugar
¼ teaspoon baking soda
3 sticks unsalted butter, chilled
    and cut into pea-size pieces
1¾ cups buttermilk, chilled
1 large egg, beaten until blended

Preheat the oven to 400°F and line a baking sheet with parchment paper.

Put the flour, baking powder, salt, sugar, and baking soda in a food processor and pulse until the ingredients are evenly distributed. Add the butter and continue to pulse until the mixture resembles the texture of coarse meal with a few pea-size pieces of butter still remaining.

➤

Transfer the mixture to a large bowl. Add the buttermilk and fold it into the dry mixture with a fork, then gently knead using your hands just until a soft, shaggy dough comes together.

Turn out the dough onto a lightly floured surface. Pat it out with your fingers until it is 1¼ inches thick. Cut out as many biscuits as you can using a 3-inch round biscuit cutter. Re-roll the scraps once and cut out more biscuits.

Arrange the biscuits on the prepared baking sheet, making sure to leave some space between each one, as they will expand during cooking. Brush the tops of the biscuits with the beaten egg and bake until golden brown, 25–30 minutes, rotating the tray once after 10 minutes of cooking time.

Spicy Black-Eyed Peas (serves 4)

Black-eyed peas are a staple of southern cooking, and we use them in a fresh, bright, and spicy salad. If smoked jalapeños aren't available, seed a fresh jalapeño, then use tongs to char it over your cooktop. Throw the blackened pepper into a brown paper bag, close the bag tightly, then let it sit for 5 minutes to help persuade the skin to loosen. Peel and finely dice.

For the black-eyed peas
1 cup dried black-eyed peas, picked through and rinsed
1 bay leaf
1 tablespoon salt, plus more as needed

For the vinaigrette
1 teaspoon ground cumin
1 teaspoon ground cayenne pepper
1 teaspoon salt
1 teaspoon dark brown sugar
1 tablespoon lime juice
¼ cup apple cider vinegar
2 teaspoons hot sauce (preferably Frank's)
1 teaspoon soy sauce
2 teaspoons tomato ketchup
¼ cup extra-virgin olive oil
¼ cup canola oil

For the salad
2 tablespoons finely diced red onion
1 tablespoon chopped fresh cilantro leaves
2 tablespoons finely diced, fresh jalapeño pepper
2 tablespoons finely diced smoked jalapeños, or 1 medium deseeded, charred, and peeled jalapeño pepper (see introduction)
1 teaspoon minced fresh garlic

Place the dried peas in a large bowl. Pour cold water over, making sure to cover the peas by about 2 inches, and leave to soak overnight, about 8–12 hours. Drain the peas, discarding the soaking water.

Place the rehydrated beans in a large pot and cover with fresh water. Add the bay leaf and bring to a boil. Lower the heat to a simmer and cook until the peas are tender, about 20–30 minutes. Add the salt to the beans and stir well. (Adding salt at the beginning of cooking can stop the starches from breaking down properly and the beans from becoming tender.)

Taste the bean cooking liquid and adjust the salt if necessary so you have a nice, lightly seasoned cooking liquid. Let the beans cool completely in their liquid.

Meanwhile, make the vinaigrette. Combine the cumin, cayenne, salt, and dark brown sugar in a small bowl, and set aside. In a medium bowl, whisk together the lime juice, vinegar, hot sauce, soy sauce, ketchup, and olive and canola oils. Add the spice and sugar mix and whisk thoroughly. Set aside.

When the beans are cool, drain, then rinse under cold running water and drain again. Transfer the beans to a large bowl. Pour ¼ cup of the vinaigrette over the black-eyed peas, mixing well. Taste and add more dressing in small increments, tasting between each addition, until you are satisfied. You will not need to use all of it and can store any leftover dressing in the refrigerator in an airtight container for up to a week.

Stir the remaining salad ingredients into the dressed black-eyed peas. The salad can be made beforehand and refrigerated for up to 2 days.

CORNED BEEF

SERVES 10

We make our own sourdough rye bread, sauerkraut, and corned beef for our Reuben sandwich. (But you can take a shortcut and use the best store-bought bread and kraut you can find!) Our servers often say, "We make everything but the cheese!" Maybe someday we'll make the cheese...

For the brine

2½ quarts water
1 cup coarse salt
½ cup dark brown sugar
1 tablespoon pink curing salt (see suppliers, page 286)
1 cinnamon stick, crushed
1 teaspoon mustard seeds
1 teaspoon black peppercorns
6 cloves
6 allspice berries
2 dried bay leaves, crushed
½ teaspoon ground ginger
1 teaspoon whole coriander seeds
½ large onion, peeled and quartered
1 pound ice (about 16–18 medium-size cubes)

5 pounds beef brisket, trimmed of excess fat

Make the brine by combining all the ingredients except the ice in a large pot. Place over high heat and bring to a boil. Simmer until the salts and sugar have dissolved. Remove from the heat and add the ice to cool down the brine. If the ice doesn't cool it down sufficiently—it needs to be 45°F or cooler—leave it overnight in the fridge.

Pour the cool brine into a large, nonreactive container and add the brisket. Cover with a weighted plate to keep the brisket completely submerged. Leave to brine for 7–10 days in the refrigerator.

When ready to cook the brisket, preheat the oven to 275°F. Remove the brisket from the brine, making sure to save the brining liquid. Rinse the brisket and place in a large pot or roasting pan. Pour over enough of the reserved brining liquid to reach halfway up the brisket. Cook, covered with foil or a tight-fitting lid, for 6 hours, then check if it is cooked sufficiently. When the corned beef is ready, a knife will slide in and out of it without resistance. If the meat is still a little tough, continue to cook, checking regularly.

Remove the brisket from the oven and leave to cool in the pot. To speed things up, we place the whole pot in an ice bath to bring the temperature down. Once cool, pop it in the fridge and chill for 8 hours (or overnight).

To serve, reheat in the braising liquid until piping hot all the way through, then thinly slice. Eat as is, or use in classic Reuben sandwiches with sourdough rye bread and sauerkraut.

LEMON BLACKBERRY PIE

MAKES ONE 9–INCH PIE

Tart and fresh and irresistible, this pie captures the brightness of spring. The "tart" comes from the combination of blackberry and lemon curds. The lemon curd is an adaptation of Sherry Yard's delicious recipe, but the blackberry curd is all ours. The addition of fresh berries tossed in sugar to pull out their juices and "melt" the fruit a little adds an extra-special touch and a more formal look.

Note

For greater accuracy, we use weight, rather than volume, measurements for the dry ingredients in this recipe.

For the shortbread crust

1 stick unsalted butter, cold and cut into small cubes
4½ ounces all-purpose flour
pinch of salt
1½ ounces confectioners' sugar, preferably 10x, sifted
finely grated zest of ¼ lemon

For the lemon curd

5 ounces granulated sugar
2 tablespoons lemon zest
3 whole eggs plus 2 egg yolks, beaten
¼ cup plus 2 tablespoons fresh lemon juice
¼ cup plus 2 tablespoons fresh lime juice
¼ teaspoon citric acid (optional)
2 tablespoons unsalted butter, cold and cut into cubes

For the blackberry curd

3 ounces blackberries
1 egg plus 2 egg yolks, beaten
2 tablespoons fresh lemon juice
1½ ounces granulated sugar
2 tablespoons unsalted butter, cold and cut into cubes

To decorate

fresh blackberries tossed in a pinch of granulated sugar

Equipment

A kitchen scale (see suppliers, page 286)

Preheat the oven to 375°F.

Begin by making the piecrust. Place all the ingredients in the bowl of a stand mixer fitted with the paddle attachment, and mix on medium until the ingredients are just combined and come together to form large clumps of dough. Be careful not to overwork the crust. Press the dough evenly into the base and up the sides of a standard 9-inch pie plate. Place the crust in the freezer for about 30 minutes, or until firm.

While the crust is chilling, make the lemon curd. First, set a small bowl over another slightly larger bowl filled with ice and cold water; set aside. In a food processor, combine the sugar and lemon zest and process until thoroughly mixed. Transfer the mixture to a double boiler or a bowl set above a pan of simmering water.

Add the beaten eggs and yolks and whisk to combine. Continue to whisk until the sugar dissolves, then add the lemon and lime juices, and the citric acid, if using. Cook until the mixture is thickened, then whisk in the cold, cubed butter, one piece at a time, making sure that each piece is fully incorporated before adding the next. Remove the curd from the heat and strain into the prepared bowl set over the ice bath. Whisk the curd until it's cold and thick. Place a piece of plastic wrap directly on the surface of the curd. Set aside.

When the piecrust is firm, remove from the freezer, line with parchment paper, and fill with baking beans. Bake the crust for 10 minutes, then remove the parchment paper and beans and return the crust to the oven for another 10 minutes until the bottom is dry to the touch and a light golden, sandy color.

Turn the heat down to 325°F.

Fill the crust with the cold lemon curd, spreading it out evenly. Return the filled pie to the oven and bake for 20–25 minutes or until the filling is set but not colored. Leave to cool on a wire rack.

Meanwhile, prepare the blackberry curd. Set a small bowl over another, slightly larger bowl filled with ice and cold water; set aside.

Place the blackberries in a small saucepan and add just enough water to cover them. Bring to a boil over medium heat and cook for 15 minutes, or until the fruit has completely broken down. Strain the

mixture through a sieve, pushing down on it with the back of a wooden spoon to extract as much juice and pulp as possible. Set aside, and discard the leftover solids.

Whisk together the beaten eggs, lemon juice, and sugar in a double boiler or a small bowl set above a pan of simmering water. Once the sugar has dissolved, add the butter (for this curd this need not be done gradually) and cook, whisking, until the butter melts. Add the blackberry juice and continue to whisk until a thick curd forms. Strain into the bowl set over the ice bath and whisk until cold.

With the lemon-curd-filled pie at room temperature, top the center of the pie with a generous scoop of the blackberry curd (either still cold or at room temperature), leaving a ring of baked lemon curd visible around the edge. Top with the fresh sweetened blackberries.

APRIL BLOOMFIELD

Fans of The Spotted Pig may be aghast to learn that this West Village gastropub, one of New York City's best-known eateries, almost never was. In 2003 a young British cook, April Bloomfield, flew from England to meet with Ken Friedman, then a would-be restaurateur who had recently relinquished his music industry career, and Mario Batali, a maestro of Italian cuisine stateside. She had spoken with Friedman several times but had no inkling as to who Batali was. A tour of the city's gastronomic delights ensued. To Bloomfield it felt as though her taste buds were being auditioned. "We didn't talk a lot about cooking," she recalls. Friedman was looking for a chef and co-owner to helm his first restaurant, and Bloomfield's friend Jamie Oliver had recommended her. She had a jolly enough time sampling the city's best, and Batali gave her his full endorsement. Once back in London, she received an email from Friedman laying out his business plan and his vision for the restaurant. But there was a problem. The menu he described simply didn't jibe with the kind of food Bloomfield wanted to cook—what she defines as "food cooked from the soul." "Thanks for the opportunity but I think I might pass," she wrote back.

Luckily for New York, Friedman replied, "OK, you can cook whatever you want." This is precisely what Bloomfield does at her (now four) New York restaurants. There's The Spotted Pig, a hip, cozy West Village gastropub; The John Dory Oyster Bar, convivial and turn-of-the-century in spirit; Salvation Taco, Bloomfield's take on a Mexican cantina; and The Breslin, a nose-to-tail meat lover's haven. Apart from Salvation Taco, with its globally inspired taquería fare, her menus are united by their showcasing of her favorite foods from home and the influence of old-school Italian cooking. So, along with Scotch eggs, kedgeree, beef and Stilton pie, scrumpets, and crisp pig's ears there's an abundance of grilled and roasted proteins and vegetables, hearty soups, fresh pasta coated in unctuous sauces, and crunchy, varied salads tossed with slick, salty dressings. Sometimes she seeks inspiration from elsewhere in Europe, and so you'll see merguez sausage, spaetzle, and aioli served with her squid stew toast.

Born and bred in industrial Birmingham, in the heart of England, Bloomfield originally fancied herself as a policewoman. When that didn't work out, she applied to the Birmingham College of Food, Tourism and Creative Studies (now University College Birmingham). Her older sisters were both at culinary school, and when Bloomfield's mother pushed her to pick a career, on a whim she picked chefdom. "I liked the look of my sisters' chef's whites," she says. By the time she left her initial interview at the school, the buzz of the kitchens and the aromas of the spices had filled her with genuine zeal for her future career.

After graduation, wanting to be among the vanguard of the Modern British culinary movement that was making the world sit up and take notice, Bloomfield moved to London. She worked with the country's top chefs at places like Bibendum and Kensington Place, eventually landing at the famous River Café, where she says she "really" learned to cook. She stayed for four years under the tutelage of two extraordinary cooks, Ruth Rogers and Rose Gray, before leaving to take on the Big Apple.

And take it on, she has. Since she opened The Spotted Pig in 2004, Bloomfield has acquired two Michelin stars, won a James Beard Award for Best Chef NYC, and written two acclaimed cookbooks. Some say she even serves up the best burger in town. Not bad for a British lass.

You're known for being extremely fussy in the kitchen—what one thing do you insist on that makes your kitchen crew groan the loudest?
I wouldn't say I am fussy. I'm particular because I have high standards. I suppose not being organized or wasting energy are two things that bother me. Everything filters down in the kitchen—so starting with the simplest things, like organization, plays a role in making sure everything is well executed and balanced.

In your opinion what is the most underrated cut of meat, and how do you prepare it best?
I think I'd have to go with pork collar. This is my favorite cut. It is perfect for braising or roasting. Fresh pork shoulder with cured coppa works really well, and they actually complement each other.

What's your favorite off-the-beaten-track, hole-in-the-wall eatery in NYC, and what's your go-to order there?
Jing Fong. I love to go for dim sum. I love everything on the menu, from char siu bao (pork buns) to shumai (dumplings). It's really a place where you can't go wrong.

WARM BACON-AND-EGG SALAD

SERVES 4

I love a fried egg, especially when it is fried in bacon fat. This is my take on a classic French brasserie favorite, *salade frisée aux lardons.* Considering that it consists of eggs and bacon, it's surprisingly quite light—hearty, but not overly heavy.

¼ cup plus 3 tablespoons extra-virgin olive oil
2 garlic cloves, halved lengthwise
1 generous cup ½-inch crustless bread cubes
8 slices of lean bacon
4 anchovy fillets, chopped
2 tablespoons Banyuls vinegar or red wine vinegar
2 teaspoons Dijon mustard
4 large eggs
5 ounces baby arugula
¼ cup chopped fresh chives
salt and freshly ground black pepper, as needed

In a large nonstick skillet, heat 2 tablespoons of the olive oil. Add the garlic and cook over medium heat until golden brown, about 2 minutes. Using a slotted spoon, transfer the garlic to a mini food processor. Set aside.

Add the bread cubes to the skillet and cook over medium heat, stirring, until browned and crisp, 3 minutes; transfer to a plate. Heat another tablespoon of the oil in the skillet. Add the bacon and cook over medium heat until crisp. Transfer the bacon to a plate and keep warm. Reserve the bacon fat in the skillet.

Add the anchovies, vinegar, mustard, and the remaining ¼ cup of oil to the garlic and process to form a smooth dressing. Season with salt, to taste, and set aside.

Re-heat the bacon fat in the skillet. When hot, crack the eggs into the skillet and fry over medium-high heat until over easy, 1½ minutes on the first side and 30 seconds on the other side. Transfer to a plate and keep warm.

In a large bowl, toss the arugula and croutons with the dressing. To serve, mound the salad on plates and sprinkle with the chives. Top with the bacon and the fried eggs, season with pepper and serve right away.

CHICKPEA AND LENTIL SALAD WITH FETA, CILANTRO, AND ONIONS

SERVES 4

There are no rules to salad. I love one that is well seasoned and well dressed. This salad is a delight with all its different textures and flavors; sometimes I serve it as a side to grilled sausages or a nice rack of lamb, but I'll also turn it into a meal in itself with a bowl of freshly marinated roasted peppers.

2 cups dried lentils
1 clove garlic, peeled
1 sprig of sage
1 red chili
Maldon salt, as needed
*2 cans (15–16 ounces each) good-
    quality cooked chickpeas, drained
    and rinsed*
1 tablespoon toasted ground cumin
3 tablespoons tahini
*3 tablespoons extra-virgin olive oil,
    plus more as needed*
freshly squeezed juice of 1 lemon
1 bunch of picked cilantro
1 medium red onion, thinly sliced
4 ounces goat milk feta

Cook the lentils. Rinse the lentils then place in a pot with just enough cold water to cover. Set the pot over medium-high heat and bring to a gentle boil, stirring occasionally, then reduce the heat immediately. Add the garlic, sage, and red chili and simmer gently, partially covered, for about 20–30 minutes or until the lentils are just tender; do not boil or the lentils will break up. Cool the lentils in their cooking liquid and then season with salt, to taste. Drain well and set aside.

To assemble the salad, in a large bowl combine the rinsed chickpeas, cooked lentils, cumin, tahini, the 3 tablespoons of olive oil, half of the lemon juice, and salt, to taste. Toss gently, being careful not to crush the chickpeas and making sure not to remove their skins.

In a separate, small bowl, combine the cilantro and sliced red onion. Dress with the remaining lemon juice, salt, and a little olive oil.

To serve, transfer the lentil and chickpea mixture to a large serving bowl and top with the cilantro and onion mixture. Sprinkle over the crumbled feta and drizzle with olive oil to garnish.

ROASTED PORK SHOULDER WITH CHIANTI

SERVES 4

Italians love their pork, and one of the most prized cuts is coppa. The balance between meat and fat in coppa is perfect for our recipe. Coppa comes from the forward shoulder of the pig (often referred to as a Boston butt). Chat up your local butcher—if he's up to the task, you'll receive a beautifully marbled cut similar to tenderloin, but with much more character. While you're at it, ask him for half a pound of fatback, from above the belly; this will make a paste to beautifully baste your roast.

1 pound very thinly sliced cured
    coppa, alternatively you can
    substitute prosciutto, speck, or
    Serrano ham
½ pound fresh pork fatback
¼ cup dried bay leaves, ground to a
    fine powder in a spice grinder
2 tablespoons fresh rosemary
    leaves, picked off the stem
8 cloves spring or regular garlic, 5
    crushed and 3 left whole
1 teaspoon salt
2–3 pounds fresh coppa in one piece
4 tablespoons olive oil
1 tablespoon cold butter
1 bottle Chianti wine (enough for 2¼
    cups for cooking and a glass for
    you while prepping!)
squeeze of fresh lemon juice

Tear off a sheet of plastic wrap about 18 x 12 inches. Lay the plastic wrap out flat and line it with the cured coppa; you want enough surface area of cured meat to wrap fully around the cut of raw coppa. Transfer to the refrigerator so it doesn't begin to melt.

In a food processor, combine the fatback, ground bay leaf, rosemary leaves, and the 5 crushed cloves of garlic with the teaspoon of salt. Process until whipped. Any small remaining chunks of fat will crisp up beautifully and add a nice surprising pop to your finished dish.

Remove the cured coppa from the fridge. Using a pastry brush, smear the fatback spread over the cured meat making sure to coat it all the way to the edges. Place the raw coppa cut across the plastic wrap along the length of the longer measurement, leaving about 2 inches of the fat-coated cured coppa exposed at the bottom.

Grab the edges of the plastic wrap and fold up and over your raw coppa so that the cured coppa meets on both sides. Don't worry if your cured coppa has some naked patches; it's simply there to add a nice savory, salty flavor. Remove and discard the plastic wrap.

Once rolled, rest the prepared coppa roast in the refrigerator for about 2 hours to give the fatback spread mix time to solidify and stick to the meat. You now have coppa wrapped in coppa, sealed with pork

fat; there's nothing better! Truss the roast with some string, using a basic butcher's tie.

Preheat the oven to 400°F.

Heat a large, heavy-bottomed skillet with the olive oil until it just begins to smoke. Place the coppa in the skillet and sear the roast on all sides. Toss the remaining 3 whole cloves of fresh spring garlic and the butter into the pan right at the end, allowing it to brown a little and take on a nutty flavor. Baste the coppa with the fat in the skillet then transfer the meat and all the drippings to a roasting pan and place in the oven. After 20 minutes, pour 2 cups of the Chianti over the top. Reduce the oven to 325°F, and cook until medium, or until the internal temperature registers at 155°F on a digital thermometer.

Remove the coppa from the oven and let it rest in the pan for about 15 minutes, turning it once or twice so the juices in the pan continue to baste the meat.

Remove the string from the roast and pour the pan drippings into a small saucepan. Bring to a boil then reduce to a simmer and add a splash of Chianti. Slice the pork about ¼-inch thick; I prefer it thicker than thin. Arrange the slices on a platter and drizzle the drippings on top, along with a squeeze of fresh lemon juice. Serve alongside a nice vegetable medley of peas, favas, and scallions.

BALSAMIC-GLAZED DUCK

SERVES 8

This is a dish I cook every Thanksgiving or Christmas. I love to balance fat with acidity and this is a classic example—the combination of balsamic and lemon juice cuts through the fat in the dish beautifully.

2 (5–6-pound) Long Island or Peking ducks, giblets and wings reserved
6 tablespoons olive oil
2 heads garlic
4 fennel bulbs, trimmed, outer layers only, chopped (reserve the tender inner parts to roast and serve as an accompaniment to the duck)
6 cups chicken stock
1 lemon, halved crosswise, plus juice of 1 lemon
1 bunch of fresh thyme
1 cup balsamic vinegar
coarse sea salt and freshly ground black pepper, as needed

Preheat the oven to 350°F. Prick the duck skin all over with the tines of a fork, taking care not to pierce the flesh, and season with sea salt. Place the ducks on a rack in a large roasting pan, and let stand for 30 minutes.

Meanwhile make the sauce. Chop the duck wings and necks into pieces. Heat the oil in a large heavy-bottomed saucepan set over medium-high heat, adding the duck wings and necks and stirring until brown. Separate and peel 1 head of garlic; reduce the heat to low, and add the fennel and garlic to the saucepan. Cook, stirring occasionally, until the vegetables have softened and caramelized. Add the stock and cook until the liquid has reduced by half, about 40 minutes. Strain into a clean saucepan, skim the fat from surface, and set aside.

Halve the remaining head of garlic crosswise, and crush it slightly. Divide the lemon, thyme, and garlic evenly between the duck cavities. Place the ducks in the oven, and roast, turning every 25 minutes, until they begin to brown, about 1 hour. Mix together the balsamic vinegar and lemon juice, and baste or brush the ducks with the mixture every 20 minutes. Cook until the skin is dark brown and the meat begins to come away from the breastbone, 2–3 hours in total.

Remove from the oven, and allow the ducks to stand for 20 minutes. Add some defatted pan juices to the sauce and reheat over medium heat until the sauce is reduced to your desired consistency; season to taste with salt and pepper. Carve the duck and serve with the sauce and roasted vegetables, if you like.

AMANDA COHEN

rom its opening in 2008 until its closing in 2014, chef Amanda Cohen's East Village fixture, Dirt Candy, commanded serious respect. The pint-size, vegetable-focused restaurant received an enviable two-star review from the *New York Times* and was widely acknowledged as the most innovative modern American vegetarian restaurant within as wide a radius as you could imagine.

The 18-seat restaurant ended its run on East 9th Street on August 30, 2014. Cohen was sad to abandon the enterprise that had thrust her into the spotlight, but sanguine nonetheless. Just six months later, Dirt Candy 2.0 reopened in its new 60-seat space in the Lower East Side on the border of Chinatown.

On Cohen's menu, every dish is a celebration of a single vegetable. (She was a vegetarian for 16 years but now does eat fish.) Her point is to push quotidian greens, roots, and tubers beyond their comfort zone. She showcases them in unexpected ways—never simply for the sake of novelty but because, for example, bright, fresh carrot juice makes a divine carrot meringue pie and roasted cucumber produces a broth of astonishing complexity, perfect for an Asian-style hot and sour soup.

Though she takes her food extremely seriously, Cohen's intentions are often lighthearted. With whimsical creations like cauliflower and waffles—a riff on classic fried chicken 'n' waffles—and smoked broccoli "dogs," Cohen wants to make her diners smile. Indeed, humor comes easily to her. In 2009, her stridently opinionated restaurant blog won *Gourmet* magazine's "Funniest In-House Restaurant Blog" award. Then there's her unconventional comic-book-style cookbook and memoir.

After she graduated from New York University, Toronto-native Cohen and her writer husband, Grady Hendrix, hotfooted it to Hong Kong for a year and a half. When they returned to NYC, Cohen enrolled at the Natural Gourmet Institute in 1998, then cruised through the city's top vegetarian restaurants. First there was Blanche's Organic Café, followed by Other Foods. A brief interlude of meat cookery at Diner Bar came next before she took charge of TeaNY, a Lower East Side vegan café owned by musician Moby. When Pure Food and Wine hit the scene with its creative raw food cuisine, Cohen—not missing a beat—jumped on board. That same instinct took her to Heirloom, which under her leadership won *Time Out* New York's Reader's Choice Award for Best New Vegetarian Restaurant in 2006.

Yet brighter pastures beckoned when Cohen was recruited to open a restaurant from the ground up. But after a conflict with the owners, she was let go. "After that I had an almost instantaneous realization that I wasn't supposed to work for anybody again." And so Dirt Candy was born. Turning over tables three times a night, plus low overheads (she had no pricey proteins to contend with and just one server—Cohen herself helped to serve and take reservations) translated to a satisfyingly profitable business.

Still, its success was double edged. Six years on, customers forced to wait two months to eat at Dirt Candy were becoming ex-customers, eventually prompting Cohen to seek larger quarters. This upgrade doesn't signal the end of her journey, though. "I am so understanding of why people make sex tapes. You get some fame and the phone starts ringing, or you get more followers on Twitter. Then one day it slows down, so you think, 'Okay, what do I have to do now?'" If her past record is anything to go by, no doubt Cohen has a lot more culinary tricks up her sleeve to keep diners coming back, and keep her clothes on!

What's your earliest memory of cooking?
I've blocked out my childhood, but my therapist thinks with a lot of hard work I'm due for a breakthrough this year.

What would your last meal consist of?
An all-you-can-eat buffet. I could keep that meal rolling on for weeks.

What dish that you've created are you most proud of and why—what makes it so special?
The Portobello Mousse, because it won me $10,000, and I needed the money to fix the restaurant's air-conditioning.

What's been your most embarrassing kitchen disaster?
I dumped a giant pot of boiling soup down my pants and had to strip immediately and be pants-less on the line. It was embarrassing, but the alternative was skin grafts.

Ultimate chef's perk—what's your favorite morsel you reserve just for yourself?
Gin.

What has been your most memorable moment professionally?
Dirt Candy not failing.

PORTOBELLO MOUSSE WITH TRUFFLED TOAST AND GRILLED PORTOBELLOS

SERVES 6–8

Earthy, rich, dense, and smooth, mushrooms have a meatiness to them—a heft and a nice chew that are hard to find in other vegetarian options. Potatoes can have that same smooth, dense feel, but they come with a heavy starchiness, whereas mushrooms land on your tongue as gracefully as butterflies.

Portobello mushrooms are a truly fantastic variety. Back in the 1980s, they were widely promoted; then in the following decade they fell out of fashion. But when prepared the right way, they still offer a silky mouthfeel, unique in the world of fungi.

For the portobello mousse
2 sticks unsalted butter
1 cup finely chopped white onions
½ cup heavy cream
1¾ teaspoons agar-agar powder
6 cups chopped portobello mushroom caps with gills scraped out and stems removed
1½ teaspoons salt
½ teaspoon freshly ground black pepper
½ teaspoon truffle oil

For the fennel pear compote
½ cup diced fennel
2 cups chopped (½-inch pieces) unripe pears: peeled and seeded
1 tablespoon agave nectar
1 tablespoon apple cider vinegar
½ tablespoon ground fennel
2 tablespoons chopped crystallized ginger
3 tablespoons chopped, soaked, and rehydrated dried sour cherries
salt, as needed

For the balsamic reduction
4 cups balsamic vinegar

For the truffled toast
½ cup olive oil
1 tablespoon truffle oil
1 baguette, sliced very thinly on the diagonal

For the grilled portobello mushrooms
10 large portobello mushrooms
½ cup olive oil
1 teaspoon salt

Equipment
A silicone ice cube tray with at least 15 (1½-inch) cube molds, or a nonstick silicone loaf pan
A squeezy bottle
A meat slicer (optional)
A chinois (optional)

Make the mousse. In a small saucepan over medium heat, melt 2 tablespoons of the butter. Add the onions and cook until very soft, about 10–12 minutes.

Add the cream and the rest of the butter, and cook over low heat for about 10 minutes. Add the agar-agar and bring the mixture to a boil. Transfer to the blender and process briefly. Add the mushrooms and continue to blend. When the mixture starts to look smooth, add the salt, pepper, and truffle oil. Continue to blend until extremely smooth. Strain the mixture through a chinois or a very fine sieve into a pitcher.

Carefully pour the mixture into the cube molds or the loaf pan mold.

Refrigerate for at least 1 hour until set.

Meanwhile, make the pear compote. In a medium saucepan, sweat the fennel until soft but not mushy, about 10–15 minutes. Add the pears and cook until the fruit is partially soft. Next, add the agave nectar, cider vinegar, ground fennel, ginger, and cherries. Season with salt to taste and cook for an additional 30 minutes, or until everything is tender. Remove from the heat and set aside.

Next, make the balsamic reduction. Place the vinegar in a small saucepan and place over a medium-high heat; bring to a boil. Reduce the vinegar until there is only about ½ cup left. Remove from the heat and set aside.

When the mousse has set and you're ready to serve, prepare the truffled toast. Preheat the grill or grill pan. Combine the olive oil and truffle oil in a small bowl and lightly brush each slice of baguette with this. Grill the baguette slices on both sides until grill marks form and the bread is crisp.

Using either a mandoline set to the thinnest setting, a vegetable peeler, or, ideally, a meat slicer, slice the portobello mushrooms, working from the smooth top to the gills; you want very thin strips. Do not slice the gills. In a large bowl, toss the mushroom strips with the oil and salt.

Preheat a grill, a grill pan, or a griddle until very hot. Sear the mushrooms until softened and cooked through.

To serve, unmold the mousse. If using the loaf pan, cut the mousse into 1-inch cubes. Pipe a zigzag of balsamic reduction across the surface of 6–8 large plates using a squeezy bottle. In one corner of each plate, place a cube of the mousse. Then, working clockwise, place in each subsequent corner a mound of grilled mushrooms, then a spoonful of the compote, and finally a few pieces of toast. Extra mousse will keep in the fridge in an airtight container for up to 1 week, and extra balsamic glaze can be stored in the fridge indefinitely.

CHARD GNOCCHI WITH GOAT CHEESE SAUCE AND GRILLED CHARD

SERVES 4

Grilled greens are one of my favorite things. The grill gives them a lot of char, making them meaty, chewy, and smoky. It simultaneously brings out the greens' bitterness and their sweetness while making them really juicy—the perfect winter food. Swiss chard is heartier than spinach, but not as tough as collards or kale, and of all the greens I've experimented with, it stands up to grilling the best.

For the green Swiss chard gnocchi
2 large russet potatoes
1 bunch of green Swiss chard (about 1 pound), leaves only
1 large egg
6 tablespoons all-purpose flour
salt, to taste
olive oil, as needed

For the garlic granola
1 cup flat-leaf parsley leaves
1 garlic clove, peeled
½ teaspoon salt
1 cup olive oil
5 cups rolled oats
¾ cup plus 1 tablespoon corn syrup

For the pickled red Swiss chard stems
1¼ cups washed and finely diced red Swiss chard stems
2 tablespoons lime juice
2 teaspoons salt

For the goat cheese sauce
¼ pound soft goat cheese
¼ cup plus 2 tablespoons milk

For the grilled chard
2 bunches of red Swiss chard (about 2 pounds) cleaned and de-stemmed (reserve stems for pickling)
¼ cup olive oil
salt, to taste

To assemble
1 tablespoon minced garlic
2 tablespoons unsalted butter
salt, to taste

Equipment
A potato ricer

Note
A food processor can be substituted for a blender in this recipe, although a blender makes a smoother purée.

First make the garlic granola. Preheat the oven to 325°F. Put the parsley, garlic, salt, and oil in a blender, and process until smooth. Transfer to a bowl and set aside.

On a sheet pan, combine the oats and corn syrup until well mixed. Bake for 20 minutes, stirring the mixture every 5 minutes. Add ¾ cup of the parsley and garlic oil mixture, and mix thoroughly. Bake for another 5 minutes, or until the granola is crunchy. Remove from the oven, leave to cool completely and store in an airtight container until ready to use.

Now bake the potatoes. Preheat the oven to 375°F. Wrap the potatoes in aluminum foil and bake for 1½ hours or until fork tender.

Next, pickle the red Swiss chard stems. Bring a small pan of lightly salted water to a boil. Prepare a bowl of ice water and set aside. Add the chard stems to a boiling water and blanch for 3 minutes. Drain and throw the chard stems into the ice water bath to shock them. Drain thoroughly and combine with the lime juice and salt in a bowl. Cover with a piece of plastic wrap and let them sit for at least 30 minutes.

Now make the cheese sauce: place the goat cheese and milk in a blender or food processor and blend until smooth. Transfer to a bowl, cover, and refrigerate until ready to use.

When the potatoes are nearly done cooking, make the green chard purée for the gnocchi. Bring a pan of salted water to a boil. Prepare a bowl of ice water and set aside. Blanch the Swiss chard leaves for 3 minutes, drain, and submerge in the ice water to shock. Drain well, then transfer to a blender (or food processor; a blender produces a smoother purée) and blend until smooth and shiny. Transfer to a bowl, cover with plastic wrap, and set aside. You need 6 tablespoons of green chard purée.

While the cooked potatoes are still hot (but just cool enough to handle), peel them. The skins should pull away easily. Cut the potatoes into large chunks and pass them through a ricer into a bowl.

Bring a large pan of water to a boil.

Place about 1½ cups (generous) of mashed potato in a mound on a clean surface or in a bowl. Make a well in the center and break the egg into it. Add the 6 tablespoons of chard purée to the well, and lightly mix the egg with the chard, then gently fold the potato into the liquid. Once thoroughly combined, lightly work the flour and salt into the potato mixture, being sure not to knead the dough, which would make the gnocchi tough.

Once the dough has come together, form it into a ball and divide it into 6 portions. Roll each portion out into a rope about ¾ inch thick. Cut each rope into 1-inch pieces. Immediately drop the pieces into the pot of boiling water; when they are cooked through, they will rise to the top. Remove them with a slotted spoon and toss them on a tray with a little olive oil. Keep the water on a boil while you prepare the grilled chard.

Preheat your grill, or a grill pan placed on the cooktop, until very hot. Meanwhile, in a bowl combine the red Swiss chard leaves, olive oil, and salt, to taste. Grill the chard until it turns bright green and grill marks form.

To serve, heat the butter and garlic together in a skillet and cook for 1–2 minutes. Stir in the goat cheese sauce and cook until thoroughly heated through. Taste and adjust the seasoning as needed.

Drop the gnocchi back into the boiling water for 30 seconds then drain well. Add the gnocchi to the skillet and toss to coat in the sauce.

Divide the grilled chard between four plates and spoon over the gnocchi mixture. Sprinkle the pickled stems around the chard and gnocchi, along with the garlic granola. Serve immediately.

SMOKED CAULIFLOWER WITH BUTTERMILK WAFFLES AND HORSERADISH CREAM

SERVES 4

This dish was inspired by the classic soul food combination of fried chicken and waffles. Instead of chicken, though, I use smoked cauliflower. Smoking brings out the best in cauliflower, and the horseradish sauce gives it some bite.

Smoking is going to step up your kitchen game, and it's a lot easier than you think it is. You can either buy a cheap smoker online or improvise one easily using my instructions, below.

For the horseradish cream
¼ cup grated fresh horseradish or ¼ cup bottled horseradish (not the pink kind!)
2 cups heavy cream
salt

For the waffles
¾ cup all-purpose flour
¼ cup cornstarch
½ teaspoon baking powder
¼ teaspoon baking soda
½ teaspoon table salt
1½ teaspoons granulated sugar
½ cup whole milk
½ cup buttermilk
⅓ cup vegetable oil, such as canola oil
1 large egg, lightly beaten

(Alternatively you can use store-bought frozen waffles.)

For the fried smoked cauliflower
½ cup cornstarch, plus extra for dredging
2 tablespoons all-purpose flour
1½ cups buttermilk
1 egg
4 cups cornflakes
4 tablespoons smoked paprika
1 tablespoon salt
1 tablespoon garlic powder
1 tablespoon onion powder
canola oil for frying
1 quantity Smoked Cauliflower (see recipe below, page 48)

Equipment
A small blender or a pestle and mortar
A waffle iron
A deep fryer or deep-frying/candy thermometer
A chinois (optional)
A smoker (optional)

First make the horseradish cream. Put the grated fresh horseradish (if using) in a small blender and add a little water, unless it's already really juicy. (If the amount is too small for your blender, use a pestle and mortar.) Blend until it's a thick paste. (Warning: do not put your face over the blender when you open it. The fumes will knock you out!)

Put the horseradish paste (or bottled horseradish) and heavy cream in a small saucepan and bring to a boil over medium heat. Reduce heat to low and simmer for 30 minutes. Remove from the heat and let cool.

Pass the mixture through a chinois or a fine sieve into a bowl, shoving any bits of horseradish into the holes with a large spoon or spatula to break them up and extract as much horseradish flavor as possible. Throw out the horseradish pulp. Salt to taste, cover with plastic wrap, and set aside.

Make the waffle batter. In a medium-size bowl, combine the flour, cornstarch, baking powder, baking soda, salt, and sugar. Whisk well. In a separate bowl or measuring cup, combine the remaining wet ingredients and pour this into the flour mixture. Whisk to blend well, so that few, if any, lumps remain. Set the batter aside to rest for 30 minutes.

Meanwhile prepare the batter for the cauliflower. Combine the cornstarch and flour in a bowl, then whisk in the buttermilk and the egg and beat until thoroughly combined. Set aside. Place the cornflakes in a food processor with the paprika, salt, garlic powder, and onion powder and pulse until the cornflakes are roughly the size of half a pea. Transfer into a separate bowl and set aside.

Preheat your waffle iron. I would use a medium-high setting, but the instructions for your own waffle iron may differ. There's no need to grease the waffle iron; simply pour on an appropriate amount of batter for your waffle maker once it's hot. Plan to use your first waffle as a test (or a chef's perk!). Cook it until golden and crisp, then keep it warm wrapped in foil in a low oven. Repeat until you use up all

➤

the waffle batter or have enough waffles for the recipe. If using frozen waffles, cook them according to the directions on the box.

Fry the smoked cauliflower. Heat about 3–4 inches of canola oil in a large heavy-based pan until it reaches 350°F on a deep-frying or candy thermometer (or use a deep fryer). Place some cornstarch in a bowl for dredging. Dip a piece of smoked cauliflower in the cornstarch, then in the buttermilk mixture, shaking off the excess liquid, and finally roll it in the cornflake mixture to coat. Place the battered cauliflower on a sheet pan, and repeat until all the cauliflower wedges have been coated.

Deep-fry the cauliflower pieces until they're golden brown. The cauliflower is more or less entirely cooked, from the smoking, before it goes into the hot oil—it's just a case of crisping the batter. Transfer to a tray lined with paper towels to drain.

When ready to serve, cut the waffles into quarters. Place two waffle quarters on each dinner plate. Put a wedge of cauliflower on top of each piece of waffle, and pour the horseradish sauce over to coat the bottom of the plate. Serve immediately.

Smoked Cauliflower
1 medium head of cauliflower, trimmed and cut into wedges, with as much of the stem removed as possible
Maple wood chips

Either use a smoker, following the manufacturer's instructions (and using maple wood chips), or follow the instructions given here.

First, in a bowl of water place enough maple wood chips to fill the bottom 1 inch of a large, heavy-bottomed saucepan or pot; leave them to soak for at least 1 hour (you can't over-soak them). This ensures that the chips won't burst into flames when you smoke with them. Next, line the pan with aluminum foil so you don't char it. Lift the wood chips out of the water, soaking wet, and spread them evenly along the bottom of the pan.

Now make a little tray out of foil and poke a few holes in it. Drop that directly on top of the wood chips. Cover the pan, and place it on the stove over high heat. Wait until the pan fills with really thick clouds of smoke; this should take about 30 minutes.

Add the cauliflower wedges to the foil tray you prepared and spread them out evenly (you may have to smoke the cauliflower in batches depending on the size of your pot). Cover the pan and bring it back up to a full smoke. Turn off the heat and let the cauliflower rest, covered, for about 20 minutes.

Turn the heat back on and let the pan fill with heavy clouds of smoke again. Once it has reached this point, turn off the heat and let it rest for 20 minutes. Check the cauliflower; it should slowly be darkening and changing color as it smokes, turning a caramel color. You don't want to taste it, because it would burn your tongue! Smoke, rest, and repeat until the cauliflower develops a light caramel coating.

Once smoked, the cauliflower wedges can be stored in the fridge overnight or used right away.

POTATO NOODLE SALAD

SERVES 4–6

Boiled potatoes, fried potatoes, mashed potatoes. Everyone cooks their potatoes until they transform into something else, but I wanted to take potatoes and barely cook them, so that they keep some of their raw, natural crunch. Usually we think of them as big, heavy, starchy monsters, but in this deconstructed potato salad they're light, crisp, and refreshing.

1 cup Japanese yam spiral ribbons
(see Equipment)
4 cups Idaho potato spiral ribbons
canola oil, for deep-frying
2 tablespoons sliced black olives
¾ cup very thinly sliced kale
2 tablespoons thinly sliced scallions
¼ cup thinly sliced green apple
matchsticks
3 tablespoons sour cream, salted
to taste
2 tablespoons extra-virgin olive oil
½ cup distilled white vinegar

Equipment
A candy/deep-frying thermometer
A spiral slicing machine (such as the Paderno Spiralizer; this is one of the most fun kitchen tools you'll ever meet; see suppliers, page 286)

First make the yam ribbons, following the manufacturer's instructions. Place the yam ribbons in a bowl of salted water. In a separate bowl, do the same with the potato ribbons. Leave both to soak for at least 24 hours, then drain well, keeping them separate. Pat dry the yam ribbons.

Heat 3–4 inches of canola oil in a heavy-based saucepan. When the temperature reaches 350°F on a candy or deep-frying thermometer, drop in the yam ribbons and fry until crisp. Remove and leave to drain on a plate or tray lined with paper towels.

Next rinse the Idaho potato ribbons. Drain well and set aside. In a large bowl, mix together the olives, kale, scallions, apples, and sour cream.

Heat the olive oil in a nonstick pan over high heat until you can see ripples in it. Add the potato ribbons and quickly shake the pan for about 2 minutes, then add the vinegar. Keep stirring for 1 more minute; the potatoes should be only parcooked and still crunchy.

Remove the potato ribbons from the heat and add them to the bowl with the kale, olive, and sour cream mixture. Toss until thoroughly combined. To serve, divide the potato salad between the plates in mounds and top with the ribbons of crisp Japanese yam.

AMANDA FREITAG

fter she graduated from the Culinary Institute of America, Food Network star and chef/restaurateur Amanda Freitag headed to the Florida Keys to acquaint herself with seafood cookery. On returning to her home state of New Jersey, she worked a few stints in somewhat unnotable restaurants, then turned her sights to New York City. "In New Jersey there were really no good places, except for diners." But she had no intention of working in diners, even the best ones. Freitag was instead drawn to the elegance and exactitude of fine dining. When she secured a job at Jean-Georges Vongerichten's Vong, with its fusion of Asian and French components, Freitag couldn't have been more thrilled.

So it really is with a spoonful of irony that when Freitag opened her first restaurant in January 2014, it was a diner. But hers wasn't just any diner. Freitag and her partners brought back to life one of Manhattan's most iconic culinary landmarks, Empire Diner, in Chelsea, which had closed in 2010 following nearly 35 years of business. The newly resuscitated Art-Moderne diner car is something of a refined, chic cousin to the no-frills archetypal Jersey institution, but there are no tasting menus or pristine white tablecloths in its beautifully restored retro black and white interior.

Freitag's modern diner caters to all walks of life, or at least all that traverse Chelsea, and soon it will do so 24 hours a day. For old-fashioned diner fans, there are all-day buttermilk pancakes, a patty melt to die for, and an unctuous grilled cheese made with Cheddar and fontina. For the sophisticate there are new dishes that are all Freitag's, as well as inventive riffs on diner classics that never stray too far from their prototypes. She sells a lamb burger adorned with whipped goat cheese, watercress, and chili jam; and her matzo ball soup is enriched with bone marrow. As for the local children, an afterschool menu quells their grumbling tummies.

After Vong, Freitag moved to Diane Forley's Verbena, near Gramercy Park. A champion of the green market, Forley instilled in the young Freitag the importance of fresh, local produce and the benefits of cooking it in season. During her six years there, Freitag made the bread (served warm with a crock of butter), the ice cream, and a lot else besides. Then she held a sous-chef position at Il Buco working under Sara Jenkins, adding an understanding of Tuscan cuisine to her repertoire.

Not that she sought out women bosses, but Freitag appreciated the more thoughtful, sharply focused kitchens they ran—a practice she emulated as chef de cuisine of 'Cesca, on the Upper West Side; at Gusto, in the West Village; and later at The Harrison, in TriBeCa, as Executive Chef.

It was while cooking "New American" fare (a catch-phrase for just about anything!) at The Harrison that Freitag was introduced to television when invited to pit her skills against Bobby Flay in the TV series *Iron Chef America*. Despite losing by one point, she displayed notable talents in front of the camera. Freitag is now a frequent judge on the Food Network's reality cooking show *Chopped* and has competed twice for the title of Next Iron Chef on the series of that name. With the Food Network situated down the road at Chelsea Market, Freitag splits her time between the studio kitchen and her diner's kitchen, with an occasional diversion to her bed. Perhaps for efficiency's sake, she will carve out a spot for sleep when Empire Diner launches its 24-hour-opening schedule.

What dish have you created that you are most proud of, and why?
Now this is truly impossible to answer! Every part of my career has produced different types of foods and inspirations. With each new project or endeavor my goal was always to create something new and top what I had done in the past. I'm still working on this every day.

What's the most disgusting combination of ingredients you've ever eaten?
The most disgusting combination of ingredients I've ever eaten, of course, was on *Chopped*. It was a "viewer's choice" episode, and I ate four lovely appetizers made out of durian fruit, lime Jell-O, and Cheetos. I survived!

What's the worst thing about watching yourself on television?
Oh, there are many things. The worst is watching and wanting to change something about myself ... the way I ate or the way I said something or wanting to change the way I look. It's torturous sometimes.

Your culinary arsenal of kitchen shortcuts must be full to the brim; can you share one of them with us?
I use herb purées as sauces very often. They are quick to make, bright in flavor, and can be layered in with other sauces to create endless flavor combinations.

BUTTERMILK PANCAKES

SERVES 2–3 (MAKES 6–7 PANCAKES)

Everyone should have a tried-and-true, made-from-scratch pancake in their collection of recipes. This one—which we serve all day at Empire Diner—has been through the test of many different cooks and has been made in batches that would feed 500 people. It works!!! The key is whipping the eggs to a fluffy, airy mass; it makes for a perfect pancake every time.

2 large eggs
1½ cups all-purpose flour
1½ tablespoons baking powder
½ teaspoon salt
3 tablespoons granulated sugar
1½ cups buttermilk
3 tablespoons melted butter, cooled to room temperature
½ stick cold butter

To serve
butter and maple syrup or fruit

Place the eggs in the bowl of a stand mixer and beat with the paddle attachment until they are pale yellow and frothy and doubled in size. This will take about 10 minutes. Alternatively, you can use a hand-held electric mixer. Set aside.

Mix together the flour, baking powder, salt, and sugar in a separate bowl. Whisk the buttermilk into the dry ingredients and blend to a smooth paste. Add the melted butter to the mixture and whisk well to incorporate. Now switch to a rubber spatula and fold the beaten eggs into the rest of the batter. Keep the batter at room temperature until ready to cook.

Heat a large skillet or a griddle pan to medium-high heat. Place a dab of cold butter on the pan and ladle out ¼ cup of batter. When the top of the pancake is aerated and small bubbles form at the surface, after 1–2 minutes, turn it over with a large metal spatula and cook for another 2–3 minutes until the underside of the pancake is a rich golden brown and the pancake is cooked through. Transfer to a roasting pan, cover with foil, and keep warm. Repeat with the rest of the batter, adding more butter to the pan as needed.

Serve the pancakes stacked on top of each other with butter and maple syrup.

Alternatively, top them with fresh seasonal fruit or with a blueberry compote: simply warm fresh blueberries in a pan until some of the berries burst their skins and release their juices.

CHARRED OCTOPUS SALAD, "GREEK STYLE"

SERVES 3–4

This salad has been a staple on many menus of mine. It fits in perfectly with the "diner" theme and truly is in a Greek style. I am a huge fan of feta cheese, and although it may seem strange to add feta to a salad containing octopus, the salty, creamy qualities of both give a unity to this dish.

For the octopus
1¼ pound raw baby octopus, pre-tenderized, if possible, and cleaned, with eyes and beaks removed
3 or 4 used wine corks
salt, as needed
2 tablespoons olive oil

For the chili oil (makes 1 cup)
½ red bell pepper, finely diced
2 Fresno chili peppers, finely diced
1½ tablespoons olive oil
6 tablespoons tomato paste
1 cup canola and olive oil blend

For the lemon vinaigrette
¼ cup lemon juice
¼ cup extra-virgin olive oil
salt, as needed

To assemble
2 cups baby arugula
½ cup (rounded) thinly sliced celery
½ cup (rounded) thinly sliced cucumber crescents
1 cup (scant) crumbled feta cheese
1 tablespoon shredded fresh mint leaves
1 tablespoon chopped fresh oregano leaves

Begin by cooking the octopus. Place the octopus in a large heavy-bottomed pot and cover with water. Add the corks to the pot; these will help to tenderize the octopus. Cook over medium heat at a gentle simmer for 1½ hours or until tender. Drain the octopus, then lay it in a single layer on a sheet tray and allow to cool.

Meanwhile make the chili oil. In a skillet set over medium heat, sauté the diced red bell pepper and Fresno peppers in the olive oil until the vegetables are softened, about 3–4 minutes. Add the tomato paste and stir to coat the peppers thoroughly; continue to cook for another 2–3 minutes. Add the canola and olive oil blend and stir to distribute the vegetable mixture throughout the oil. Cook for 5 more minutes. Remove the skillet from the heat and leave the mixture to steep for at least 1 hour. Strain and set aside.

Next make the lemon vinaigrette. Place the lemon juice in a small bowl and whisk in the extra-virgin olive oil. Season with salt to taste, then set aside.

Once the octopus has cooled, season it with salt. Heat a skillet over high heat until very hot, add the 2 tablespoons of olive oil to the pan, then sear the octopus until the skin is crisp and charred, turning as necessary. Remove from the pan and keep warm.

When ready to assemble the salad, place the arugula, celery, cucumber, feta, half the mint, and all the oregano in a large bowl. Toss with 4 tablespoons of the lemon vinaigrette, then taste and add more vinaigrette, as needed. Transfer to a platter. Top with the warm, charred octopus, then garnish with the remaining mint and drizzle with the chili oil. (Leftover chili oil can be kept in an airtight container in the refrigerator for a couple of weeks.)

EMPIRE DINER PATTY MELT

SERVES 4

As an experienced chef, it has been so much fun to create a "diner" menu for my latest project, the Empire Diner. This patty melt is pretty traditional and is one of my favorite late-night snacks.

1 tablespoon unsalted butter
1 tablespoon olive oil
2 large onions, about 2½ pounds total, halved crosswise and thinly sliced to yield half rings
a pinch of granulated sugar
1¼ pounds ground chuck (a blend of 80% lean meat and 20% fat) or 4 ready-made 5-ounce burger patties using the same proportions of lean and fat meat
freshly ground black pepper, as needed
canola oil, as needed
8 slices Swiss cheese
4 slices Cheddar cheese
8 slices seedless rye bread
1 stick unsalted butter
salt, as needed

Equipment
A steak weight (optional)

First, caramelize the onions. Place the butter and olive oil in a large heavy-bottomed skillet over medium-low heat. Once the butter has melted, add the onions and cook, stirring occasionally, for about 10 minutes. When the onions are softened, add the sugar and a pinch of salt. Reduce the heat to low, and continue to cook for another 35–45 minutes, stirring every now and then, until the onions are a deep golden brown color. Remove from the heat, transfer the onions to a bowl, and allow to cool. You should have about 1 cup of caramelized onions.

Meanwhile, make (if necessary) and cook the beef patties. If starting with ground chuck, divide the meat into 4 equal portions and form into patties, being sure not to make them too dense.

To cook the patties, first season them with salt and pepper. Then lightly oil a large skillet with canola oil and place over medium-high heat until the pan is very hot. Add the patties, in batches if necessary, and sear until they are medium-rare in the center and well browned on the outside, about 2½ minutes on each side. Transfer the patties onto a sheet pan and let cool to room temperature.

To assemble the sandwiches, arrange 2 slices of Swiss cheese and a slice of Cheddar on a slice of rye bread, then top with 3–4 tablespoons of caramelized onions. Place the beef patty on a second slice of bread, then close to create a sandwich.

Heat a 12-inch skillet over medium heat. Add 4 tablespoons of butter to the pan and, once melted, carefully place 2 sandwiches in the pan. Press down on the sandwich with a steak weight or another pan to compress the ingredients, melt the cheese, and brown the bottom. Turn the sandwiches over and repeat until golden brown on top.

Remove the sandwiches from the pan and keep warm. Repeat with the remaining sandwiches, adding more butter as needed. Cut each sandwich in half and serve immediately with salad or French fries.

ORZO "MAC 'N' CHEESE" WITH ASPARAGUS AND BLACK TRUFFLE BUTTER

SERVES 4

This is my version of an adult "mac 'n' cheese." It is quite a stretch from the traditional, but there IS pasta and there IS cheese. My regulars and fans have come to know and love this version, and I have even converted some discerning young palates into preferring this to the "orange" pasta they are used to eating. Now that is something for a chef to be proud of.

1 bunch of standard-size asparagus (about 1 pound), cleaned but untrimmed
1½ cups orzo pasta
extra-virgin olive oil, as needed
3 garlic cloves, sliced thinly
1½ cups heavy cream
2 tablespoons unsalted butter
6 tablespoons grated Parmesan cheese, plus more as needed
3 tablespoons grated pecorino romano
1–2 tablespoons black truffle butter (can be found in the dairy section of Whole Foods or gourmet markets. Do not use truffle oil.)
salt and fresh cracked black pepper, as needed

Fill a 5-quart pot with salted water and bring to a rolling boil. Add the asparagus and blanch for 1 minute. Remove the asparagus from the pot with tongs, transfer to a plate, and set aside. Bring the pot of water back up to a boil, then add the orzo and cook for 7–9 minutes until al dente. Drain in a colander, then drizzle a little olive oil over, tossing to coat all the pasta, and set aside.

Trim the tough stem ends off the asparagus and discard. Cut the remaining asparagus stalks into ¼-inch-thick diagonal slices and set aside.

In a good-size (about 10-inch) skillet, heat 2 tablespoons of extra-virgin olive oil over medium heat; add the garlic. Cook until the garlic starts to brown lightly, then add the sliced asparagus to the pan and stir well to coat it with the garlic and oil. Stir in the cooked orzo, reduce the heat to low, and cook for 1 minute. Add the heavy cream and butter, stirring constantly. Next, add the Parmesan and pecorino, and keep stirring until they melt and the mixture thickens. Add the black truffle butter to the pasta mixture, to taste, and season generously with salt and black pepper. Remove from the heat.

Spoon the pasta into a large bowl and serve family style, or portion out into ramekins. Top with a sprinkling of extra Parmesan cheese before serving.

GABRIELLE HAMILTON

In 2011, Gabrielle Hamilton won the James Beard Award for Best Chef NYC. In 2014 she was shortlisted for the title of Outstanding Chef. Many chefs credit their success to a celebrated mentor; others, to hard graft; still others, to good old-fashioned luck. Hamilton attributes hers to an experience of visceral hunger.

A decade or so before opening her 30-seat East Village restaurant, Prune, in 1999, Hamilton traveled the world with a backpack. When money was at its most sparse, she didn't—or rather, couldn't—eat. She intensely craved not only the delicious foods around her but also much-missed foods from home. "For me appetite is never unspecific; I might want something fatty or plain grilled fish or salty broth." So when she opened Prune, her manifesto was to cook homey food that would satisfy at an elemental level.

It's no coincidence that her menu articulates the same ethos as the unfussy but forthrightly flavorsome meals her French mother would prepare. Hamilton grew up eating innards as a matter of course; and so among her signature dishes at Prune for the first 15 years were sweetbreads that simulated chicken-fried steak and dripped with a caper and bacon sauce. (As a kind of abbreviated mission statement, the name "Prune" echoes the childhood nickname Hamilton's mother bestowed upon her.)

In 2014, in tandem with the publication of her acclaimed cookbook *Prune*, Hamilton overhauled her menu; and today the sweetbreads have gone. However, she couldn't bear to part with the bar snack of sardines, Dijon mustard, cornichons, and Triscuits that had virtually become her trademark. Part of Hamilton's skill is locating those pleasure points where diners experience a gratifying fusion of nostalgia and taste. Unlike many of her peers, she is unashamedly honest about using store-bought ingredients. The crackers aside, there are also Thomas brand English muffins cradling her lamb burgers and the Grape-Nuts cereal she served with maple syrup and an upturned vanilla ice cream cone. Her point? As if she could make Grape-Nuts from scratch better than the people at Post Foods...

By the time she opened Prune, Hamilton had already lived an incident-crammed, improbable life, which she describes in her brilliant, best-selling memoir, *Blood, Bones & Butter: The Inadvertent Education of a Reluctant Chef* (2011). A bucolic early childhood in Pennsylvania's bohemian enclave New Hope came to an end when her mother left and the family disintegrated. The 13-year-old Gabrielle was left to fend for herself—cobbling meals from paltry pantry staples and dishwashing for money, and for amusement joyriding and shoplifting. At 16, she left for New York City. While working there in the Lone Star Cafe and coked up to the hilt, she was almost charged with grand larceny. Next came a distinctly unfulfilling career in catering.

At the age of 30, Hamilton got out of the kitchen. She headed to the University of Michigan to study fiction writing—a long-cherished passion—and determine if it wasn't too late to salvage that dream.

Despite a Master of Fine Arts in hand and a passion retrieved, Hamilton fell back into cooking. When an East Village space became available, the confluence of purpose and opportunity it offered proved too enticing to reject. Hamilton has since reconciled herself to the career that chose her but her flair for writing has not been neglected. She has been published prolifically and her work has been anthologized in eight volumes of *Best Food Writing*. She is that rare breed of human who is supremely good at two things. Make no mistake, though: Hamilton is not a "great food writer." She is a great chef and a great writer.

In your book *Blood, Bones & Butter*, you sing the praises of your (ex-) mother-in-law as a culinary inspiration. What lesson that she taught you informs how you cook to this day?
To maintain your personal, eccentric, imperfect, humane, often self-contradictory thumbprint and to leave its mark on every plate.

You're at home at 1:00 a.m. after a long night of service and you're starving ... what do you reach for?
Like college students the world over, I eat oodles of noodles, three for a dollar—in my case, with a spoonful of Tom Yum Paste stirred in and a poached egg (which I recommend to college students the world over).

Is there an ingredient/seasoning that you detest and that we'll never see on the menu at Prune?
Lemon verbena, which tastes exactly like Pledge furniture polish.

Share a culinary secret that will make some unenviable kitchen task easier?
Clean as you go.

CANNED SARDINES WITH TRISCUITS, DIJON MUSTARD, AND CORNICHONS

SERVES 1

Everything I cook at the restaurant has a connection to some aspect or era of my life, and these canned sardines mark the period when I moved to NYC as a 16-year-old. I lived in a roach-infested Hell's Kitchen apartment, and had nothing but a large jar of change for money. Canned sardines in oil were 35 cents a piece at the bodega. I lived for months on them. I still, some 30 years later, eat a few cans a week even though I now have a bank account and a (mostly) roach-free home.

1 can boneless, skinless sardines
* in oil*
1 dollop Dijon mustard
small handful cornichons
small handful Triscuit crackers
1 parsley branch

Buckle the can after you open it to make it easier to lift the sardines out of the oil without breaking them.

Stack the sardines on the plate the same way they looked in the can—more or less. Don't crisscross or zigzag or otherwise make "restaurant-y."

Arrange mustard, cornichons, and Triscuits neatly on the plate. Garnish with the parsley branch.

Commit to the full stem of parsley, not just the leaf. Chewing the stems freshens the breath—especially useful after eating oily sardines.

CELERY HEARTS VICTOR

SERVES 6

Be sure to let the celery drain thoroughly after the braise, so the marinade will not be diluted in any way.

6 celery heads
3 quarts College Inn chicken broth
whole black peppercorns, as needed
2 bay leaves
flat-leaf parsley, to garnish

For the celery marinade
6 oil-packed anchovies, minced
4 cloves fresh garlic, minced
big pinch red pepper flakes
2 tablespoons fresh lemon juice
4 tablespoons extra-virgin olive oil
kosher salt and freshly cracked
  black pepper, as needed

Remove the big, fibrous outer stalks of each head of celery and shave off the dirty, browned bit at the root end to reveal clean white flesh. Keep head intact.

Trim the tops without losing the interior bright yellow leaves. Wash thoroughly, rinsing deep into the heads by holding directly under the faucet.

Place the celery heads in single layer in a roasting pan and cover with the chicken broth. Scatter with some peppercorns and add the bay leaves. Don't salt. The celery itself has some salinity.

Cover with parchment paper and then foil and bring to a simmer on the stovetop over two burners, if necessary. Lower the heat to the barest flame possible and let braise for 15–20 minutes on the stovetop until the celery is tender when you pierce deep into the base with a blade or skewer.

Remove seal and lift the cooked celery out onto a rack set over a sheet pan to fully drain and cool. If you think you'll make use of it, save the celery braising liquid—well labeled and accurately dated—to braise your next batch of celery. It will get better each time.

When cool enough to handle, pull off the green outer stalks to reveal the celadon, tender, beautiful hearts. Leave the hearts as natural and "as is" as possible. Cut crosswise into 2½-inch medallions and pack neatly and tightly into a shallow container to be marinated. Don't let them fall apart.

Whisk together the olive oil, lemon juice, minced anchovy, and garlic and season with the chili flakes, kosher salt, and freshly ground black pepper. The flavor should be bright, assertive, and bracing. Chill the celery hearts in the marinade for at least a few hours. Arrange 1 heart's worth of medallions per person in the shallow small bowl, keep nestled closely together so they hold their shape without falling open. Be sure much of the dressing is spooned over and really drenching the cold celery. Add freshly chopped parsley as you plate and allow to temper briefly to shake the dulling cold from the celery.

COD IN SAFFRON BROTH WITH LEEKS, POTATOES, AND SAVOY CABBAGE

SERVES 4

Fish is expensive and overcooks very quickly and I imagine that discourages a lot of people. Cod has such a generous window of time between cooked and ruined; I think it's one of the most forgiving fish for beginning cooks.

1 dozen Yukon gold potatoes, scrubbed, skin-on, sliced into ½-inch discs
2 medium leeks, sliced into ½-inch discs as far up into green as viable, completely free of sand
generous ½ pound savoy cabbage, cut into attractive wide ribbons
1 cup fish stock
1 medium shallot, finely diced
2 thyme branches, long and thin, not the bushy, woody ones
3 small pinches saffron
1 cinnamon stick
clarified butter, for cooking
2 pounds cod, filleted, skin-on, and butchered to 5 ounce portions
2 tablespoons Berbere Ethiopian spice mixture
3–4 tablespoons cold unsalted butter

Bring 8 quarts of well-salted water to a boil in a large pot. Add the potatoes to boiling water and cook until nearly done, keeping in mind they will carry over residual heat while they drain. Gently remove with a slotted spoon or spider and lay out to drain and cool. Repeat with the leeks and then the cabbage.

Bring the fish stock, minced shallot, thyme branches, saffron threads, and cinnamon stick to a simmer in a saucepan over medium heat. Let it slightly reduce and come together while you cook the fish.

Heat a moderate ladle of clarified butter in a flat-bottomed sauté pan, over medium-high heat.

Season the portioned codfish on both sides with the Berbere spice rub. Take care with your seasoning—it wants to be bold and have a point of view, but not be aggressive or unbalanced.

Sear the codfish, skin-side down, in the hot pan and take it all the way on the stove top, flipping once—get a good, crisp, golden-brown skin, with opaque flesh. You want the natural flake line to start to open, but don't take it so far that you lose all that milky enzyme as it weeps into the pan.

Look at what you have in your saucepot—further reduce or build back up slightly with more fish stock, depending on what you see. You want fragrant, full-bodied, slightly viscous saffron broth that can still receive a few nuts of cold, mounted butter, and is still hot and brothy enough to be able to warm through a few ribbons of juicy cabbage, several coins of watery leeks and a few waxy potato slices without totally thinning out into body-less liquid.

Spoon the finished broth and all the veg into the wide bowl; leave nothing in the pan. Center the cod, flesh-side up.

Fish out the cinnamon stick and the thyme branch and make sure they are visible in the bowl, like a garnish.

ROASTED CAPON
ON GARLIC CROUTON

SERVES 8–10

We work in a horrible, basement kitchen in a 115-year-old East Village tenement building, and not, as I would wish, in a countryside farmhouse with a wood-burning hearth where we could spit-roast capons in front of an open fire, and toast croutons over glowing embers. So we do this instead, and we manage some pretty incredible succulence and deliciousness in spite of our unfavorable conditions.

1 cup sugar
2 cups kosher salt
1 gallon hot tap water, plus 1 gallon very cold water
1 8-pound capon
blended canola and olive oil, as needed
freshly ground black pepper, as needed
2-day-old peasant bread, thickly sliced
peeled fresh garlic, 1 clove per slice of bread

In a clean large container place the sugar and the salt. Add 1 gallon hot tap water to dissolve the salt and sugar and whisk until completely dissolved. Add 1 gallon of very cold water. Stir the brine and submerge the capon in it. Let brine for a full 24 hours, refrigerated.

After 24 hours, remove the capon from the brine. Set the capon in a roasting pan and glug a little blended oil over the bird, rubbing it to coat until slick and slippery. Season all over with black pepper only.

Set the bird in a 350°F oven directly onto the oven rack—breast-side down. Quickly fill the oily roasting pan ½ way with water and set on oven floor directly under the bird. Take care to place it well to collect the fat and juice that drips down throughout the roasting; you don't want a grease fire in your oven.

Roast for 2 hours and 10 minutes, until the juices run clear when pierced with a skewer.

While roasting, cut thick slices of 2-day-old peasant bread and lay them out on a baker's drying rack. Rub each one on both sides with raw cloves of garlic until you have worn the cloves down to nothing—use one whole clove per slab of bread. For the last 40 minutes of roasting, set the croutons still on their rack into the oven, directly under the bird, and directly above the pan of water collecting juices. They will toast here and absorb fat and juice. Check them occasionally to see they aren't burning and conversely, to see that they are in fact toasting. Some birds are so juicy that the croutons can become too soggy before they have a chance to toast.

Remove the capon from the oven, carefully. I think it's best to pull out the rack as far as you can without it tipping and then confidently grab the bird with a clean dish towel folded up in each hand. Place it directly into a waiting pan and let all the juice that has accumulated in the cavity pour out into the pan.

Remove the croutons. Remove the roasting pan of accumulated water/juice and fat from the oven floor and strain into a heatproof container. Add any juices from the capon cavities. Skim the fat off the top and keep warm.

Butcher the bird into 10 parts—2 wings, 2 legs, 2 thighs, 2 breasts cut in half creating 4 pieces of breast meat. It's tricky, but leave the skin intact to the best of your ability.

Place portioned meat on top of croutons and spoon a generous amount of the collected, strained, and defatted juices over each portion.

Recipes originally published in *Prune* (Random House; 2014)

MEXICAN, SPANISH, AND LATIN FLAVORS

SASHA MIRANDA 73

Basil Pesto-infused Polenta Tamales · Ensalada del Mar (Seafood Salad) · Tinga de Pollo con Cilantro "Ñoqui" (Chipotle-braised Chicken with Cilantro Gnocchi) · Pastelón de Plátano (Sweet Plantain and Beef Casserole)

ALEX RAIJ 83

Berenjena con Miel (Crisp Eggplant with Honey and Nigella Seeds) · Pericana con Sopes (Valencian Salt Cod Dip with Bread Rusks) · Fricandó (Catalan Veal Stew with Porcini Mushrooms) · Lacón con Grelos (Galician Pork Chops with Turnip Greens)

BARBARA SIBLEY 93

Sopes con Cabrito en Adobo de Tres Chiles (Sopes with Braised Goat Shanks in Three-Chilies Adobo) · Queso Fundido con Huitlacoche y Langosta (Baked Cheese with Huitlacoche and Lobster) · Pato con Salsa Borracha de Chabacano y Pasilla (Grilled Duck with Rustic "Drunken" Salsa of Roasted Apricots and Pasilla Chilies) · Tacos de Huachinango con Salsa Xnipec (Red Snapper Tacos with Adobo and Red Onion Habañero Salsa)

IVY STARK 103

Chayote Salad with Hibiscus Vinaigrette · Albóndigas in Chipotle Salsa · Butternut Squash Enchiladas with Baby Spinach and Guajillo Salsa · Grilled Salmon with Avocado Pipian, Black Bean Pico de Gallo, and Oyster Mushrooms

SASHA MIRANDA

rowing up in the New York borough of Queens, with its vast cultural diversity, Sasha Rodriguez Miranda was exposed to myriad food experiences. She would feast on midweek, five-course dinners with the families of her Italian friends; on exotic, spicy meals with her Korean neighbors; and on traditional Dominican food cooked by her immigrant grandmother, who lived down the hallway.

It's not surprising, then, that this chef, formally trained at the Culinary Institute of America (C.I.A.), where she specialized in Italian cooking, owns a restaurant whose offerings escape the margins of a single culinary tradition. But this is not to say that she cooks without boundaries altogether. When Miranda and her Mexican-born-and-bred husband, Mauricio Miranda, began dating in 2002, their courtship blossomed around dreams of one day opening a restaurant. Revels were fueled with jointly prepared repasts, mingling flavors the couple were most familiar with—the dishes of their youth and of Sasha's training. Naturally, a unique form of Latinized Italian fare emerged. When the restaurant dream became a reality, and thoughts turned to the menu, the couple chose this familiar, innovative cuisine as their signature style. For Sasha, it was the obvious way to go, to stake their livelihood on food they really believed in.

Miranda Restaurant opened its doors in 2007 on a quiet Williamsburg corner, with Mauricio running the front of house and Sasha the kitchen. Dishes such as house-made pappardelle with a ragu of lamb braised in mole sauce, mussels steamed in Pinot Grigio and served with a chile pulla, and grilled branzino featuring Sicilian capers and a lemon-achiote oil showcase a subtle and deft melding of Mediterranean and Hispanic notes in a synthesis that is seamless, novel, and delicious. The restaurant draws regulars from the neighborhood, as well as fans who make the trip to Brooklyn from as far away as New Jersey and Connecticut every weekend. The atmosphere is easygoing—evoking an Italian trattoria without laboring the point.

Following her graduation from the C.I.A.'s Italian program, Miranda was one of only two students in her class awarded a gastronomic tour of Italy. A fellowship at the school's student-run restaurant came next. Miranda's career began in earnest when she joined Verbena, in Manhattan (where she met Mauricio). It was no coincidence that Verbena was owned and operated by a woman, the revered chef Diane Forley. Miranda, disheartened by the male-chauvinist attitudes of her instructors at school, had actively sought out kitchens run by women. Her instinct served her well, and she rose through the ranks quickly. Still, mindful that the end goal was to open her own place, Miranda mastered all aspects of restaurant management, emerging from the kitchen after two years to become Verbena's dining room manager. Subsequent roles at Café Gray, Raoul's, and Alto (all in NYC) followed before Miranda and Mauricio found their spot in Williamsburg.

With a new baby at home, Miranda is determined to prove that she can have it all: family, restaurant, and success in both. "We have a rule," she says, of how she and Mauricio balance the personal and the professional. "We live in Astoria [Queens] and so have to cross a bridge to get home... work stays in Brooklyn."

What meal have you recently eaten that was especially memorable, and where was it?
Sik Gaek Chun Ha Korean restaurant in Flushing. Atmosphere, ritual—fried egg to start the meal. "Steampot" of fish and chili pepper stew.

What cookbook do you keep referring to and why?
It's not actually a cookbook but rather an illustrated guide to ingredients in Italian. As I mentioned, recipe/menu development for me starts with an ingredient, so I thumb through this book when I need some inspiration or if I want to name a dish in Italian and need some help with the language. It's called *Guida illustrata agli alimenti*.

Is there a food that you hate no matter how hard you try to like it?
Tripe, also fruit-flavored candy.

What moment—good or bad—in your professional career will you never forget?
Being offered less money for a job than a male colleague was offered, even though he had less experience.

What's the best thing about being a chef?
Being able to create what I want, how I want, and experimenting with different flavors.

What's the worst thing about being a chef?
Difficulty in disconnecting when I am not at work.

If you could change one thing about your restaurant, what would it be?
Size of the kitchen; it's too small.

BASIL PESTO-INFUSED POLENTA TAMALES

SERVES 4–6

Tamales are a special treat eaten most abundantly around Christmas in Mexico and Central America. Large quantities are usually prepared by groups of friends or family, while engrossed in conversation. For our staff holiday party last year, we made a few hundred tamales together—it was a great time! I give my tamales a hint of Italian flavor by starting with cooked polenta, rather than the traditional raw masa (finely ground corn flour), and flavoring the sauce with basil as for a traditional pesto.

1 pack corn husks (you'll need about 25 husks); these can be found at most large supermarkets and at Mexican grocery stores.

For the sauce
10 cups (about 3 ounces) fresh basil leaves
¼ cup extra-virgin olive oil
¼ teaspoon red chili flakes
1 teaspoon kosher salt

For the polenta
3 cups water
½ teaspoon kosher salt
⅓ cup (rounded) polenta
6 tablespoons freshly grated Parmigiano-Reggiano cheese

To assemble
¼ cup extra-virgin olive oil
8 ounces fresh mozzarella, cut into ¼- x 3-inch pieces
⅝ cup thinly sliced sun-dried tomatoes

Sort through the corn husks, separating the whole husks from the ripped ones. Place about 16 whole corn husks in a large bowl and cover with hot water. Set these aside. From the remaining corn husks (you can use the ripped ones for this) prepare at least 32 strips of corn husk, each about ¼ inch wide, to use as "ribbons" for tying off ends; simply tear the husk along the grain. Soak these also to make them pliable.

To prepare the sauce, combine all the ingredients in a blender or food processor and purée until smooth. If your blender has trouble getting through all of the basil leaves, add half a cup of water, but be sure to reduce the amount of water added to the polenta by that much.

To prepare the polenta, bring the 3 cups of water, seasoned with the salt, to a boil in a 2-quart pan over medium heat, then stir in the sauce. Reduce the heat to medium-low and slowly pour in the polenta in a steady stream, whisking all the time. Stir the polenta almost constantly for about 20 minutes until the mixture thickens. Stir in the cheese and remove from the heat.

Drain the corn husks and squeeze out the excess water.

To assemble each tamale, dip your fingers in the olive oil and spread a little oil on the inner side of a single whole husk. Spread 1½–2 tablespoons of the polenta in the center of the husk, at least 1½ inches from the edge. Place a slice of mozzarella and several slices of sun-dried tomatoes in the middle, then roll the corn husk around the filling as tightly as possible, and tie off each end with a corn husk "ribbon." The finished tamale should look like a wrapped bonbon. Repeat with the remaining corn husks. If the polenta stiffens as you get toward the end, return the pan to the stove and whisk in a little bit more water until it becomes spreadable again. Uncooked tamales can be prepared and stored in the refrigerator, tightly wrapped, up to 1 day ahead of serving.

To cook the tamales, place a steamer basket in a deep 6-quart pot (or in a pot large enough for the quantity you are cooking). Fill the pot with water until it reaches just below the steamer basket and bring the water to a boil. Using tongs, carefully arrange the tamales in the basket and cook, covered, for 15–20 minutes on low heat (adding extra boiling water if the water beneath the basket runs too low).

Serve the tamales immediately, letting your guests unwrap them at the table.

ENSALADA DEL MAR
(SEAFOOD SALAD)

SERVES 6

This chilled seafood salad is a favorite of mine, especially on hot summer days. The fennel is refreshing, and the avocado adds richness. Some items need to be prepared the night before, so plan ahead and use a timer when preparing the seafood since overcooking will make it rubbery.

¼ pound dried salt cod (bacalao), boneless

For the shrimp
6 ounces large shrimp, peeled, deveined, and sliced in half lengthwise
1 tablespoon extra-virgin olive oil
1 teaspoon chopped fresh rosemary leaves
1 teaspoon freshly grated lemon zest
1 teaspoon minced garlic

For the dressing
6 tablespoons grapefruit juice
3 tablespoons lemon juice
3 tablespoons lime juice
4 small garlic cloves, peeled and mashed
salt and freshly ground black pepper, as needed

For the rest of the salad
2 pounds fresh octopus (preferably Iberian), cleaned, with head, beak, and internal organs removed; your fishmonger will do this for you
½ cup (rounded) small-diced, trimmed fennel bulb
½ medium-large mango (about 1 pound), peeled, stoned, and flesh cut into small dice
1 teaspoon minced serrano chili pepper
2 tablespoons chopped fresh cilantro leaves
½ large avocado, peeled, stoned, and chopped into small dice
salt and freshly ground black pepper, as needed

To serve
lettuce of choice

Rinse the salt cod, then place it in a large bowl and cover with cold water. Cover with plastic wrap and refrigerate for 12 hours, changing the water 3 times.

In a medium nonmetallic bowl, marinate the shrimp with the olive oil, rosemary, lemon zest, and minced garlic. Cover with plastic wrap and refrigerate for 8–12 hours, or overnight. In another bowl, combine the citrus juices for the dressing with the mashed garlic, and season to taste with salt and pepper. Cover with plastic wrap and refrigerate for 8–12 hours or overnight.

Fill a 6-quart pot three-quarters of the way up with water, place on high heat, and bring to a boil. Rinse the octopus well in cold water, then, using tongs, dunk the octopus in and out of the pot of boiling water 3 times. Drop the octopus in the boiling water again, then leave it to cook at a gentle simmer for 40 minutes or until tender, lowering the heat as necessary. Fill a large bowl halfway with ice and very cold water and set aside. Transfer the octopus to the bowl of ice water to stop it from overcooking.

In the same pot of simmering water, gently poach the marinated shrimp for 3 minutes. Transfer to the ice water. Next cook the drained salt cod in the same water for 5 minutes and shock in the ice bath as well. Once the seafood has cooled, drain it well.

Slice the octopus legs into 1-inch pieces, and flake the salt cod into bite-size pieces. In a large bowl combine all the seafood with the remaining salad ingredients and toss together with the citrus dressing until thoroughly combined. Taste, and adjust the seasoning as needed.

Serve the salad at room temperature or chilled, over a bed of lettuce.

TINGA DE POLLO CON CILANTRO "ÑOQUI"
(CHIPOTLE-BRAISED CHICKEN WITH CILANTRO GNOCCHI)

SERVES 6

I tried Tinga de Pollo for the first time when my husband made it for me the traditional way, served on top of crisp corn tortillas with beans, cotija cheese, sour cream, cilantro leaves, and shredded romaine lettuce. I always tell him that it was that dish that made me fall for him. We now serve it at the restaurant with a twist, accompanied with gnocchi, and it's a favorite of our guests. Gnocchi can be a very tricky thing to master, so read through the entire recipe before beginning, to be sure you time it just right.

For the gnocchi
4 Idaho potatoes (about 1¾ pounds)
1 bunch of fresh cilantro, well rinsed
1 cup cold water
2 tablespoons extra-virgin olive oil
1 teaspoon kosher salt
¼ teaspoon freshly ground black pepper
½ cup freshly grated Parmigiano-Reggiano
1 egg, beaten
1⅜ cups unbleached, all-purpose flour, plus more for dusting

For the chicken
1½ cups large-diced red onion
1 teaspoon kosher salt, plus more as needed
1 pound plum tomatoes
¾ pound boneless, skinless chicken breast (about 2 large breasts)
1 teaspoon whole cumin seeds
2 tablespoons canola oil
4 large garlic cloves, peeled and mashed

2 or 3 chipotle chilies in adobo sauce (depending on how much heat you like)
1 tablespoon extra-virgin olive oil
freshly ground black pepper, as needed

To serve
¼ cup freshly grated Parmigiano-Reggiano

Equipment
An instant-read thermometer

Preheat the oven to 425°F.

Using the tines of a fork, stab the potatoes for the gnocchi all over several times, then arrange on a parchment paper-lined sheet tray and cook for 40–50 minutes until fork tender all the way through.

Meanwhile, start preparing the chicken. Place a 6-quart pot on the stove and fill it three-quarters full of water. Add 2 tablespoons of the diced red onion and 1 teaspoon of the salt; bring to a simmer.

To peel the tomatoes, score an "X" in the bottom of each one and remove the stem end with a paring knife. Have ready a medium-size bowl of ice water and a slotted spoon. Drop the tomatoes into the simmering water, remove after about 1 minute, using the slotted spoon, and transfer to the ice water bath. Once cool enough to handle, slip off the loosened skins; set the tomatoes aside.

Using the same pot of simmering water, carefully slide in the chicken breasts and poach for about 20 minutes until cooked through or until an internal temperature of 165°F is reached on an instant-read thermometer. Remove the chicken from the pot and set it aside. Reserve 2 cups of the poaching liquid.

Meanwhile, heat a 10-inch pan over medium heat and add the cumin seeds. Stirring frequently, cook until the seeds are fragrant and start to "jump." Transfer the seeds to a small bowl and set aside. In the same pan (which by now should be quite hot) carefully pour in 1 tablespoon of the canola oil and then add the remaining red onion. Cook the onion, stirring, until translucent, then add the garlic and cook until lightly browned. Remove from the heat and leave to cool slightly.

Next, combine the peeled tomatoes, toasted cumin seeds, chipotle chilies, and the extra-virgin olive oil in a blender and purée. Add the cooked onion and garlic and blend again until smooth.

Shred the cooked chicken into bite-size pieces. Add the remaining 1 tablespoon of canola oil to a saucepan, cover with a lid, and place over medium-high heat. Once the oil is hot, add the puréed mixture along with 1 cup of the reserved chicken-poaching liquid. Cover immediately and reduce the heat—stand back, as this water and oil mix will create some intense bubbles! Once the spitting has died down, bring the mix back to a simmer and add the shredded chicken. Cook uncovered for 15 minutes, stirring occasionally and adding more of the reserved poaching liquid if the mixture becomes too dry; it should have a saucelike consistency to coat the gnocchi. Season with salt and pepper to taste, then remove from the heat and set aside.

While the chicken is cooking, continue with the gnocchi. It is important to work quickly and have all your prep done in advance so the potatoes don't cool down too much—you need the gnocchi mixture to be warm. So have ready the remaining ingredients for the gnocchi, along with a tablespoon, a ricer or food mill, a large bowl, a large cutting board, a knife, and a baking parchment-lined sheet tray dusted with flour.

Begin by blending the cilantro with the cold water until finely puréed. Strain, reserving the solids. (The intense green water can be saved to be added into a cilantro vinaigrette, if desired.)

Remove the potatoes from the oven. When just cool enough to handle (they should still feel quite hot—use gloves, if necessary), peel the potatoes by simply pulling away the loosened skin. Roughly chop the peeled potatoes and pass through the ricer or food mill placed over the bowl. Add the strained cilantro solids, olive oil, salt, and pepper to the potato mixture, and mix by hand until just combined but still

"shaggy." Add the egg, ¼ cup of the Parmigiano cheese, and the flour, and mix again to form a dough ball. Handle the dough as little as possible and as lightly as possible, as over-mixed gnocchi becomes very dense.

Transfer the dough to a large, clean chopping board and cut into 8 equal pieces. Dust your hands and the cutting board with flour and roll out one piece of dough into a log about 12–13 inches long and about ¾–1 inch wide, trying to keep the thickness the same throughout. Slice the log into ½-inch pieces. Spread out the gnocchi on the prepared sheet tray and cover with plastic wrap.

Continue until all the dough has been used up, dusting the board with flour as needed to prevent the dough from sticking. Refrigerate it, wrapped well in plastic, until ready to cook. (The gnocchi can be made, arranged in a single layer on a lined tray and placed in the freezer until solid. Once fully frozen, it can be stored in an airtight container in the freezer for a few weeks.)

To cook the gnocchi, bring a large pan of water to a rapid boil. Reheat the tinga de pollo if necessary.

Add the gnocchi to a boiling water and cook until they float to the surface; drain well. Add the gnocchi to the chicken and toss to combine.

Serve immediately with the remaining Parmigiano-Reggiano sprinkled over the top.

PASTELÓN DE PLÁTANO
(SWEET PLANTAIN AND BEEF CASSEROLE)

SERVES 6

This is a popular Dominican meal, one I grew up eating. Depending on who made the picadillo (seasoned ground beef), the flavor was always a little different, as every cook has his or her own *sazón*, or "seasoning." The ripeness of the plantains is very important for this dish: medium-ripe is what you want. Look for yellow plantains with some black spots—but not too much black—and avoid any with green on any part of the fruit.

For the picadillo
1½ tablespoons canola oil
¾ cup small-diced peeled onion
1 tablespoon minced garlic
1½ pounds ground sirloin
1 tablespoon Worcestershire sauce
1 tablespoon soy sauce
1½ tablespoons tomato sauce
1 teaspoon ground cumin
1 tablespoon dried oregano
½ (rounded) cup raisins
2 tablespoons capers
2 hard-boiled eggs, peeled and
   chopped
salt and freshly ground black
   pepper, as needed

For the plantain topping
3 tablespoons unsalted butter
3½ pounds medium-ripe plantains
   (about 7 or 8 small or 4 large
   ones)
salt and freshly ground black
   pepper, as needed

To assemble
1 pound string beans, trimmed
   and steamed until tender and
   chopped into 2-inch pieces
½ cup freshly grated Parmigiano-
   Reggiano cheese
6 ounces fresh mozzarella, sliced

Bring a 6-quart pot of water to a boil and season with 1 teaspoon salt.

Preheat the oven to 400°F.

Meanwhile, begin preparing the ground beef picadillo. Heat the oil in a 12-inch heavy-bottomed skillet over medium-high heat. Sauté the onion until translucent, then add the garlic and cook until fragrant. Add the ground sirloin and the Worcestershire and soy sauces and continue to cook, stirring, for 7–10 minutes, until the meat is lightly browned. Add the remaining ingredients and cook for an additional 5 minutes. Season the picadillo with salt and pepper to taste. Remove from the heat and set aside.

Butter a deep 9- x 13-inch baking dish (or any baker with a 3½-quart capacity) using 1 tablespoon of the butter; set aside.

Peel and cut the plantains in half. Add the plantains to the pot of boiling water and cook until very soft but not falling apart, about 25 minutes. Drain the plantains, but reserve at least 1½ cups of the cooking liquid. Using a potato masher, roughly mash the plantains.

Add the remaining 2 tablespoons of butter and 1 cup of the reserved cooking liquid and continue to mash to create a smooth mixture. The plantain mash should be spreadable, so depending on their ripeness you may need to add a little more of the cooking liquid. Season with salt and pepper to taste.

To assemble the pastelón, spoon half of the plantain mash into the baking dish and spread it to the edges. Top evenly with the picadillo and follow with the string beans. Add the remaining plantain, spread to the edges, and sprinkle the Parmigiano cheese over it. Finally arrange the slices of mozzarella on top. Cover with aluminum foil and bake 20 minutes. Carefully remove the foil and bake for an additional 10 minutes until the cheese is fully melted and golden brown. Alternatively, place the dish under a hot broiler for a few minutes until bubbly and golden.

ALEX RAIJ

The uni panini at chef Alex Raij's Chelsea tapas joint El Quinto Pino is as near perfect as food can be. Within a slender, toasted ficelle, or mini baguette, the distinctive marine funk of creamy sea urchin melds with sweet butter and pungent Korean mustard oil. The rest of Raij's menu, devised as a road trip through regional Spanish tapas, stands up to this delectable bocadillo, or sandwich, with admirable finesse. Raij's mastery of the tapas genre is most palpable when she innovates. Sometimes she introduces Hispanic influences, as in the Bikini de Huitlacoche, a Catalonian pressed sandwich spiked with roasted poblano peppers and corn fungus; at other times she plays with Asian flavors.

In 2004, Raij, who had trained at the Culinary Institute of America, and her husband, the chef Eder Montero, a native of Bilbao in Spain's Basque Country, teamed up at Tía Pol to bring authentic tapas bar culture to New York (they have since sold their interest there). In 2007, the pair, who had met at Meigas in 1999, a high-concept Spanish eatery in SoHo where he was the sous-chef and she a line cook, refined their vision with the tiny El Quinto Pino in Chelsea. Standing room only was the lot for most patrons too slow to land one of the 16 stools that ringed the curved bar. Just as in Spain, customers would graze on highly flavored bites while they sipped on wines and Iberian-inspired cocktails until they moved to another bar or elsewhere for their main meal. In 2014, Raij and Montero added an adjoining dining room.

From when she worked at her local Baskin Robbins as a teen, Raij, raised in Minneapolis to Argentinian parents, aspired to own an intimate eatery. Raij fell in love with food by way of her mother's homey renditions of Mediterranean and South American cooking, but it was an extended trip to Spain with Montero after leaving Meigas in 2002 that ignited her passion for real-world, nuanced Iberian cuisine.

After Meigas, Raij landed at Gabrielle Hamilton's Prune which embodied precisely the sensibility of the intimacy she envisioned. Once she found her niche in Spanish cuisine, however, her dream evolved to comprise not one but several small restaurants. Where El Quinto Pino was to introduce New York City to the breadth of regional Spanish food beyond paella, the next projects would be more focused.

With Txikito, which opened in 2009 around the corner from El Quinto Pino, the husband and wife team settled on the Basque region as their next frontier. "Don't expect Mediterranean food," she cautions. "It's not tomatoes, saffron, or pretty colors. It's kind of ugly but in the best possible way in that it respects the flavors of the ingredients." This unapologetic ethos is reflected in the dining room, with its greying clapboard walls and garage-door entrance, where wait staff bring out dishes of beef tendons, tripe and trotters, house-cured pork loin, head-on shrimp, veal jowl terrine, octopus carpaccio, and fries with a spicy cod roe mayonnaise for dipping.

When her daughter turned two, Raij readied herself for the next chapter. Looking toward the Arab and Sephardic legacies in Spanish cuisine, Raij (herself Jewish) relished the opportunity to explore the food of the Moriscos and Marranos (Moorish and Jewish converts, respectively, to Christianity during the Spanish Inquisition). In 2012, Raij and Montero moved out of Chelsea to conquer Brooklyn. They opened La Vara (meaning "branch" in Judeo-Spanish) on a leafy street in Cobble Hill, reinforcing their status as the undisputed rulers of New York City's Spanish empire.

What do you think is the biggest misconception that exists about Spanish food in the U.S.?
That paella is Spain's national dish.

What is your favorite month to cook in, and why?
August—it's just so bountiful. I do well in a box, so it's even more challenging to have so many options and try to reflect the season.

Is there one rule of conduct in your kitchen that above all others has to be abided by/that you enforce most strictly?
Taste and season your food, and do not waste.

What's the best thing about working with your husband?
That he protects me and challenges me.

What's the worst thing about working with your husband?
Our personal life is often interrupted by work demands.

What's in your fridge at home?
Charcuterie, pork chops, chicken, organic broccoli, pickles, apple juice, eggs, and lots of milk ... And kid food.

If you weren't a chef, you'd be ...
A textile buyer.

BERENJENA CON MIEL
(CRISP EGGPLANT WITH HONEY AND NIGELLA SEEDS)

SERVES 6

Sweet, light, and crisp, these eggplant "fries" are a super crowd pleaser. I first ate them in Barcelona at a friend's house. In developing my own version, I incorporated my husband Eder's experience in preparing Japanese "age tofu" (soft tofu coated with cornstarch and deep fried) to give it the ultimate crunch. I have been making this dish for a long time, adding the nigella seeds to give it a Middle Eastern flair for La Vara.

2½ quarts lukewarm water
½ cup kosher salt, plus more as needed
2 medium eggplants, about 1 pound each
8 cups vegetable oil, for frying
1 cup cornstarch
¼ cup clover honey
nigella seeds, to taste

Place the lukewarm water in a large bowl and add the salt, then stir until dissolved.

Cut each eggplant into 2 pieces crosswise so that the narrow elongated top is separated from the round bottom part. Placing the flat side of each eggplant half on a cutting board, square them off with a sharp knife, removing most of the skin. Cut into slices 3–4 inches long and ½–¾ inch thick, then slice those pieces lengthwise so that you end up with about 40 eggplant sticks.

Soak the sticks in the salted water for 2–4 hours. This will season the eggplant on the inside and also remove some of the stinging sensation that some people experience.

After soaking, drain the eggplant and pat dry. In a heavy-based medium sauté pan or other pan with tall sides, heat the vegetable oil until it reaches 375°F. Toss the eggplant in the cornstarch in a large bowl or in a large Ziploc bag, then, using a colander, shake off the excess cornstarch to prevent any clumps.

Dividing the sticks into 2 or 3 batches, fry them until they become a light yellow color (not golden brown), about 2–3 minutes. Transfer them to a platter lined with paper towels. Season with a little salt.

To serve, arrange 7 or 8 eggplant fries on each plate, drizzle with the honey, and finish with a sprinkling of nigella seeds.

PERICANA CON SOPES
(VALENCIAN SALT COD DIP WITH BREAD RUSKS)

SERVES 8–10

I love this recipe; part dip and part sauce, it is a condiment of the first order. Although Valencian in origin, it has an Asian-like umami flavor. Use the best-quality ingredients you can find for this dish.

For the pericana

1½ pounds salt cod

3 dried guajillo peppers, deseeded and stems removed

⅜ cup sun-dried tomatoes, canned in oil

3 garlic cloves, very thinly sliced

1¼ cups best-quality Arbequina olive oil from Spain, plus more as needed

½ teaspoon smoked hot paprika

For the bread rusks

1 baguette, chilled in the freezer for 30 minutes or until firm

A day or two before you plan to make and serve the dip, soak the salt cod in plenty of water in a large pot for 16–36 hours, changing the water 3 or 4 times. The soaking time depends on the thickness of the cod pieces and how aged they are. To test that the cod has been soaked enough, tear off a small piece and taste it; if it is pleasantly seasoned but not overly salty, it is ready to be drained. Put the drained cod back into the pan or into a bowl; set aside.

Prepare the bread rusks. Preheat the oven to 260°F. Thinly slice the chilled baguette, then arrange the slices in a single layer on 2 rimmed baking sheets. Bake until very lightly golden and oven dried, about 40 minutes. Leave the slices to cool; they should be crisp and fragile. (The rusks can be made in advance and stored in an airtight container for up to 3 days.)

When ready to make the dip, first drain the cod and dry well with paper towels. Use your fingers to tear it up into very small pieces; or tear it into long, thin shreds then chop these into very small pieces. Transfer to a large bowl and set aside.

Toast the guajillo peppers for 20 seconds in a dry skillet until aromatic; set aside.

Drain the sun-dried tomatoes, reserving the oil, and chop them finely; set aside.

In a small saucepan set over low heat, combine the garlic and olive oil. Cook, stirring, until the garlic starts to become golden. Remove the pan from the heat and crumble the toasted guajillo peppers into the oil. Add the sun-dried tomatoes, along with 2 tablespoons of their oil and the paprika. Stir to combine and pour over the cod.

Fold all these ingredients together. Adjust the seasoning to taste, adding more oil if needed. Transfer to a serving dish and serve with the bread rusks.

FRICANDÓ
(CATALAN VEAL STEW WITH PORCINI MUSHROOMS)

SERVES 6

The best fricandó I ever ate was in Barcelona. This excellent veal stew has a depth and complexity of flavor derived from both dried and wild mushrooms and from picada—a thick, fresh sauce of nuts, garlic, and olive oil that forms an essential component of Catalan cuisine.

For the stew
1 ounce dried porcini mushrooms
2½ pounds boneless trimmed veal breast, cut into 1-inch cubes
all-purpose flour, for dredging
olive oil, as needed
2 medium Spanish onions, finely diced
3 cloves garlic, minced
1 tablespoon tomato paste
pulp of 3 plum tomatoes grated on a box grater
⅜ cup white wine
2 cups trimmed mixed fresh wild mushrooms; chanterelles, black trumpet, and yellow foot are good choices
4 tablespoons brandy
salt and freshly ground black pepper, as needed

For the picada sauce
½ cup toasted Marcona almonds
10 hazelnuts, toasted
2 tablespoons toasted pine nuts
½ teaspoon kosher salt
2 dried guajillo peppers, deseeded
4 garlic cloves, peeled
olive oil, as needed

To garnish
chopped fresh flat-leaf parsley

Begin by soaking the dried porcini mushrooms in 1½ cups of just-boiled water for about 20 minutes or until reconstituted.

Meanwhile, in a large bowl, season the veal with salt and pepper and dredge in flour until lightly coated. Transfer to a colander or sieve and shake off the excess flour.

Heat a Dutch oven or similar pot over high heat and add enough olive oil to coat the bottom. When hot, sear the meat on all sides until golden brown. Work in batches, transferring the browned meat to a bowl or plate as you go. When all the meat has been browned, pour off and discard the fat.

Add 1 tablespoon of olive oil to the pot and reduce the heat to medium-low. Add the diced onion and cook, stirring and scraping the bottom of the pot with a wooden spoon, until the onion is translucent, about 20 minutes. Add the garlic and cook for another minute. Increase the heat to medium-high and add the tomato paste and tomato pulp. Cook, stirring every now and then, until the liquid has evaporated.

Add the wine, bring to a boil, then simmer until reduced by half, then return the meat to the pot. Arrange the reconstituted porcini mushrooms over the meat. Strain out and discard any grit remaining in their soaking liquid, then pour this into the pot. Add water to the pot to cover the meat by two-thirds.

Simmer gently, uncovered, for 20 minutes, then cover the pot and cook until the meat is tender but not falling apart, about 40 minutes more.

Meanwhile prepare the picada. Place the nuts, guajillo peppers, and salt in a food processor and quickly pulse 10 times. Add the garlic and pulse again until the garlic, peppers, and nuts are finely chopped but not a paste. Place the mixture in a small saucepan and add olive oil until three-quarters covered. Stir constantly over medium-low heat until the sauce is aromatic and light brown; be careful not to burn it. Transfer to a plate and leave to cool while you finish braising the veal.

Once the meat is tender, stir in the wild mushrooms, brandy, and picada. Return the stew to a simmer for 5 minutes. Add salt and pepper to taste, if needed, then remove the stew from the heat and leave to rest for at least 30 minutes. When ready to serve, reheat gently and garnish with chopped parsley.

LACÓN CON GRELOS
(GALICIAN PORK CHOPS WITH TURNIP GREENS)

SERVES 4

This Galician dish is a mainstay of traditional boiled dinners, called *cocidos*. Traditionally it is made with ham hocks or cured pork shoulder, requiring an extremely long cooking time, but this version uses brined pork chops for a quicker preparation. Using good-quality pork and the best starchy potatoes makes all the difference. The optional pink curing salt adds a distinctive flavor and color to the pork.

For the pork chops
8 cups water
½ cup granulated sugar
1 cup kosher salt, plus more as needed
pinch of pink curing salt (optional; see suppliers, page 286)
4 1-inch-thick, bone-in Berkshire, or Kurobuta, pork chops (make sure they are well marbled)

For the greens and potatoes
1 pound turnip greens, cleaned and stems removed (dandelion or mustard greens can be substituted)
salt, to taste
4 Carola or other yellow starchy medium-size potato, peeled and left in cold water to cover
3 cloves garlic, sliced
2 tablespoons olive oil, plus more as needed
2 ounces Spanish chorizo, cut into small coins

The day before you plan to serve the dish, brine the pork chops. Bring 4 cups of the water to a boil in a large pot. Add the sugar and salts and stir to dissolve. Remove the pot from the heat and add the remaining water. Leave to cool to room temperature. Place the pork chops in the cool brine and refrigerate overnight.

When ready to cook, remove the pork chops from the brine and pat dry. (Discard the brine.) Place the chops in a pot just large enough to hold them and cover in lightly salted cold water. Bring to a boil, then reduce to a very low simmer. Cook very gently until the meat is tender but still holding the bone, about 1½–2 hours.

Meanwhile, bring a large pot of lightly salted water to a boil. Blanch the turnip greens for 3–5 minutes, then plunge into a large bowl of ice water. Drain well, and set aside.

When the pork is cooked, carefully transfer to a platter and keep covered with foil. Drain and halve the potatoes. Using the same water used to cook the chops, simmer the potatoes until just tender. Drain, reserving 1 cup of the cooking liquid. Halve the potato pieces, if they are large, then arrange around the pork. Cover tightly and keep warm.

In a skillet set over medium heat, gently brown the garlic in the olive oil. Remove from heat and add the chorizo and the drained turnip greens. Toss to coat in the garlic-infused oil. Place the skillet over a low heat and gently reheat the greens without cooking them further. Add the reserved cooking broth to the skillet and toss the greens and chorizo in it.

To serve, remove the foil from the platter and spoon the greens and chorizo, along with the broth, onto the platter. Serve warm.

BARBARA SIBLEY

In her early 20s, Barbara Sibley worked the front of house at Bandito, in the East Village. Although its menu offered predictable Tex-Mex fare, along with margaritas topped with inedible garnishes in the shape of camels and monkeys, the staff often enjoyed a more genuine Latin experience. The kitchen crew would step aside, and Sibley, who was born and raised in Mexico City, would prepare traditional Mexican dishes for everyone. With no formal training, she had acquired her recipes and understanding of Mexican cuisine by watching the family cook and the cooks of other households that her family would visit. "I would always go into the kitchen and almost always leave with a recipe."

The daughter of American expatriates, Sibley moved to the United States at 15 to attend boarding school in Michigan. When it came time to go to college, she chose New York City, a place where she—Mexican on the inside but blond on the outside—could speak Spanish and in whose multicultural environment she would feel at home. While still studying anthropology at Barnard College, she kicked off her career in restaurants as a dishwasher in the student cafeteria and a coat check attendant at the tiny French bistro La Tulipe, in Greenwich Village.

After graduation, Sibley stayed on at La Tulipe, where she progressed to running the dining room, while also working at Bandito, first as a waitress then as manager. When Bandito's owner, Rudy Mozny, decided to open Telephone Bar and Grill, an English-themed gastropub, across town in the West Village, Sibley was there with him; eventually, in the 1990s, she took over the running of the restaurant. Already, the idea of starting her own Mexican restaurant was brewing in her mind, and Sibley took a series of classes in finance and business planning to ready herself for that next step.

In 2000, Sibley opened La Palapa Cocina Mexicana on St. Mark's Place, with menu items that read like a totally different language. "My menu was so wordy because I had to explain what everything was; I even kept a big food dictionary." Her concept was simple: she cooked and served the food she was homesick for. In place of cheesy nachos and burritos that had come to stand in for authentic Mexican fare elsewhere in the city, there were nopales, or cactus paddles; huitlacoche, the funky-tasting fungus that grows on ears of corn; barbecued pork wrapped in banana leaves; braised beef with avocado leaves; and duck seasoned with a painstakingly prepared mole sauce of 26 ingredients. Almost everything, including the Mexican-style cheeses, was made in-house, out of necessity. Whenever relatives from Mexico visited, their suitcases were padded out with chilies, cinnamon, and other spices.

Despite being enveloped by the restaurant industry, Sibley never relinquished her interest in anthropology; over the years she researched deeply into historical Hispanic cuisine, particularly into the convent kitchens of seventeenth-century Mexico. Sibley's devotion to authenticity has been richly rewarded. Fifteen years on, La Palapa is still considered among the best Mexican restaurants in New York City and Sibley among the city's foremost experts on Mexican regional cuisine and culture. In 2009, she published her first cookbook, *Antojitos: Festive and Flavorful Mexican Small Plates*; more recently she was a contributor to the anthology *The Way We Ate: 100 Chefs Celebrate a Century at the American Table*.

Still, Sibley's success, though unequivocal, has not always won the respect it deserves. When answering calls from suppliers wanting to speak with La Palapa's proprietor, the president (since 2013) of the New York Women's Culinary Alliance frequently fields the request "Honey, when does the boss get in?"

What is the most unusual or unexpected ingredient that we will find in your restaurant kitchen?
Japanese rice wine vinegar. I make a vinegar-based salsa with charred chilis serranos, and at home in Mexico I would use homemade banana or pineapple vinegar. In adapting the dish for the restaurant I could not find mild and slightly fruity vinegar. Surprisingly, after trying many combinations the rice wine vinegar was perfect.

What industry issue do you feel most strongly about, and how would you change it if you could?
I think that there is great inequality in restaurant kitchens. Luckily in New York there is some mobility, but it seems that the cooks who do most of the great work do not get the recognition they deserve.

What request(s) from diners irks you the most?
I really believe that we should make our guests happy and grant nearly any request. That being said, I find it very disheartening when people complain that we do not serve chips and salsa!

SOPES CON CABRITO EN ADOBO DE TRES CHILES
(SOPES WITH BRAISED GOAT SHANKS IN THREE-CHILIES ADOBO)

SERVES 6–8

Sopes are handmade grilled corn masa tortillas that are typically found on the streets and in markets throughout Mexico. Usually oval with a pinched rim like a small tart, they make ideal vehicles for spiced meats or salsas. An adobo is basically a chili marinade, rub, or salsa. It is used to season meats for braising and grilling and can also be served as a salsa. Here the smoky, bright guajillo, the sweet chili ancho, and the spicy chili de arbol create a pungent marinade to stand up against rich goat meat.

For the Adobo de Tres Chiles
10 dried guajillo chilies, stemmed, seeded, and wiped clean
2 dried ancho chilies, stemmed, seeded, and wiped clean
4 dried de arbol chilies, stemmed, seeded, and wiped clean
1 tablespoon white vinegar
½ medium white onion, chopped
6 garlic cloves, peeled
½ teaspoon ground cumin
1 teaspoon kosher salt

For the goat meat
6 avocado leaves, fresh or dried
4 (1–1¼-pound) goat shanks
1 medium onion, sliced, about 1 cup
1½ cups water
kosher salt, as needed

For the sopes
3¾ cups powdered masa harina
1½ teaspoons salt
3 cups plus 6 tablespoons warm water
canola oil, as needed

Make the adobo. Heat a large, dry cast-iron skillet or griddle over medium heat.

When hot, toast the guajillo chilies in the pan until they become aromatic and flexible—about 30 seconds to 1 minute. They burn very quickly, so keep an eye on them. Transfer the chilies to a nonreactive bowl. Repeat the process with the ancho and the de arbol chilies. Pour over enough boiling water to cover the chilies and leave them to soak for about 20 minutes until they soften. Transfer the chilies to a blender, reserving the soaking water. Pulse until the chilies are liquefied into a smooth paste. Add the vinegar, onion, garlic, cumin, and salt to the chili purée, and pulse until the mixture is blended and smooth, adding the reserved water as necessary to create a paste. Transfer to a bowl and set aside. The adobo can be stored, covered, in the refrigerator for 1 week or frozen.

Prepare the goat meat. Preheat the oven to 350°F. Heat a large, dry cast-iron skillet or griddle over medium heat. When hot, toast the avocado leaves in the pan until they become aromatic—about 30 seconds. Set aside.

Rinse the goat shanks, pat dry with paper towels, then salt the meat all over. Rub the adobo marinade over the goat shanks and place them in a large Dutch oven, with the meat side down and the bone side up. They should fill most of the bottom of the pan without crowding. Place the avocado leaves, onion slices, and water at the bottom of the pot around the meat of the shanks. Cover the pot and place it in the oven. Allow the meat to braise for about 3 hours or until it is falling off the bone.

When cooked, let the goat cool slightly, then remove the meat from the bones and chop it coarsely. Discard the bones as well as very fatty pieces and tendons. Transfer the meat to a bowl, cover, and set aside. Reserve the braising adobo liquid and onions to serve with the sopes. Discard the (inedible) avocado leaves.

Make the masa dough for the sopes. In a large mixing bowl, stir together the masa harina and salt. Slowly add the water and, as you do, work the masa into a dough with your hands. Knead the dough for 3–5 minutes or until it is moist and smooth but not sticky. If the dough seems too dry, moisten your hands with water and knead some more. If it seems too wet, add a little more masa harina, no more than 1 tablespoon at a time. You want a moist, smooth dough. The dough may be used immediately or rested for up to 2 hours covered with a damp cloth or plastic wrap so it does not dry out.

When ready to form and cook the sopes, divide the masa dough into 18 equal-size balls. Shape the balls into oval discs about 2 x 3 inches and ½-inch thick. Heat a dry griddle or cast-iron pan over medium-high heat, and when hot cook each disc for about 2 minutes on each side. Do not move the sopes until a crust forms on the outside; otherwise they will stick to the pan and break when you try to flip them. It is best to work with about 3 sopes at a time in the pan.

As you remove the discs from the pan, and while they are still warm, pinch all the way around the edges, forming a rim about ½-inch high. The steam inside the sopes may be very hot, so be careful. Transfer them to a plate. The sopes can be made ahead of time up until this point, cooled, and covered with plastic wrap until ready to serve.

If necessary, reheat the goat meat in a 350°F oven in a baking dish covered with a lid or with foil. Place the adobo braising liquid in a small saucepan and heat through on the stove.

Meanwhile, crisp up the sopes in a skillet in a small amount of oil, frying them gently for about 1 minute on each side, or until slightly crisp and with the undersides lightly golden. Do not brown the sopes, as they will be too hard. With a slotted spoon, remove from the oil and place on paper towels to drain.

When ready to serve, fill each of the sopes with a spoonful of the goat meat and drizzle over a little of the adobo braising liquid. Offer the remaining adobo liquid alongside for your guests to help themselves. Serve immediately.

QUESO FUNDIDO CON HUITLACOCHE Y LANGOSTA
(BAKED CHEESE WITH HUITLACOCHE AND LOBSTER)

SERVES 6

This dish brings together several parts of Mexico: lobster from the Pacific, huitlacoche (a highly prized, naturally occurring corn fungus) from the central Sierras, and queso Chihuahua from the northern state of that name, where it was first produced by Mennonite settlers. The method for preparing the lobster tails is very simple and the cooking time brief, as the tails will continue to cook as they bake with the tangy cheese.

For the lobster
3 small lobster tails about 6 ounces each, or 2 large ones (smaller lobsters will be more tender and flavorful), fresh or frozen
3 cups water

For the huitlacoche
1½ cups fresh huitlacoche kernels, or 2 cobs with huitlacoche (alternatively you can substitute canned, preserved huitlacoche)
3 tablespoons corn oil
¼ cup diced onion, preferably a sweet variety such as Vidalia
1 clove garlic, chopped
1 serrano chili, deseeded and finely chopped
2 tablespoons chopped fresh or dried epazote leaves
salt, as needed

To assemble
2 tablespoons corn oil
½ cup Crema Mexicana (see recipe below, page 98)
3 cups grated queso Chihuahua or other melting cheese

To serve
flour tortillas
Salsa Verde (see recipe below, page 98)

Poach the lobsters. If you are using frozen tails, first thaw them for 24 hours in a covered nonreactive bowl in your refrigerator. Bring the tails up to room temperature by setting on your kitchen counter for about 20 minutes.

Fill a 2-quart stockpot with the 3 cups of water and bring to a low boil over medium heat. Add the tails to the water and reduce to a simmer. Poach the lobster tails for about 6 minutes until the shells turn red and the steam smells deliciously of lobster. Remove the lobster tails from the stockpot and allow them to cool for about 5 minutes. Wrap the tails in plastic wrap and set aside.

Prepare the huitlacoche. If using whole cobs with the huitlacoche still attached, gently remove the husk, rinse the cobs under cold water, then pat dry with a paper towel. Standing the corn on its flat end, gently cut off the kernels with a serrated knife, starting at the top and using a gentle sawing motion to remove them as close to the cob as possible. This will keep most of the kernels intact while cooking. Also cut off any regular corn kernels and add to the huitlacoche. If using canned huitlacoche, drain off the liquid, gently squeezing out the excess, and discard it.

In a large sauté pan set over medium heat, warm the corn oil and then add the onion, garlic, and serrano chili. Once the onion looks transparent, add the huitlacoche to the pan and continue to cook, stirring gently with a spatula. Reduce the heat to medium-low and sauté until the huitlacoche is tender when pressed, about 5 minutes. Some of the kernels will release a delicious black juice. If the huitlacoche is very watery, allow some of the juices to cook off for about 3 more minutes. Stir in the epazote leaves and salt and remove from the heat. Set aside.

Remove the lobster meat from the shells and cut it into 1-inch pieces.

To assemble the queso fundido you will need a 10-inch cast-iron pan or 6 ramekins, about 4-inches in diameter; I prefer to make one large serving for guests to share.

Preheat the oven to 375°F. Oil the bottom of the pan or ramekins with a small amount of the corn oil, using a paper towel. Over it spread a layer, about ¼-inch thick, of Crema Mexicana. Add about 1½ cups of lobster tail meat evenly over the crema. Next add the huitlacoche mixture. Sprinkle the cheese over this in a layer about ½-inch thick, covering the huitlacoche and lobster mixture completely. Bake for about 15 minutes or until the cheese is bubbling and beginning to brown slightly. Serve immediately with warm flour tortillas and salsa verde.

Note
With canned or frozen huitlacoche the covering of the kernels becomes very soft and your huitlacoche will ➤

be very watery. It will still taste delicious but the texture imparted by fresh, whole kernels will be lost.

Crema Mexicana (makes 1½ cups)
½ cup sour cream
1 cup heavy cream
1 teaspoon salt

Mix the sour cream, heavy cream, and salt in a nonreactive bowl. Cover and refrigerate for at least 8 hours—or up to 1 week.

Salsa Verde (makes 2 cups)
6 tomatillos, roughly chopped
¼ cup chopped sweet onion
2 serrano chilies
½ cup fresh cilantro leaves, rinsed and patted dry
1 teaspoon kosher salt, plus more as needed

Place the tomatillos, onion, serrano chilies, cilantro, and salt in a blender. Pulse until the mixture is a thick liquid. Taste to check the salt and adjust as needed, bearing in mind that kosher salt takes some time to dissolve. Pour into a nonreactive bowl and use immediately, or cover and refrigerate for up to 5 days.

PATO CON SALSA BORRACHA DE CHABACANO Y PASILLA
(GRILLED DUCK WITH RUSTIC "DRUNKEN" SALSA OF ROASTED APRICOTS AND PASILLA CHILIES)

SERVES 6

This recipe is based on one that was a favorite of Emilio "El Indio" Fernández, a talented director of the golden age of Mexican cinema in the 1940s and 1950s. Said to have been the model for the Oscar statuette, he was a great artist but also a great eater, and he was known for his dinner parties in Coyoacán, a neighborhood in Mexico City.

The original recipe uses peaches. Small and hard, Mexican peaches have an intense, almost wild flavor. Because American peaches are generally too juicy for this recipe, I've substituted apricots (chabacanos) for my version. "Borracha" refers to the pulque or beer added to the sauce.

For the Salsa Borracha
5 pasilla chilies, stemmed, seeded, and wiped clean
1 cup boiling water
3 whole fresh apricots or small, firm peaches
2 whole tomatillos
1 medium white onion, peeled and cut into quarters
3 garlic cloves, peeled
⅓ cup pulque or beer, such as Tecate
2 teaspoons (or less) kosher salt, as needed
½ cup fresh cilantro leaves, finely chopped (optional)

For the duck
6 (8-ounce) Peking duck breasts
½ cup olive oil
salt and freshly ground pepper, as needed

To serve
warm corn tortillas

Make the Salsa Borracha. Heat a dry large cast-iron skillet or griddle over medium heat. When the pan is hot, toast the chilies in it until they become aromatic and flexible, about 30 seconds to 1 minute. They burn very quickly, so keep an eye on them.

Transfer the chilies to a nonreactive bowl and pour the cup of boiling water over them. Leave them to soak for about 20 minutes until they soften. Using the same cast-iron pan, turn the heat back up to medium and place the apricots, tomatillos, onion, and garlic in it; roast them until slightly charred, turning them with tongs as needed so they char on all sides evenly. Once lightly browned, remove and set aside on a plate. Usually the onion and garlic will be ready first. The skin on the apricots and tomatillos will bubble slightly and may come off in places.

Transfer the chilies to a blender, reserving the soaking liquid. Add the pulque or beer to the blender and pulse until the chilies are liquefied to a smooth paste, adding some of the soaking liquid, if necessary. Next, add the apricots, tomatillos, onion, and garlic to the purée and pulse until the mixture is blended but still slightly chunky. Turn out into a nonreactive bowl and add salt to taste and the cilantro, if using.

Allow the salsa to rest for about 30 minutes and then taste and adjust the salt again. Serve immediately or store covered in the refrigerator for up to 1 week. This salsa is best at room temperature.

To prepare the duck, first rinse the duck breasts under cool tap water and pat dry with a paper towel. Using a sharp knife, remove some of the fatty skin from the side edges of each breast, leaving a central 2-inch-wide strip of skin along the length. This will keep the meat from becoming dry when cooked. Score this remaining skin with diagonal slits.

Season both sides of the duck breast with salt and pepper, then rub all over with the olive oil. Using a grill pan preheated over medium-high heat, cook the duck breasts skin-side down for 2–3 minutes to sear and brown the skin. Flip and sear on the flesh side for an additional 3 minutes. Lower the heat to medium and continue to cook until medium-rare or when a digital thermometer reads 135°F when inserted into the center of each breast (they will continue to cook as they rest). Allow the duck to rest for 5–10 minutes, then slice diagonally and against the grain into ½-inch-thick slices.

Serve the duck with a generous covering of the Salsa Borracha and warm corn tortillas for wrapping. Saffron rice and sautéed Swiss chard would also make delicious accompaniments. Any leftover salsa can be stored in the refrigerator for up to 1 week.

TACOS DE HUACHINANGO CON SALSA XNIPEC
(RED SNAPPER TACOS WITH ADOBO AND RED ONION HABAÑERO SALSA)

SERVES 6

In Yucatán, most dishes are basically quite mild because they are served with very fiery salsas on the side. The name Xnipec is derived from the Mayan for "dog's nose"—possibly evoking a dog's wet muzzle and the sinus-clearing effect of the habañero chili. The red onion colors this salsa a beautiful magenta, and the lime juice it soaks in becomes infused with the habañero chili. This particular adobo, or marinade, also comes from Yucatán. The red snapper fillets are first coated in the red paste then baked in the oven.

For the Xnipec salsa
1 cup finely diced red onion
1 habañero chili, seeded (using gloves) and finely diced
¼ cup freshly squeezed lime juice
2 tablespoons grapefruit juice
2 tablespoons orange juice
1 teaspoon salt

Optional additions to the salsa
½ cup diced slightly under-ripe avocado
½ cup diced mango
½ cup diced white peach
½ cup diced firm papaya

For the Achiote Adobo
2 tablespoons annatto seeds
½ cup water
2 dried ancho chilies, stemmed, deseeded, and wiped clean
1 teaspoon freshly ground allspice
2 teaspoons freshly ground black pepper
1 tablespoon kosher salt

1 tablespoon dried Mexican oregano
2 cloves garlic, peeled
½ white onion, thickly sliced
1 tablespoon apple cider vinegar
½ cup freshly squeezed orange juice
¼ cup freshly squeezed lemon juice

For the fish
3 (8-ounce) boneless red snapper fillets
¼ cup corn oil
salt, as needed

To serve
warm corn tortillas

Make the salsa. Place the onion, habañero chili, citrus juices, and salt in a nonreactive bowl; mix thoroughly, then allow to macerate in the refrigerator for an hour. Add one or more of the optional ingredients and allow to chill for another 30 minutes. The basic Xnipec without the addition of fruits will keep for 1 week, well covered, in the refrigerator. After adding the fruit, the salsa should be eaten within 1 day.

Make the Achiote Adobo. Put the annatto seeds and water in a small saucepan and place over high heat. Bring to a boil, cover, and reduce to a gentle simmer. Cook for 30 minutes. Remove from the heat and let steep for 20 minutes, or until the seeds are softened.

Meanwhile, toast the ancho chilies in a preheated cast-iron pan until they become aromatic and flexible, about 30 seconds to 1 minute. They burn very quickly, so keep an

eye on them. Transfer the chilies to a nonreactive bowl. Cover with water and leave to soak for about 20 minutes or until softened.

Drain the annatto seeds and ancho chilies, discarding the liquid, and transfer to a blender or food processor along with the remaining adobo ingredients. Blend until smooth. The adobo will keep, tightly covered, for up to 5 days in the refrigerator.

When ready to cook the fish, rinse the red snapper fillets, pat dry with paper towels, and season lightly all over with salt. Preheat the oven to 350°F.

Set a large heavy-bottomed sauté pan over medium heat and add 2 tablespoons of the corn oil. When very hot, place the red snapper fillets in the pan skin-side down and cook until the skin is golden brown, about 1 minute, then flip and cook until the flesh side is just seared but not cooked through. Cook in batches if necessary, as the fillets will steam instead of sear if the pan is overcrowded. Transfer the seared fish to a sheet pan lined with parchment paper. Spoon over some of the Achiote marinade to cover the fish and place the pan in the oven. Bake for 8–10 minutes or until the fish is cooked through.

Flake the cooked snapper meat off the skin and spoon the fish into warm corn tortillas. Serve the tacos with the Xnipec salsa on the side.

IVY STARK

vy Stark, executive chef of Dos Caminos, tasted her first jalapeño chili pepper on a Mexicana flight to the beach resort city of Puerta Vallarta when she was five. Although this fiery bite might have turned many youngsters off, for Stark it was the beginning of a love affair with the myriad flavors and tastes of Mexican food. Growing up in Colorado, with its large Hispanic population, there were ample opportunities to enjoy south-of-the-border cuisine closer to home. To this day, she vividly recalls the frequent trips to Casa Bonita, her family's favorite Mexican eating place in Denver. While studying history at the University of California, Los Angeles (UCLA), Stark experienced a more authentic version of Latino cuisine by way of a wonderful Mexican home cook, Alegría, the mother of her then boyfriend. Addicted to her prodigious and comforting repasts, Stark fixed herself at the stove by Alegría's side to learn all she could.

Even today, as Stark oversees the kitchens of an upscale Mexican restaurant chain with four locations in Manhattan, one in Atlantic City, New Jersey, and one in Florida, her recipes are informed by Alegría's deft seasoning. With Dos Caminos' high-energy atmosphere and reputation for throwing a great party, Stark's menu has much to compete with (there are more than 100 varieties of tequila offered). No matter—she embraces the challenge, and her food trumps the margaritas any day of the week.

Since she joined the Dos Caminos empire in 2003, Stark's ethos has been unwavering: to present diners with genuine Mexican cuisine made from the freshest, most authentic ingredients. To this end, the tortillas are made from scratch every day at every location, and each order of guacamole is prepared tableside. What has evolved, however, is the degree of sophistication of Stark's creations. Barbecued goat enchiladas are offered alongside the more usual beef and chicken options. The guacamole comes with the choice of adding chapulines (Oaxacan grasshoppers). The shrimp quesadilla is accompanied by smoked wild mushrooms. Of course, while familiar ingredients still feature strongly on her menu, informed by her annual research trips to the lesser-traveled regions of Mexico, Stark treats her patrons to unexpected preparations such as the Yucatan-style roast pork and the Tecate battered rock shrimp.

Stark arrived at her present position by a circuitous route. After UCLA she enrolled at the Peter Kump's New York Cooking School (now the Institute of Culinary Education) in New York City. Post graduation, she headed back westward, landing in Santa Monica, California. Despite her recently acquired training in classic French cuisine, she took on a job at the Border Grill under the formidably talented doyennes of modern Mexican cuisine Mary Sue Milliken and Susan Feniger. Two years later, New York beckoned once more. There, Stark first established a reputation outside the field of Mexican cooking, working at some of the city's top kitchens, including the opulent Sign of the Dove. Still, she couldn't escape the allure of Latin flavors; and in between stints at NYC hotspots Cena and Match Uptown, she opened Ciudad for Milliken and Feniger in Los Angeles. In an unexpected turn, Stark then took on a role as beverage director and sommelier at Manhattan's Brasserie 8½ before returning to her true calling as chef. Now firmly planted in New York, she continued to seek out her culinary home, taking on positions at Zocalo, Amalia, and Rosa Mexicano. Finally, the folks at Dos Caminos came knocking, and the itinerant chef settled down.

What dish have you created that you are most proud of?
Sautéed calamari with roasted garlic and piquillo peppers and grilled country bread.

What's the secret of making a great guacamole?
Creating a paste in the molcajete (mortar) with the chilies and onions before adding the avocado.

What's in your fridge at home?
Milk, wine, hummus, cheese, bacon, eggs, and hot sauces.

What's your favorite place to order take-out and what do you order?
Sushi from Nanatori—Hamachi Don

Who or what has most influenced your cooking?
The Mexican culture.

Do you have a cookbook that you keep going back to time and time again?
Culinary Artistry by Andrew Dornenburg and Karen Page.

What's your favorite thing to do on your day off?
Run, hang out with my dogs, eat out with my friends.

What moment—good or bad—in your professional career will you never forget?
Being nominated for the Women Chefs & Restaurateurs' Golden Whisk Award.

CHAYOTE SALAD WITH HIBISCUS VINAIGRETTE

SERVES 4

A quick, simple, and elegant salad made from an exotic but inexpensive squash native to Mexico. With its crisp, apple-like crunch, the mild-flavored chayote adds great texture to this appetizer. And its kaleidoscope of color makes the dish a beauty on the plate.

1 large chayote, peeled and thinly sliced lengthwise
4 radishes, thinly sliced into coins
8 tablespoons Hibiscus Flower Vinaigrette (see recipe below)
1 cup packed baby spinach leaves
½ avocado, stoned, peeled, and thinly sliced
2 teaspoons toasted chopped peanuts
1 ounce crumbled queso fresco

In a medium bowl, gently toss the chayote and the radish slices with 6 tablespoons of the vinaigrette. Place the baby spinach leaves in a salad bowl and drizzle the leaves with more of the remaining dressing, to taste. Top with the dressed chayote and radishes, then garnish with the sliced avocado, toasted peanuts, and queso fresco. Serve immediately.

Hibiscus Flower Vinaigrette

2 tablespoons rice vinegar
2 tablespoons fresh lime juice
1 garlic clove, peeled
2 teaspoons sugar, plus more as needed
1 teaspoon kosher salt, plus more as needed
½ teaspoon freshly ground black pepper, plus more as needed
½ cup vegetable oil
½ cup olive oil
¾ cup dried hibiscus flowers

In a blender, combine the vinegar, lime juice, garlic, sugar, salt, and pepper.

Blend on low speed until smooth. Combine the oils in a measuring pitcher and pour into the blender in a thin stream, with the motor running, until the mixture is emulsified. With the blender turned off, add the hibiscus flowers and allow to soften in the liquid for a couple of minutes, then blend until roughly chopped. Adjust the sugar, salt, and pepper to taste. This dressing can be stored in the refrigerator in an airtight container for up to 4 days.

ALBÓNDIGAS IN CHIPOTLE SALSA

SERVES 6–8

These Albóndigas (Mexican meatballs) are light as air, and they are especially delicious paired with smoky, spicy chipotle chili sauce.

For the meatballs
½ cup chicken stock
1 small onion, roughly chopped
5 garlic cloves, roughly chopped
½ bunch of flat-leaf parsley (about 1½ ounces), roughly chopped, plus extra to garnish
½ pound ground beef
½ pound ground pork
½ pound ground veal
2 tablespoons bread crumbs
2 whole eggs plus 1 yolk, lightly beaten
½ cup grated cotija cheese (an aged Mexican cheese; pecorino romano may be substituted), plus extra to garnish
1–2 tablespoons chili powder, depending on the heat level of your chosen chili powder
½ tablespoon cumin seeds, toasted and ground
½ teaspoon crushed red pepper flakes
½ tablespoon salt
2–4 tablespoons olive oil, for cooking

For the chipotle sauce
1 medium onion
4 garlic cloves
1 (28-ounce) can peeled tomatoes
2 canned chipotle chilis in adobo sauce
1 bay leaf
1 teaspoon cumin seeds, toasted and ground

1 teaspoon crushed, dried epazote (a leafy Mexican herb; basil may be substituted)
1 teaspoon dried oregano
1 teaspoon freshly ground cinnamon
⅛ teaspoon freshly ground allspice
½ teaspoon freshly ground black pepper
¼ cup olive oil, plus more for cooking
salt, to taste

To garnish
¼ cup grated cojita cheese
2–3 tablespoons chopped fresh flat-leaf parsley

To make the meatballs, first place the chicken stock, onion, garlic, and parsley in a blender and purée to form a paste. Set aside.

Place the three meats, the bread crumbs, eggs, cheese, chili powder, cumin, red pepper flakes, and salt in a large bowl. Add the puréed mixture and mix gently until just combined. Form the mixture into golf-ball-size meatballs and arrange on a tray. Refrigerate the meatballs for at least 30 minutes to firm up.

Meanwhile, cook the onion and garlic for the chipotle salsa. Preheat the broiler. Place the onion on a baking sheet lined with foil and broil for 15–20 minutes until somewhat softened. Add the garlic cloves to the baking sheet, flip over the onion, and continue to cook for another 15–20 minutes until the onion and garlic are both very soft. Remove from the oven and leave to cool slightly.

For the chipotle salsa, combine all the ingredients in a blender, and purée until smooth. Heat 1 tablespoon olive oil in a large saucepan over medium heat, add the salsa, and simmer for 20 minutes. Taste and adjust the seasoning with salt.

To finish the dish, first brown the meatballs. Heat 2 tablespoons olive oil in a large casserole pot over medium-high heat. When hot, add the meatballs and brown evenly on all sides. Cook the meatballs in batches if necessary, adding more oil as needed.

Return all the meatballs to the casserole, add the chipotle salsa, and bring to a simmer. Cook gently, partially covered, until the meatballs are completely cooked through, about 15 minutes.

Serve hot, garnished with grated cotija cheese and chopped fresh parsley. The dish can also be served over rice or pasta to make a hearty entrée.

BUTTERNUT SQUASH ENCHILADAS WITH BABY SPINACH AND GUAJILLO SALSA

MAKES 6 ENCHILADAS

A nontraditional take on a Mexican favorite, these hearty vegetarian enchiladas bathed in a bright red and spicy guajillo chili salsa will satisfy meat eaters too.

For the butternut squash
½ cup olive oil
1 tablespoon chipotle chili powder
2 teaspoons ground cumin
2 teaspoons garlic powder
2 sprigs of fresh thyme, chopped
2 sprigs of fresh oregano, chopped
1 tablespoon brown sugar
1 large or 2 small butternut squash (about 3 pounds total weight), peeled, deseeded, and cut into 1-inch cubes; or 2½ pounds already peeled, deseeded, and cubed squash
salt and freshly ground black pepper, as needed

For the sautéed spinach
1 tablespoon olive oil
2 cloves of garlic, minced
6 ounces fresh baby spinach
salt, as needed

To assemble
2 cups guajillo salsa, reheated if cold (see recipe below)
vegetable oil, as needed
1 dozen 6-inch blue corn tortillas
3 cups shredded cheese blend

To garnish
¼ cup matchstick-cut radishes
¼–⅓ cup shredded lettuce
2–4 tablespoons sour cream

Equipment
2 rimmed 18- x 13-inch baking sheets

Preheat the oven to 400°F.

Prepare the butternut squash filling. Mix the olive oil, chili powder, cumin, garlic, thyme, oregano, and sugar in a small bowl, then add salt and pepper to taste.

Place the squash in a large roasting pan and pour the oil and spice mixture over it. Bake for 40–50 minutes until tender and browned. Remove from the oven and mash the squash cubes with a fork, leaving some chunks behind. Transfer to a bowl and set aside.

Meanwhile, cook the spinach. Add the olive oil to a medium skillet set on medium heat. When the oil shimmers, add the garlic and sauté for a minute until translucent but not browned; be careful not to burn it. Throw in the spinach and sauté until wilted. Remove from the heat, season with salt to taste, and set aside.

When ready to assemble the dish, pour the warm guajillo salsa into a shallow bowl (reheat first, if necessary), and lightly grease both baking sheets with the vegetable oil. Assemble each enchilada completely before moving on to the next. (Each baking sheet will hold 3 enchiladas.) Dip a tortilla in the salsa to coat it completely and place it on the sheet. Add about ½ cup of the squash mixture to the center of the tortilla, then a spoonful of the spinach; spread these out evenly. Add a few teaspoons of the shredded cheese. Dip another tortilla in the salsa and place it on top. Sprinkle the tortilla with cheese to cover completely.

Place the baking sheets on two oven shelves and bake the enchiladas for 15–20 minutes until the cheese is bubbly and browned in spots, swapping the baking sheets' positions halfway through the cooking time.

Serve the enchiladas garnished with matchstick-cut radishes, shredded lettuce, and a dollop of sour cream.

Guajillo Salsa
12 garlic cloves, with skins left on
32 large dried guajillo chilies
½ tablespoon dried Mexican oregano
½ teaspoon whole black peppercorns
½ teaspoon whole cumin seeds
4 cups chicken stock
3 tablespoons vegetable oil, or a mixture of canola and olive oil
1½ tablespoons sugar, or to taste
salt, to taste

Equipment
A chinois (optional)

Place a griddle or large cast-iron skillet over medium heat. When hot, toast the garlic, turning occasionally, until blackened in spots and softened, about 15 minutes. Cool and roughly chop.

While the garlic is toasting, break the stems off the chilies, tear the

chilies open, and remove and discard the seeds. After the garlic is done, toast the chilies, in batches, on the hot griddle until fragrant, about 20 seconds per side. Transfer to a bowl, cover with hot water, and leave to rehydrate for 30 minutes, stirring regularly to ensure even soaking. Drain and discard the water.

Place the oregano, peppercorns, and cumin seeds in a spice grinder or mortar and pulverize until ground. Transfer to a blender along with the drained chilies, toasted garlic, and ⅔ cup of the chicken stock. Purée until you have a smooth consistency, scraping down the sides of the blender and stirring the mixture every few seconds.

Use a rubber spatula to push the purée through a fine sieve or chinois into a bowl, discarding the remaining solids. Stir in up to 1 more cup of the chicken stock if the purée is too thick to go through the sieve. Taste, and season with salt.

Heat the oil in a medium-size pot or saucepan over medium-high heat. When hot enough so that a drop of the purée will sizzle sharply on the surface, add the purée to the pot. Cook, stirring constantly, until the mixture reduces, thickens, and darkens, about 8–12 minutes, depending on how much stock you added to the purée.

Taste the purée; it is done once the harsh chili flavor has lessened. Stir in the remaining stock, partially cover the pot, and simmer, stirring occasionally, for about 30 minutes. Taste and season with salt and sugar. The salsa can be made ahead and will keep, covered, in the refrigerator for up to 1 week.

GRILLED SALMON WITH AVOCADO PIPIAN, BLACK BEAN PICO DE GALLO, AND OYSTER MUSHROOMS

SERVES 6

Pipian is a classic Mexican sauce made with pumpkin seeds, and the addition of avocado here adds a richness that complements the salmon beautifully. A plumped up version of the traditional pico de gallo—with black beans and roasted corn joining the classic tomato, red onion, and cilantro salsa—brings a refreshing element to the plate.

For the avocado pipian
½ cup raw pumpkin seeds
1 clove garlic, peeled and roughly chopped
zest and juice of 1 lime
½ ripe avocado, stoned and peeled
¼ cup water
3 tablespoons extra-virgin olive oil
½ cup fresh cilantro leaves, chopped
salt and freshly ground black pepper, as needed

For the black bean pico de gallo
2 cups cooked and drained black beans
1 cup grilled or toasted corn kernels
3 medium tomatoes, diced
½ cup diced red onion
½ cup chopped scallion greens
½ cup chopped fresh cilantro leaves
2 tablespoons minced jalapeño pepper
2 tablespoons fresh lime juice
1 tablespoon ancho chili powder
1 tablespoon extra-virgin olive oil
½ teaspoon salt

For the grilled oyster mushrooms
3 tablespoons fresh orange juice
1½ tablespoons fresh lemon juice
1 tablespoon red wine vinegar
½ cup olive oil
2 pounds large oyster mushrooms, stems trimmed and torn into large pieces
½ teaspoon coarse sea salt

For the salmon
6 (6–7-ounce) salmon fillets
salt and freshly ground black pepper, as needed

To make the avocado pipian, place all the ingredients in a blender or food processor and blend until smooth, scraping down the sides if necessary. The pipian should be the consistency of a thick salad dressing. If it is too thick, add cold water, one tablespoon at a time, while blending, until the desired consistency is reached. Season to taste with salt and pepper, then pour into a bowl and set aside.

Now prepare the pico de gallo by combining all the ingredients in a bowl. Taste and adjust the seasoning. Set aside.

Preheat the grill to medium-high.

For the grilled oyster mushrooms, first whisk together the orange juice, lemon juice, vinegar, and oil in a small bowl to make a vinaigrette. Transfer two-thirds of the vinaigrette to a large bowl (reserving the rest), add the mushrooms, and toss well. Leave to marinate for 15 minutes.

Grill the mushrooms on an oiled grill sheet set on the preheated grill, turning frequently, until golden brown, about 5 minutes. Immediately transfer to the bowl with the reserved vinaigrette. Sprinkle the sea salt over the mushrooms and toss well.

Season the salmon fillets on both sides with salt and pepper. Grill over medium-high heat until just opaque in the center, about 4 minutes per side. Transfer to a platter and keep warm.

To serve, spoon a little avocado pipian onto 6 dinner plates. Place a piece of salmon in the center of each plate and top with the black bean pico de gallo. Finally, arrange the grilled oyster mushrooms alongside the salmon.

ASIAN FUSION

LEAH COHEN 115

Grilled Pork Jowl and Watermelon Salad · Curry Lamb Ribs with Pickled Beets, Yogurt, and Wholewheat Roti · Whole Fried Fish with Hot and Sour Broth · Quail Adobo

SOHUI KIM 125

Pork and Shrimp Dumplings with Water Chestnuts and Chives · Salt-broiled Mackerel with Daikon and Frisée Salad · Soy-braised Short Ribs with Chestnuts and Kimchi · Korean-style Bouillabaisse

SAWAKO OKOCHI 135

Chilled Corn Soup with Ikura, Crème Fraîche, and Potato Chips · Berkshire Pork Belly with Heirloom Tomatoes and Udon · Smoked Duck 'n' Soba · Tuna Tataki with Black Tahini

ANN REDDING 145

Chu Chee Scallops with Red Curry and Kaffir Lime Leaves · Plaa Muk Tod Kamin (Baby Squid with Fresh Turmeric and Garlic) · Massaman Curry with Wild Boar and Green Peppercorns · Khao Gun Jiin (Jasmine Rice with Pork, Blood, and Herbs Steamed in Banana Leaves)

LEAH COHEN

orn in New York of mixed Filipino and Russian-Romanian-Jewish parentage, Leah Cohen already had a wealth of culinary resources at her disposal when she conceived the idea of opening her first restaurant. Her initial inclination was to incorporate none of the culinary influences of her heritage, but not without good reason.

Nearing the end of a 15-month-long tour of Southeast Asia in 2010, Cohen decided that her restaurant would instead focus solely on Thai cuisine. It was in Thailand that she had spent the most time during this trip and where she had worked in several restaurants, while also hopping across to Vietnam, Cambodia, the Philippines, Bali, and other regional gastronomic hot spots. However, her Filipino mother was horrified that her daughter would neglect her culinary legacy. So Cohen promptly tweaked her menu, opting instead for a pork-heavy, pan-Asian approach centered mostly on Filipino and Thai fare. Recalling the noisy potluck parties of her childhood with her Filipino relatives, she knew she had plenty of family recipes to call upon.

Indeed, the sisig, made the traditional way, with pig's head chopped and sautéed with ginger, chilies, and spices; the modern variant of crispy pata, consisting of braised, air-dried, then deep-fried pork shank; and the addictive banana fritters, or turón, served at Cohen's Lower East Side restaurant Pig & Khao constitute some of the best Filipino food in New York City. It has become something of a culinary badge of honor for Cohen that she will put a dish on the menu only if she has studied its making in its country of origin. She has just started serving little-known Burmese dishes following her recent travels to that faraway locale.

As a girl, Cohen had often enjoyed the Jewish food prepared by her paternal grandmother, a home economics teacher, on religious holidays—notably her "killer" matzo ball soup and brisket. Everyday meals, though, were mostly Italian. When Cohen graduated from the Culinary Institute of America (C.I.A.), she had already completed a six-month externship with David Burke, at his (now closed) Park Avenue Café, where the menu featured Mediterranean-style dishes. Feeling most comfortable working with ingredients from that region, she attended Italy's Slow Food program in Le Marche. Then, capping her experience in Italy with a year at the Michelin-starred La Madia in Sicily, she entered a kitchen of men skeptical that a girl could actually cook. She

began her stint peeling shrimp and washing dishes; but quickly proving herself a bona fide chef, she ended it by mastering all aspects of the menu, allowed to make even the fresh pasta—an achievement, indeed, for a novice.

Her father's enticing promise to secure her an apartment in New York City brought her back to the United States (he was motivated by an intense dislike of her Sicilian boyfriend). Back on home turf, she continued her fine-dining experience at Eleven Madison Park. Next she opted for an altogether different beat when she took on a sous-chef role at the fashionable (now closed) neighborhood joint Centro Vinoteca in 2008. While there, the 26-year-old Cohen was recruited for a spot on season five of the Bravo network's *Top Chef* show.

When the show aired, Cohen was already planning her trip to Asia, excited at the prospect of immersing herself in a distinctly different genre of cooking techniques and flavor profiles that she had merely sampled growing up. She hated the competitive cooking of *Top Chef*, but the popular series offered a showcase for her skills and the limelight required to open a successful restaurant in Manhattan. She ran with the opportunity, opening Pig & Khao in 2012, with her father as an investor. The rest, as they say, is history.

What's the most unexpected, even embarrassing ingredient that's a regular part of your kitchen must-haves?
Mushroom powder.

What kitchen pet peeve is bound to get you really riled up?
People who combine salt and pepper to make it "easier and faster" to season food.

Which chef or food figure, famous or not-so-famous, do you most admire?
Anita Lo. She is a badass in the kitchen, and her food is amazing! I also love that she is actually in her kitchen on most nights.

What's in your fridge at home?
A bottle of sriracha, Laughing Cow French onion cheese, water, and beer.

What has been your most memorable moment professionally?
Getting a two-star review from the *New York Times*.

Is there a food that no matter how hard you've tried to like it, you just can't stand it?
Calf liver—I just can't get down with it.

GRILLED PORK JOWL AND WATERMELON SALAD

SERVES 6

This dish was inspired by a street vendor right around the corner from my apartment in Bangkok. I added the watermelon to this salad because I felt that its sweetness makes the dish more balanced and complex.

2½ pounds pork jowl

For the marinade
1½ ounces chopped cilantro root
3 large garlic cloves, roughly chopped
1 teaspoon salt
1½ (14-ounce) cans coconut milk
5 tablespoons fish sauce
2½ tablespoons granulated sugar
½ teaspoon ground white pepper

For the watermelon salad
2 shallots, sliced
¼ cup mint leaves, picked from the stem
¼ cup whole cilantro leaves
cubed flesh of 1 small seedless watermelon
⅓ cup Pig and Khao House Dressing (see recipe below)

To garnish
2–3 tablespoons toasted rice powder (available from Filipino and other Asian grocery stores; or toast raw rice in a skillet until light brown, then grind in a coffee grinder)
¼ cup chicharron (crisp pork rinds, available from Filipino and Latino grocery stores)

Equipment
An immersion circulator or sous vide water oven (optional)

If you have a sous vide water oven or immersion circulator, cook the pork jowl in a vacuum-sealed bag in the water bath for 12 hours at 145°F. When the jowl is cooked, place the bag in a bowl of ice water to cool it down. Alternatively, you can oven-braise the pork jowl submerged in water in a roasting pan, covered tightly with foil, for about 6 hours at 210°F or until fork tender but not mushy.

Make the marinade for the pork. Combine all the ingredients in a small blender or the small bowl of a food processor and process until smooth. Transfer to a large bowl. Once the pork is cool, submerge it in the marinade. Place in the fridge and leave to marinate for at least 3 hours, or overnight.

When ready to assemble the dish, preheat the grill to high. Remove the jowl from the marinade and shake off the excess. When the grill is very hot, grill the pork until slightly charred and heated through, about 3–5 minutes on each side. Remove from the heat, leave to rest for a couple of minutes, then slice thinly.

Combine all the watermelon salad ingredients in a bowl. Mix well, then season with salt to taste. Serve the sliced pork alongside the watermelon salad and garnish with toasted rice powder and chicharron.

Pig and Khao House Dressing
½ red jalapeño chili, roughly chopped
1 small garlic clove, smashed
6 tablespoons lime juice
3½ tablespoons fish sauce
2 tablespoons granulated sugar
3 tablespoons water

Using a pestle and mortar, grind the chili and garlic until you have a paste. Transfer to a medium bowl, then add all the remaining ingredients and stir until the sugar dissolves. Leftover dressing will keep in the refrigerator in an airtight container for up to 1 week.

CURRY LAMB RIBS WITH PICKLED BEETS, YOGURT, AND WHOLEWHEAT ROTI

SERVES 6

These lamb ribs are one of my favorites among the dishes I serve at Pig and Khao. The dish is fun and playful and works especially well with the family-style sharing at the restaurant.

For the lamb ribs
4–6 garlic cloves, peeled
½ (rounded) cup peeled and chopped fresh ginger
3 lamb breasts, cleaned, trimmed, and cut into individual ribs (your butcher can do this; about 6 pounds trimmed weight)
⅓ cup canola oil
salt and freshly ground black pepper, as needed

For the pickled beets and onions
1¼ cups peeled and thinly sliced Spanish onion
1 tablespoon salt
1½ cups red beet, peeled and cut into thin matchsticks (about 5 ounces)
½ cup distilled white vinegar
1 tablespoon granulated sugar

For the wholewheat roti
4 cups wholewheat flour, plus more as needed
1 tablespoon salt
2 cups water
olive oil, to cook

For the spice mix
2 teaspoons whole coriander seeds
1 tablespoon whole cumin seeds
2 small cinnamon sticks
2½ (slightly rounded) tablespoons garam masala
¼ teaspoon salt
pinch of garlic powder
½ teaspoon chili powder

For the yogurt sauce
2 cups plain full-fat Greek yogurt
1½ tablespoons toasted cumin seeds, ground
4 tablespoons fresh lime juice
2 teaspoons minced fresh garlic
salt, as needed

To garnish
1 lime, cut into wedges
¼ cup finely shredded mint

Equipment
A spice grinder
A grill

Preheat the oven to 300°F. Using a pestle and mortar, pound the garlic and ginger with a pinch of salt until a paste forms, or use a small blender. Place the lamb ribs in a shallow bowl and season all over with salt and pepper. Spoon the garlic and ginger paste on top and rub all over the ribs with your hands. Completely wrap the ribs in aluminum foil to form a well-sealed parcel, then place in a roasting pan and cook for approximately 3 hours or until fork tender. Remove from the oven, open up the parcel, and leave the ribs to cool in their juices.

Meanwhile make the pickles. Place the sliced onions in a bowl with the salt and toss. Let sit for 30 minutes for the onions to release their liquid. Using your hands, squeeze out as much of the juice from the onion as possible, then dry with paper towels. Combine the salted onions with the rest of the ingredients in a small bowl, mix well, and set aside.

Next prepare the roti dough. Combine the flour and salt in the bowl of a stand mixer fitted with a dough hook attachment. Turn the machine on to a slow setting and slowly pour in the water. Once all the water is incorporated, keep mixing the dough until it forms a ball. (Alternatively, you can do this by hand.) Transfer the dough to a clean surface and knead for 3–5 minutes until smooth and elastic, flouring your hands and the surface as necessary. Wrap the dough in plastic and let it rest for at least 30 minutes.

Make the spice mix for the ribs. In a small sauté pan toast the coriander seeds, cumin seeds, and cinnamon sticks over medium-low heat, stirring, until the spices are fragrant. Remove from the heat. When the spices are cool, combine with the garam masala, salt, garlic powder, and chili powder. Tip the mixture into a spice grinder and grind to a fine powder.

For the yogurt sauce, place all the ingredients together in a small bowl and whisk until thoroughly combined. Cover with plastic wrap and refrigerate until ready to use. **➤**

When ready to grill the lamb, pour the canola oil over the cooled ribs and rub all over with your hands. Season the ribs with 4–6 tablespoons of the spice mix, depending on your taste. Any leftover spice mix will keep in an airtight container indefinitely.

Light the grill. While waiting for it to heat up, cook the roti. On a lightly floured surface, work the ball of dough into a long log and then divide into 24 equal balls. Heat up an 8-inch-diameter nonstick pan over medium heat. Add about 1½ teaspoons olive oil to the pan and wipe the oil around the pan with a folded paper towel. Roll out one ball of dough to a ⅛inch-thick disc, then transfer to the pan. Cook each side of the roti about 1½ minutes until slightly puffed and browned in spots. Transfer to a baking sheet, cover with foil, and keep warm in a very low oven. Repeat with the remaining dough balls.

Grill the ribs over moderately high heat, turning every now and then, until nicely charred outside (remember that they are already cooked through). Transfer to a platter, squeeze the lime wedges over the ribs and garnish with the mint. Serve with the roti, pickled beets and onions, and yogurt sauce. Tell your guests to pull the lamb meat off the bone with their hands, place it in a piece of roti, top with the pickles and yogurt, then roll it all up and eat!

WHOLE FRIED FISH WITH HOT AND SOUR BROTH

SERVES 4

One of my favorite ways to eat fish is served whole on the bone and fried. This dish is a version of something I had while I was living in Thailand. The broth is the star of the dish and pairs really well with the fried fish.

For the hot and sour broth
1 cup roughly chopped cilantro roots
10–12 fresh kaffir lime leaves
bottom 4 inches of 3 lemongrass stalks, bruised
½ cup (rounded) chopped fresh galangal
2½ tablespoons tamarind paste
3 tablespoons oyster sauce
3½ tablespoons chili jam
2 tablespoons fish sauce, plus more as needed
4 cups chicken stock, ideally homemade or low-sodium canned broth
½ cup medium-diced shallots
½ cup halved cherry tomatoes
1 cup cleaned and torn oyster mushrooms
juice of 1 lime

For the fish
canola oil, for frying
1 (2-pound) whole branzino, scaled and gutted but with head and tail left on
½ cup rice flour
salt, as needed

To serve
½ cup Thai basil leaves, picked off the stem
¼ cup cilantro leaves

Equipment
A deep fryer or wok large enough to hold the fish

Make the broth. Combine the cilantro roots, kaffir lime leaves, lemongrass, galangal, tamarind paste, oyster sauce, chili jam, fish sauce, and chicken stock in a 4-quart saucepan and bring to a boil over medium-high heat. Turn the heat off and let the aromatics steep inside the liquid for 1 hour. Strain the liquid, discarding the solids. Return the broth to a clean 4-quart saucepan and set aside.

Prepare the fish. Preheat the canola oil in a deep fryer to 350°F. Alternatively, preheat 2½–3 inches of oil in a wok and use a deep-frying or candy thermometer to make sure the oil reaches the correct temperature.

Rinse the fish under cold running water, then dry it very well. Score both sides of the fish with 3 slits about 2 inches long. Make sure you don't cut all the way into the bone; cut just ⅔ of the way into the flesh.

Place the rice flour in a shallow bowl or rimmed platter. Season the fish liberally with salt, then dredge on all sides with the rice flour, shaking off any excess.

When the oil is hot enough, gently lower the fish into the fryer or wok. Be careful, as it may splatter. Cook until golden brown and completely cooked through, about 8–10 minutes. If using a wok, flip the fish over halfway through the cooking time, using tongs or a couple of heatproof spatulas. Remove the fish from the wok or the fryer and drain on a tray lined with paper towels. Season again with a sprinkling of salt.

When ready to serve, return the saucepan with the broth to the stove and add the shallots, tomatoes, and mushrooms. Bring to a boil, then reduce to a simmer and cook over low heat for 5 minutes until the shallots and tomatoes soften. Remove from the heat and stir in half the lime juice. Taste and add more lime juice and fish sauce if needed.

To plate, place the Thai basil leaves in a serving bowl, pour the broth over, and place the fish on top. Garnish with the cilantro leaves.

QUAIL ADOBO

SERVES 6

When people think of Filipino food one of the first dishes that comes to mind is an adobo. Traditionally, the main ingredient is pork or chicken, which is braised in the piquant adobo sauce. My version of this dish uses quail; and instead of braising the quail, I fry it and serve it like Buffalo chicken wings.

For the adobo sauce
1¼ cups low-sodium soy sauce
1¼ cups coconut milk (preferably
   Chaokoh brand)
½ cup coconut vinegar
½ cup water
1½ tablespoons canola oil
3 tablespoons granulated sugar
5 garlic cloves, smashed
¾ tablespoon freshly ground black
   pepper
½ teaspoon ground bay leaf powder

For the quail
1½ cups rice flour
½ teaspoon salt
1¼ cups water
6 whole quail, semi-deboned
2 quarts canola oil, for frying

To garnish
4 quail eggs
crisp-fried garlic (make your own
   or buy in an Asian grocery store),
   to taste
2 scallions, green part only, thinly
   sliced
2 tablespoons whole cilantro leaves
bay leaf powder, to taste
Szechuan peppercorns, to taste

Equipment
A deep fryer (optional)

First make the adobo sauce. Combine all the ingredients in a medium saucepan and bring to a boil. Reduce to a simmer and cook for 20–30 minutes until the sauce has thickened enough to coat the back of a wooden spoon. You should have about 1¼–1½ cups of sauce; be careful not to over-reduce it or it will be very salty.

Meanwhile, prepare the quail eggs for the garnish. Half-fill a small bowl with ice and cold water. Bring a small saucepan of water to a boil. Gently lower in the eggs, and cook them for 2 minutes exactly, so that they are soft-boiled. Remove and immediately dunk them into the ice water bath. Once the eggs are cool, peel and halve them. Transfer to a bowl and set aside.

Make the batter for the deep-fried quail: place the rice flour in a medium bowl with the salt and whisk in the water to form a smooth batter. You may not need to use all the water, or you may need to add a little extra. The batter should be slightly thinner than pancake batter. Leave to sit for 15 minutes.

When ready to fry your quail, heat the canola oil in a deep fryer to 350°F. Alternatively, fill a heavy-based saucepan with the oil and use a deep-frying or candy thermometer to make sure the oil reaches the correct temperature.

When the oil is ready, season the quail all over with salt, then dip each one into the bowl of batter and coat evenly. Lightly shake off any excess batter, then, using tongs, gently lower them into the hot oil. Fry until golden brown and cooked through, about 5–7 minutes, turning if necessary. Remove from the oil, drain well on paper towels, then transfer to a large bowl. Pour over them all but a few tablespoons of the adobo sauce and toss to coat.

To serve, spoon the reserved adobo sauce into a serving bowl, then arrange the fried quail on top. Garnish with the crisp garlic, scallions, cilantro, bay leaf powder, Szechuan peppercorns, and the quail eggs. This dish is best eaten with a bowl of hot jasmine rice.

SOHUI KIM

The arc of Sohui Kim's life reads like the narrative of a novel. As a young girl in Seoul, Korea, she lived a very comfortable, even privileged life. Her father ran a successful construction company at the time. The family had household staff and her mother enjoyed cooking as a hobby. On important Buddhist holidays, Kim's grandmother would take her deep into the countryside to a remote temple. There they would scour the mountains with the monks, foraging for mushrooms, tree bark, and dandelions for their meals.

But in the mid-1970s, the economy stalled and Kim's father lost his business. The family relocated to New York City to start afresh from a tiny apartment in the Bronx. There were no maids and her father cleaned vegetables in a Korean grocery store until he had saved enough money for his own vegetable stand. Kim was a dedicated student and exemplary daughter. When her father—determined his children would become doctors and lawyers—told her to give up a scholarship to study clarinet at the Fiorello H. LaGuardia High School of Music & Art and Performing Arts, she listened.

With a political science degree from Barnard College, Kim had every intention of fulfilling her father's dream, eventually. But her father had died some years back in a car accident, and her motivation waned. First she worked in publishing. Then she took on a second job in the evenings as a hostess at a trendy SoHo restaurant to fund her newfound penchant for fine dining. When she wasn't eating out, she cooked for friends, who slipped her $20 each to feast on fancy French recipes from her cookbooks.

At 29, Kim finally conceded that her career would lie in the kitchen, not the law courts, and she enrolled at Peter Kump's New York Cooking School (now the Institute of Culinary Education). She interned at the Blue Hill Restaurant, in Greenwich Village, and then worked briefly for Peter Hoffman at a neighborhood bistro, Savoy, in SoHo. But no experience was more influential than Kim's year and a half at the globally inspired Annisa, under the formidable Anita Lo. "I learned that if you have a strong cooking style and a point of view then your food is going to make it."

Fast-forward a couple more jobs (working at Joe Bastianich's Italian Wine Merchants and at the Sony Club), and Kim and her husband, Ben, are homeowners in Red Hook, Brooklyn. A former deli on the better end of Van Brunt Street opens up around the corner from their house, and the couple take their chances on the tiny space.

Kim helms the kitchen and Ben, a carpenter and actor, outfits the restaurant with a curved wooden ceiling that evokes a ship's cabin. An affordable neighborhood bistro that entices diners to more adventurous plates once they've had the burger and onion rings for the umpteenth time is what Kim envisions. So on the opening menu, alongside the burger, are hot wings and roast chicken. The more intrepid diners are rewarded with crisp veal sweetbreads and Korean-style steak and eggs with kimchi fried rice. A month after its opening, The Good Fork receives excellent reviews by *New York* magazine, the *New Yorker*, and Peter Meehan of the *New York Times*.

Kim feels no pressure to limit her repertoire to the remits of her Asian roots. "I'm passionate about perfectly cooked risotto just the same way that I am about perfectly fermented homemade kimchi." But is it a coincidence that her pork and chive dumplings, her Korean braised squid with mungbean pancakes, and her soy short-ribs with forbidden rice and egg ribbons are prepared with a finesse born of an innate understanding of those flavors?

Probably not.

What piece of kitchen equipment can't you live without?
A mandoline.

What dish that you've created are you most proud of?
My Steak & Eggs Korean Style.

What's your gastronomic guilty pleasure?
Foie gras, sweetbreads, caviar.

What's your favorite season to cook during (and why)?
Spring—new life after a long winter, root vegetables. I also like fall—love to pickle the bounty.

It's your final meal; where are you, what are you eating, who are you eating it with, and what are you washing it all down with?
Korean barbecue in Seoul with my family, and drinking soju.

What has been your most memorable moment professionally?
Lots of perfect nights line cooking ... oh, and reopening The Good Fork on New Year's Eve after being hit by Sandy.

PORK AND SHRIMP DUMPLINGS WITH WATER CHESTNUTS AND CHIVES

**SERVES 4–6; MAKES
35–40 DUMPLINGS**

**Dumplings are great for so many
occasions and can be used in so
many different ways. I put a
version of this recipe on my
opening menu at The Good Fork
and it has stayed there ever since!**

For the dumplings
canola oil, as needed
½ small onion, finely chopped
1 large clove garlic, minced
*½ tablespoon finely minced fresh
    ginger*
*¾ cup finely chopped flat Chinese
    garlic chives*
2½ tablespoons hoisin sauce
½ tablespoon fish sauce
½ teaspoon salt
pinch of freshly ground black pepper
½ pound ground pork
*½ pound peeled and cleaned
    shrimp, cut into small dice*
*½ cup finely chopped water
    chestnuts (canned are fine; just
    be sure to rinse and drain them
    well)*
*1 package round dumpling
    wrappers (about 40 wrappers)*

For the dipping sauce
½ cup dark soy sauce
½ cup rice wine vinegar
¼ cup dark brown sugar
1 star anise

Make the dumpling filling. Heat a
large sauté pan or a wok over
medium heat. Add 2 teaspoons of
canola oil and sauté the onion,
garlic, and ginger until translucent
and slightly caramelized, about 4–6
minutes. Add the garlic chives and
cook a minute longer, just until
heated through. Transfer to a large
mixing bowl and leave to cool.

Once the onion mixture is at room
temperature, add the hoisin and fish
sauces and the salt and pepper, and
mix well. Then add the pork, shrimp,
and water chestnuts and combine
everything. Heat an oiled frying pan,
and cook a small spoonful of the
dumpling filling to taste it. Adjust
the seasoning with more hoisin and/
or salt and pepper, if necessary.

To make the dumplings, place a
wrapper on a clean surface or
chopping board, keeping all the
other wrappers covered with some
paper towel or a cloth so that they
don't dry out. Have a small bowl of
water ready. Place a tablespoon of
filling in the lower half of the
wrapper, leaving a rim around the
edge. Paint a little water around the
rim, using your finger. Fold the top
portion of the wrapper over the
filling and pinch close all the way
along the edge to seal. Transfer to a
platter and repeat with the
remaining dumpling wrappers until
you've used all the filling. Cover with
plastic wrap.

When ready to serve, make the
dipping sauce. Combine all the
ingredients in a small saucepan and
bring to a simmer. Remove from the

heat and allow to cool to room
temperature while you cook the
dumplings. Discard the star anise
before serving. The sauce keeps well
refrigerated, indefinitely.

To cook the dumplings, heat a
nonstick frying pan or well-seasoned
cast-iron skillet with a skim of canola
oil over medium-high heat. Working
in batches, brown the bottom of the
dumplings in the frying pan, being
careful not overcrowd the pan.

When all the dumplings are
browned, return as many of them as
will fit snugly in one layer to the
frying pan, then add about ¼-inch of
water to the pan. Cover, and steam
until nearly all the water evaporates.
Wipe out any remaining water from
the pan, and briefly pan-fry the
dumplings again, adding more oil if
necessary, for just long enough to
re-crisp their bottoms slightly.
Repeat with the remaining
dumplings. Serve immediately with
the dipping sauce.

Uncooked dumplings can be frozen
(they do not refrigerate well). Freeze
them, uncovered, on a cookie sheet
until they harden, then pack them
into zip-top bags. They will keep
frozen for up to 3 weeks. Cook them
just as you would fresh dumplings,
but with slightly more water so they
steam a little longer.

SALT-BROILED MACKEREL WITH DAIKON AND FRISÉE SALAD

SERVES 4

Packed with Omega-3 oils and with that distinctive fatty, rich taste, mackerel is one of my favorite fish. It pairs really well with this Korean-style sweet, spicy, gingery glaze, which offsets the bitter frisée and crunchy daikon. If you are pressed for time, you can omit the glaze altogether. Just cook the fish simply salted and broiled and served over rice for the simplest weeknight dinner.

For the mackerel

2 mackerel fillets, 7–8 ounces each
1 tablespoon gochujang (Korean hot pepper paste)
1 garlic clove, minced
1 teaspoon grated fresh ginger
1 tablespoon rice wine vinegar
1 teaspoon honey
1 teaspoon sesame seeds
salt and freshly ground pepper, as needed

For the salad

1 teaspoon gochogaru (Korean red chili flakes)
1 teaspoon soy sauce
1 teaspoon fish sauce
1 tablespoon rice wine vinegar
1 teaspoon sesame oil
2 packed cups washed, dried, and torn pieces of frisée lettuce
1 cup matchstick-cut daikon radish
½ cup thinly sliced scallion greens

Season the mackerel fillets on both sides with a liberal amount of salt and some freshly ground black pepper. Set aside for 30 minutes to 1 hour.

Preheat the broiler to medium-high.

In a bowl, combine the gochujang, garlic, ginger, rice wine vinegar, honey, and sesame seeds to make a sauce. Whisk until thoroughly mixed, then set aside.

Pat the mackerel fillets dry with paper towels and place skin-side up on an oiled rack set over a rimmed baking sheet lined with foil. Broil for 4–5 minutes until the skin is crisp and the flesh is cooked through. Flip the fillets, brush the sauce thickly over the flesh side, and briefly flash under the broiler for another 30 seconds.

To prepare the salad, first combine the gochogaru, soy and fish sauces, rice wine vinegar, and sesame oil in a bowl. Taste for seasoning and adjust with more soy sauce if necessary. Place the frisée, daikon, and scallion greens in a separate bowl, pour the dressing over, and toss. Serve the fish accompanied with the salad.

SOY-BRAISED SHORT RIBS WITH CHESTNUTS AND KIMCHI

SERVES 4–6

These short ribs are a play on the traditional Korean-style short ribs that I grew up with. The flavors of kimchi and sweet soy create an amazing combination. Here I suggest serving these ribs with Korean black rice, but they are also delicious served atop noodles.

For the short ribs

4–5 pounds English-style (bone-in) short ribs, chopped into 5- x 2-inch pieces—ask your butcher to do this for you
canola oil, as needed
1 large onion, cut into large dice
3 cloves of garlic, crushed
⅓ cup sliced peeled fresh ginger
2 cups red wine
½ cup packed, dark brown sugar
¾ cup soy sauce
½ cup mirin
2 cups water or chicken stock, plus more as needed
½ cup diced Korean kimchi or daikon kimchi (optional; see suppliers, page 286)
6 ounces roasted, peeled chestnuts, finely crushed
3 tablespoons cold butter, diced
salt and freshly ground black pepper, as needed

To garnish and serve

3–5 cups cooked Korean black rice prepared according to the package instructions
¼ cup thinly sliced kimchi
a paper-thin plain omelet rolled up and sliced into fine ribbons
¼ cup sliced scallion
½–1 tablespoon sesame seeds

Place the ribs in a large bowl and season them lightly with salt and pepper on all sides, bearing in mind that the soy will add a good deal of saltiness. Heat 1–2 tablespoons canola oil in a rondeau or other wide, heavy-bottomed pot over high heat. When hot, sear the ribs until well browned on all sides. Do this in batches so as not to crowd the pot. Transfer to a clean bowl and set aside.

Pour out most of the fat, then add a little more canola oil to the pot. When hot, sauté the onion, garlic, and ginger until softened, about 8–10 minutes. Add the red wine, bring to a boil, and simmer until the wine has reduced by half. Next add the brown sugar, soy sauce, and mirin, along with the water or chicken stock, and return to a boil. Taste the liquid—it should be nicely sweet and salty.

Add the kimchi, if using, then return the ribs to the pot. The liquid should cover the ribs at least three quarters of the way up. If it doesn't, add a little more water or stock, and a splash of soy, if necessary. Bring to a boil, then reduce to a low simmer, cover, and cook for about 2–2½ hours. Check after 2 hours to see if the rib meat pulls very easily off the bone but that the ribs are not falling apart. When this point is reached, remove from the heat.

Transfer the ribs to a bowl and cover to keep warm. Strain the sauce and skim off as much of the fat as possible. Return the strained sauce to the pot and heat over a medium-low flame. When hot but not boiling, stir in the crushed chestnuts, then drop in a few cubes of the cold, diced butter and whisk continuously, adding more butter as necessary, until the sauce emulsifies, thickens, and becomes shiny. Be careful not to boil the sauce at this point or it will split. Remove from the heat, taste, and adjust the seasoning, if necessary.

To plate, arrange the ribs (still on the bone) over a mound of cooked black rice on each plate. Spoon some of the sauce over, then dot some sliced kimchi around the plates. Garnish with the ribbons of omelet, sliced scallion, and a sprinkling of sesame seeds.

KOREAN-STYLE BOUILLABAISSE

SERVES 4

You can make this soup as homey or as fancy as you like. It's just another way to show how truly magical kimchi can be in all manner of different and varied applications.

1 tablespoon canola oil
1 small onion, thinly sliced (about ½ cup)
2 garlic cloves, minced
1 cup chopped Korean kimchi (the more aged the kimchi, the better), plus more if needed (see suppliers, page 286)
1 tablespoon gochogaru (Korean chili flakes)
1 teaspoon soy sauce
1 teaspoon fish sauce
1½ cups diced peeled potatoes
3½ cups dashi (homemade or reconstituted from dashi powder)
1½ cups chicken stock
½ pound mussels, scrubbed and beards removed
1 pound cod steaks (or substitute any mild, flaky fish), cut into 1-inch chunks
12 shell-on medium shrimp
3 tablespoons thinly sliced scallions
1 cup watercress leaves (only) or baby arugula
salt and freshly ground black pepper, as needed

In a large pot, heat the oil over medium-high heat. Add the onion and sauté for 3–4 minutes; add the garlic and cook for another 2 minutes until the onion is soft and translucent. Add the chopped kimchi and cook, stirring, for 3 more minutes.

Add the gochogaru, soy and fish sauces, and the potatoes. Pour in the dashi and chicken stock, then bring to a boil, lower the heat, and let the broth simmer for about 10 minutes or until the potatoes are just tender.

Discard any mussels that are open and don't close when gently tapped or are broken, then add the mussels, fish, and shrimp to the pot. Cover, and simmer until the mussels open up, about 3–5 minutes. If any mussels don't open, discard them. Taste and add salt and pepper as needed, or more chopped kimchi.

Divide the soup and seafood into 4 large bowls, and top each serving with the sliced scallions and a little watercress or arugula Serve immediately.

SAWAKO OKOCHI

When Sawako Okochi opened her first restaurant, Shalom Japan, in the summer of 2013, she cooked what seemed most natural to her. She served challah made with sake kasu, the yeasty lees left over from sake brewing, and okonomiyaki, a Japanese savory pancake accompanied by corned lamb's tongue and house-made sauerkraut.

Many initially questioned if, with its witty name, this "authentically inauthentic" Japanese and Jewish eatery in Brooklyn's South Williamsburg was a sort of culinary ethnic joke. But it was no joke; the mélange reflects how Okochi and her Jewish husband, chef Aaron Israel—co-owner of Shalom Japan—have actually come to cook and eat since meeting in 2010. In this sense, it is the most sincere fusion, an organic hybrid of gastronomic traditions.

The married duo's deft approach to their playful combinations, executed with refined skill, has since been lauded by the food press and by diners. Even their simplest dishes, such as edamame tossed in poultry fat, are born of careful consideration and hours of trials.

Raised in Hiroshima, Japan, Okochi has come a long way since she would eat only white foods: egg white omelets, rice, tofu, noodles. (She eventually grew out of this phase with the gentle coaxing of her nutritionist mother.) But it wasn't until she moved to Texas in 1995, to attend the University of North Texas, that she started to cook, re-creating dishes from home with recipes assembled from cookbooks and instructions dictated over the phone by her mother. By the time she graduated, she had abandoned her earlier plans to become a translator and had applied to the New York Restaurant School.

After two years of culinary schooling, Okochi interned at the elegant, chandelier-bedecked Chanterelle in Manhattan's TriBeCa. There, steeped in classic French cuisine, Okochi picked up her first tools of the trade. She continued in the vein of fine dining at Annisa, where she stayed for five years. Under the wing of chef Anita Lo, Okochi eventually rose to become sous-chef at this West Village establishment. "It was a truly amazing experience for me. She [Anita] has no boundaries in her cooking, literally." Perhaps the highlight of Okochi's tenure at Annisa was being part of Lo's all-female team when she defeated Mario Batali on *Iron Chef America*.

From there, Okochi joined fellow Annisa veteran Sohui Kim at her Red Hook establishment, The Good Fork. Kim was pregnant and needed a replacement to head her kitchen, a perfect scenario for Okochi, who was seeking more responsibility, creative license, and a casual dining experience to expand her repertoire.

By the summer of 2011 Okochi had left The Good Fork and was running the Otakara Supper Club, a fantastically successful dinner series with a distinctly Japanese flavor, held in the backyard of a friend's place in Fort Greene, Brooklyn. Guests made a "donation" of $100 for a meal for two, and brought their own wine.

When fall arrived it was time to get serious. A brief spell at Julie Reiner's tropical cocktail lounge, Lani Kai, followed; there Okochi was charged with overhauling the menu. Yet she was looking for something more, a place that truly defined her as much as she defined it. Then on a trip to Japan in 2012, Okochi and Aaron crystallized plans to open a restaurant together. "The food came first," she says. "It was always meant to be just our food."

What is your favorite unlikely Japanese/Jewish food or flavor combination?
Horseradish can be good with a lot of stuff. We used beet horseradish in our pork udon and it was very good and made our broth pink.

If disaster struck, and your restaurant no longer existed (you can fill in your own nightmare scenario!), which item(s) would you be most aggrieved about losing?
I hope that never happens; I would be too sad to lose the restaurant. My ice cream maker and rice cooker would be missed, not to mention all my knives I've collected over the years.

Who is the one person, living or dead, whom you would be terrified to cook for?
My grandparents.

What's the most underused/underrated seasoning/spice/pantry ingredient?
Two: salt and vinegar.

What's your favorite food memory from when you were young?
My mother got friends' kids together and taught them how to bake bread. It was so much fun, kneading and shaping dough into fun shapes and seeing them come out of the oven. She's a great cook.

CHILLED CORN SOUP WITH IKURA, CRÈME FRAÎCHE, AND POTATO CHIPS

SERVES 4

I make this soup every summer with different kinds of garnishes. It's very easy to prepare and tastes great with or without the ikura (salmon roe). I've served it with fried shrimp, with popcorn, or just simply with homemade crème fraîche on top. Be sure to use tasty corn from your local farmers' market, if you can, and season the soup generously with salt—it risks being bland if seasoned poorly.

For the dashi stock
piece of kombu seaweed (available at Japanese grocery stores), 2 x 2 inches
8 cups water
1 cup loosely packed bonito flakes (available at Japanese grocery stores)

For the soup
4 cups fresh corn kernels (from 8–10 small to medium cobs), with juices reserved
1 large potato, preferably Idaho, peeled and halved and kept in a bowl of cold water
¼ cup crème fraîche, ideally homemade (see recipe below)
pinch of cayenne pepper
½ lemon
salt and freshly ground black pepper, as needed

To garnish
2 ounces ikura (sushi-quality wild salmon roe)
deep-fried matchstick potatoes (see recipe below)
soy salt (see suppliers, page 286)
finely chopped fresh chives

First make the dashi stock. Place the kombu in a pot and add the water. Set over low heat and gently heat, without boiling or simmering, for an hour. Remove the kombu (save it for another use, or discard) and add the bonito flakes to the pot. Increase the heat and bring the stock up to a boil, then skim the top and turn the heat off. Let the bonito flakes sink to the bottom of the pot and leave to steep for 15–20 minutes. Strain the liquid through a fine strainer lined with cheesecloth and discard the solids. Set aside the stock.

Prepare the soup. Place the corn kernels in a large pot. Dice one half of the potato into small cubes and add it to the pot. (Keep the other half of the potato in cold water to prevent it from blackening.) Pour in 4 cups of dashi stock (reserving the rest) and add a few pinches of salt. Place the pot over medium-high heat and bring to a boil. Lower the heat slightly, and simmer for 15–20 minutes until the corn and diced potato are very tender.

Transfer the soup to a blender and purée on high until the soup is very smooth and velvety with a fairly thick consistency. If the purée is too thick, add more dashi to thin it a little, being careful not to make the soup too loose. Taste, and season generously with salt and pepper.

Pass the soup through a fine sieve into a large bowl. Set the bowl of soup inside another bowl half-filled with ice and ice water to quickly cool it down. Once cool, keep refrigerated while you prepare the

accompaniments. In a bowl, combine the crème fraîche and cayenne with a squeeze of lemon juice and salt and pepper to taste. Cover and refrigerate while you prepare the matchstick potatoes for garnishing the soup.

To serve the soup, dab some of the crème fraîche mixture on the inner rim of 4 soup bowls, and use the bowl of the spoon to spread it halfway around the inside. Carefully ladle in the chilled soup, making sure that the smear of crème fraîche can still be seen. Spoon some ikura onto the center of each serving and arrange some of the fried potato matchsticks next to this. Finish with a pinch of soy salt and a sprinkle of the chopped chives.

Homemade Crème Fraîche
Combine 1 part buttermilk with 3 parts heavy cream in a nonreactive container. Cover with plastic wrap and leave to sit at room temperature for 1–2 days until thickened, checking periodically. Refrigerate until ready to use. (Can be stored in the fridge for up to 1 week.)

Deep-Fried Matchstick Potatoes
Half of a large potato (left over from main recipe)
2 cups canola or vegetable oil, for frying

Using a very sharp knife, cut the half potato into very thin matchsticks. Alternatively, use a Japanese mandoline with the fine-toothed blade attached. Transfer to a bowl of cold water.

Heat the canola or vegetable oil in a heavy-based deep saucepan until it reaches 350°F on a deep-frying/candy thermometer. Drain and thoroughly dry the potato matchsticks. Working in small batches, fry the potatoes until golden and crisp. Drain on a tray lined with paper towels and sprinkle with salt while still hot. Set aside.

BERKSHIRE PORK BELLY WITH HEIRLOOM TOMATOES AND UDON

SERVES 4

Udon, a great Japanese noodle, has many varieties, originating in different parts of Japan. I like inaniwa udon, from Akita prefecture, for its silkiness. I used to make the noodles for this recipe by hand, but I'm happy that nowadays sanuki and inaniwa udon are easy to obtain from local Japanese grocery stores.

For the pork
1½ pounds Berkshire pork belly
canola oil, as needed
1 small yellow onion, cut into 8 wedges
1 small carrot, peeled and cut into small chunks
2 stalks celery, cut into 2-inch lengths
1 head of garlic, cloves separated, peeled and crushed
4 or 5 sprigs of fresh thyme
2 bay leaves
1 teaspoon coriander seeds, toasted
1 cup cooking sake, or white wine
¼ cup apple cider vinegar
¼ cup rice vinegar
4 cups chicken stock, preferably homemade
1 cup balsamic vinegar (use a lower-grade vinegar)
salt and freshly ground black pepper, as needed

For the dashi soy sauce
2 tablespoons mirin
¼ cup soy sauce
1 teaspoon granulated sugar
½ cup bonito flakes
salt, to taste

12 ounces inaniwa udon, or another high-quality udon (a silky variety of udon is best suited to this dish)
ice cubes, for chilling the noodles
2 or 3 heirloom tomatoes (ideally a combination of different varieties), halved and cut into ¼-inch-thick slices

To garnish
3 scallions, thinly sliced on the diagonal
4 shiso leaves, shredded

Begin by braising the pork belly. Preheat the oven to 300°F. Season the pork generously with salt and pepper. If there are any bones, leave them in; they'll create more flavor and will come out easily after braising.

Heat a medium Dutch oven or other heavy-based, ovenproof pot with a lid (about 5–7 quarts capacity) over high heat. Add enough oil just to coat the bottom of the pot. When the fat starts to smoke, place the pork belly in the pot skin-side down. Lower the heat to medium-high. Turn the pork over and carefully sear all sides until golden brown.

Transfer the pork to a rimmed baking sheet or platter. Add the onion, carrot, celery, garlic, thyme, bay leaves, and coriander seeds to the pot, and cook the vegetables until they are lightly browned but not quite tender, about 7–9 minutes. Pour in the sake or wine and bring to a boil. Next add the apple cider, rice vinegar, and chicken stock. Carefully return the pork belly to the pot and bring the liquid back

to a boil. Skim off any scum that forms on the surface carefully, using a slotted spoon.

Turn off the heat, cover the pot, and transfer the pork to the oven. Braise for 2½–3 hours, until the bones pull easily off the meat, or a paring knife slips easily in and out when inserted into the thickest part.

While the meat is braising, reduce the balsamic vinegar. Put the vinegar in a small saucepan and set it over high heat. When it boils, reduce the heat to low and let the vinegar reduce, checking every 5 or 10 minutes. It is ready when it coats the back of a spoon (bear in mind that the reduced balsamic will thicken considerably as it cools). The balsamic syrup will keep in an airtight container indefinitely.

When the meat is cooked, transfer it to a tray or platter to rest. Strain the braising liquid through a fine sieve into a container, cover with plastic wrap, and refrigerate. Cover the meat with plastic wrap and refrigerate, ideally for several hours before serving so that the pork belly firms up and is easier to slice. Once the braising liquid is cold, skim off the solidified fat from the surface and discard it.

Make the dashi soy sauce. Pour the mirin into a medium saucepan, set on high heat, and bring to a boil to drive off the alcohol. Add the soy sauce and sugar, reduce the heat to low, and cook for 3–5 minutes. Add about 3 cups of the defatted pork jus, and bring to a boil. Add the bonito flakes and turn off the heat. When the bonito flakes settle on the bottom of the pan, season the sauce to taste with salt, then strain through a fine sieve into a pitcher or bowl. Cover with plastic wrap and refrigerate until cold.

When ready to serve, bring a large pot of water to a boil for the udon. Preheat the oven to 400°F.

Remove the pork belly from the fridge and cut it into about ⅓- to ½-inch-thick slices. Arrange the pork on a rimmed baking sheet lined with foil, and place in the oven for about 5–7 minutes or until heated through.

Cook the udon noodles according to the package instructions. Drain through a strainer and rinse under cold running water, adding some ice to the strainer to help the udon cool down quickly. Remove the ice and drain well.

To plate, divide the cool udon equally between 4 shallow bowls or plates. Place the pork belly slices on top of the noodles. Next arrange a few tomato slices around the pork, then pour ¼ cup of the cold dashi soy sauce onto each dish. Spoon a little balsamic reduction on and around the pork and the tomatoes. Finally garnish with the scallion and shiso leaves. Serve immediately.

SMOKED DUCK 'N' SOBA

SERVES 4

I love duck, and I love noodles. I smoke the duck here, and the smokiness goes very well with the earthy buckwheat flavor of the soba. I served this version of the dish when I ran an underground supper club for one summer in Fort Greene, Brooklyn.

For the duck stock

3–4 pounds duck bones or duck necks
piece of kombu seaweed 10 x 10 inches
bunch of scallions (about 6 or 7)
2-inch piece of fresh ginger, roughly sliced
2 whole heads of garlic, unpeeled and sliced in half horizontally
8 dried shiitake mushrooms, tied up in a square of cheesecloth
zest of 1 orange
4 cups loosely packed bonito flakes
salt, as needed

For the smoked duck

4 skin-on duck breasts, preferably Long Island Peking duck (total of about 2 pounds)
salt and freshly ground black pepper, as needed
1 tablespoon vegetable oil

For the tamago (Japanese rolled omelet)

3 large eggs
¼ teaspoon salt
2 tablespoons cold dashi (you can reconstitute it from store-bought dashi powder)
2 teaspoons cornstarch
1 teaspoon soy sauce
2 teaspoons granulated sugar
freshly ground black pepper, as needed
1 tablespoon vegetable oil

12-ounce package of dried soba noodles

To garnish

1 mountain potato, or yamaimo (available at Japanese grocery stores), peeled and cut into fine matchsticks—be careful, it is very slimy!
2 tablespoons Japanese parsley, or mitsuba, leaves only (available at Japanese grocery stores)
zest of 1 orange (white pith removed), shredded
2 scallions, thinly sliced
Shichimi togarashi, a Japanese spice and chili pepper mix (available at Japanese grocery stores)

Equipment

A smoke gun and wood chips of your choice, such as cherry or apple (see suppliers, page 286)
A pair of chopsticks (optional)

Make the duck stock. Place the duck bones or necks in a large pot, together with the kombu, scallions, ginger slices, garlic, dried shiitakes, and orange zest. Pour over these enough water to cover (about 2 gallons). Place the pot over high heat and bring to a boil. Skim off the scum from the surface, lower the heat, and simmer for 3 hours.

Next add the bonito flakes and increase the heat to medium-high. Bring the stock back to a boil, then immediately turn off the heat, and let the bonito sink. Taste the stock, and season with salt. Strain twice through a fine sieve, then cool and refrigerate if not using right away.

Next prepare the duck. Using the tip of a sharp knife, score the skin of the breasts diagonally in a crisscross fashion without cutting into the flesh. Season the breasts generously all over with salt and pepper.

Heat a large skillet, ideally one with a spout, over high heat until smoking hot. Carefully place the duck breasts skin-side down into the pan. (The skin should sizzle immediately upon contact with the pan; if it doesn't, the pan isn't hot enough.) Don't overcrowd the pan; if necessary cook 2 breasts at a time.

Once the duck is in the skillet, lower the heat; once fat starts to render from the skin, carefully lift and tilt the pan and pour out the fat into an old can or bowl to cool down before discarding. Keep rendering the fat from the duck skin and discarding it for about 7–10 minutes. Keep the ➤

heat low enough so that the flesh doesn't cook. When the skin looks mostly rendered and has shrunk to half its original thickness, transfer the breasts to a plate or tray, placing them skin-side up.

Now you're ready to smoke the duck. Place the breasts in a nonreactive container. Stick the smoke gun's nozzle inside the container and tightly cover the opening with foil so no smoke can escape. Prepare the smoke gun according to the manufacturer's instructions and smoke the duck for 10–20 minutes, keeping the container covered. Periodically lift the foil and check the smokiness; if you don't smell very much smoke, keeping smoking the duck breasts. When done, remove the breasts from the container and refrigerate until to ready to cook.

Now make the tamago omelet. In a bowl, beat the eggs with the salt. In a separate small bowl, combine the dashi and cornstarch, and stir to dissolve. Add the soy sauce, sugar, and a good grinding of pepper to the dashi mixture, then add this to the egg and beat until just combined.

Heat a nonstick skillet (or a Japanese rectangular egg pan, if you have one) over low heat. Pour in the oil, swirling it around the pan. Use a folded square of paper towel to soak up the excess oil; set this aside to use later. Drop a small amount of the omelet mixture into the pan and cook it. Taste and adjust the seasoning as necessary.

When ready to cook the omelet, wipe the pan with the oiled paper and keep the pan on low heat. (A pair of chopsticks is the best implement to use when making the omelet.) Pour just enough egg mixture into the pan to coat the bottom. Once the bottom has set but there is still plenty of raw egg mixture on top, start rolling the omelet from the side of the pan that is closest to you. Roll about ¼ inch of the omelet, then let the rolled part cook through completely so that it sets and sticks together. Keep rolling in this way, ¼ inch at a time.

If the egg cooks through too quickly and there isn't enough raw mixture in the pan to act as an adhesive, add a few drops of raw egg mixture to seal the omelet as you roll it. Once the omelet is completely rolled up, draw it back to the side of the pan closest to you. Wipe the rest of the pan with the oiled paper again, and pour more raw egg mixture in to just cover the base. Lift up the cooked, rolled egg and let the raw mixture run under it. Start rolling again exactly as you did before, this time rolling the mixture around the previously cooked egg. Repeat with the rest of the egg mixture. Transfer the omelet to a plate and set aside.

Next, bring a large pot of water to a boil for the soba. Reheat the duck stock in another large pot, and adjust the seasoning if necessary.

Meanwhile, finish cooking the duck. Heat a large skillet over medium-high heat and add the 1 tablespoon of vegetable oil. When hot, place

the duck breasts into the pan, skin-side down. When the skin is crisp and well browned, flip the breasts over to the flesh side. Reduce the heat to low and cook for about 5 minutes, or until the duck meat is cooked to medium and reads 145°F on a digital thermometer. Transfer the duck breasts to a clean chopping board and leave to rest for 5–7 minutes.

Cook the soba in a boiling water according to the package instructions minus 1 minute of the stated cooking time (this is to avoid overcooking the soba during plating). Drain the noodles and divide equally between 4 deep soup bowls. Thinly slice the duck meat and the tamago omelet. Pour the hot soup over the noodles, then arrange the duck slices and tamago on top, followed by the yamaimo matchsticks.

Finally garnish with the mitsuba, orange zest, and scallions. Serve along with a small bowl of shichimi togarashi for sprinkling on top.

TUNA TATAKI WITH BLACK TAHINI

SERVES 4

This is one of the first recipes that my husband, Aaron, and I came up with, and it became one of our signature dishes. Tataki is a traditional Japanese culinary technique in which meat or fish is briefly seared over high heat until the outer surface is cooked but the inside is still raw, then served thinly sliced. Our tuna tataki is made with nerigoma, a Japanese version of tahini—ground sesame paste that is often used in Jewish and other Middle Eastern cooking. The black nerigoma looks very striking on white plates, so use these if possible for your tataki.

½ pound sushi-quality or grade 1 tuna, trimmed of skin and the dark red blood line
3 tablespoons black tahini paste or black nerigoma (available at Japanese grocery stores)
3 tablespoons honey
3 tablespoons soy sauce
½ head broccoli, thick stem removed
olive oil, as needed
1 medium red onion, trimmed, peeled, and quartered
juice of ½ lemon
salt and freshly ground black pepper, as needed

To garnish
top-quality extra-virgin olive oil
Maldon sea salt
2 shiso leaves, very thinly sliced
few threads of ito togarashi (Japanese shredded chili pepper—available from Japanese grocery stores) or a pinch of chili powder

Prepare the tuna by trimming it into a block measuring about 6½–7½ inches long, 2–3 inches wide, and 1–1¼ inches thick. (This particular cut is known as saku.) Transfer to a bowl, cover with plastic wrap, and refrigerate until ready to use.

Next make the tahini sauce. Mix the tahini paste well, as it tends to separate, then place the measured amount in a small bowl with the honey. Slowly whisk in the soy sauce until emulsified. Set aside.

Preheat the oven to 450°F and place a rimmed baking sheet inside.

Break up the broccoli head into small florets and transfer to a medium bowl; add a good drizzle of olive oil and a sprinkling of salt and black pepper. Toss well to coat. Taste a small piece of broccoli and add more salt if necessary. Scatter the broccoli onto the preheated baking sheet and give it a shake. Roast for 6–8 minutes or until the broccoli is cooked through. Remove from the oven, transfer to a bowl, and leave to cool.

Preheat the grill to high, or place a grill pan on a burner turned to high. In a small bowl, toss the onion in a little olive oil and salt and pepper. When hot, place the onion quarters on the grill or grill pan, flat-side down, and grill until just cooked through. If the onion is still a little raw on the inside and charring too much on the outside, place the quarters in a roasting pan and finish cooking them in the oven. Transfer to the bowl of broccoli and set aside.

To cook the tuna, remove from the fridge and allow to come up to room temperature. Drizzle some olive oil over it and season with salt and pepper. Use your hands to coat the tuna on all sides. Reheat the grill or grill pan until very hot, then carefully place the tuna on it. Cook for 20 seconds, then turn it to a different side and cook for another 20 seconds. Continue to do this until all the sides are cooked in this way. Transfer the tuna to a platter or tray lined with paper towels and leave it to rest.

Plate the dish. Spoon the tahini sauce onto the center of 4 plates. Season the broccoli and red onion, to taste, with the lemon juice, and give them a quick toss. Divide the vegetables equally between the plates, placing them in the center of the pool of sauce. Using a very sharp knife, slice the tuna tataki against the grain into ⅓-inch pieces and place 3 or 4 slices of tuna on each plate on top of the broccoli and red onion. Brush the olive oil onto the tuna slices, then sprinkle with Maldon sea salt flakes—1 or 2 flakes per slice. Finally, top with a few ribbons of shiso and the ito togarashi or chili powder. Serve immediately.

ANN REDDING

Life was meandering nowhere in particular for Ann Redding when she had an epiphany. She had abandoned her journalism degree at the University of Maryland after just one year and, following a spate of random jobs, moved to New York City. There, she waitressed, was an agent for makeup artists, then waitressed some more. Two years on, her sister sat her down and asked, "But what do you really love?" Redding's obsession with the Food Network came to mind. "Um … food," she replied.

That was all it took to catapult the career of one of the most dynamic young chefs in New York City. Redding enrolled at Peter Kump's New York Cooking School (now the Institute of Culinary Education). Graduating at 27, she joined some of the most challenging kitchens and honed her craft under grueling taskmasters. Her first "stage" (as an internship in the culinary world is called) was at Daniel, under the formidable Alex Lee. Next came a five-month stint at Payard. Eventually she landed at Thomas Keller's restaurant Per Se, where she stayed for two years. Starting out doing prep at the back, she ended up running the canapé station, devising and perfecting bite-size works of art.

At Per Se, Redding met Matt Danzer, now her husband, who shared her entrepreneurial ambitions. In 2008 they took on a grocery and gourmet market in Shelter Island, just east of Long Island. In addition to ensuring that the boaters could get all their dry food supplies, they had a fresh fish and butcher counter, prepared foods, and ran a café and take-out operation, making sandwiches, fish tacos, and lobster rolls to order. They'd open up Reddings around Easter and close up after Labor Day. For the rest of the year, they would travel to Thailand and hang out with Redding's family.

Redding was born in Ubon, in northeast Thailand, to a Thai mother and an American father, who was teaching English there with the Peace Corps. She recalls her childhood as one vividly punctuated with colorful food-filled experiences—from sitting with her grandmother at the wet market, selling home-grown vegetables, to enjoying grilled, just-caught seafood from beachside vendors. When Redding was seven her family moved to the Philippines; a few years later, they moved to the States. Wherever they were, Thai home cooking was the family's staple diet. Redding's mother carried her culinary traditions with her, imparting them to her daughters, who even helped her with the chopping and prepping as she made isan (Thai fermented sausages) to sell at the local fair.

After five years of catering to the warm-weather crowds at Shelter Island, Danzer and Redding decided to move on. They headed into Manhattan's Nolita neighborhood to open Uncle Boon's (named for a favorite relative). Though its décor is somewhat tongue-in-cheek—with a kitschy Asian pub feel created by a mishmash of wall coverings consisting of old-school black-and-white family portraits, photos of Thai kings, and Thai movie posters—the approach to the food is as serious as Redding's canapés for Per Se. She had scrutinized the making of local dishes during their trips to Thailand, learning particularly from an aunt who had cooked at the royal palace. Everything at Uncle Boon's is born of a genuine Thai dish, but Redding has brought in her fine dining experience to elevate dishes just enough to appeal to the city's culinary cognoscenti.

Although Redding's real Uncle Boon may be more used to eating his Mee Grob with shrimp or pork, Redding's version of the crisp noodle dish, with sweetbreads, would surely make him proud.

What is your favorite food memory from your childhood?
Sitting with my grandmother at the market as she sold the vegetables from her farm. I remember all the various vendors in the stands next to her and the dishes they sold.

If there was one person—chef/artist/writer/anyone—that you could collaborate with, whether on a pop-up restaurant, writing a book, creating a dish together, whatever you like, who would it be and what would you do?
My grandfather on my mom's side. He died before I had the chance to meet him, but by all accounts he was an incredible cook. My mother, also an incredible cook, learned from him.

What's your favorite band/album to play in the restaurant?
We play a mishmash of old Thai music we've collected, as well as some stuff I've stolen from my mother's house. And I love the band Caribou.

What's the strangest thing you've ever eaten?
Grasshoppers, in Thailand as a kid. Balut [duck embryo eaten in its shell] in the Philippines as an afternoon snack as a kid.

CHU CHEE SCALLOPS WITH RED CURRY AND KAFFIR LIME LEAVES

SERVES 2–3

Chu chee curries can be made with any seafood. The best version of this dish that I've ever had was with my Uncle Nuey in Thailand when he took me to his favorite chu chee spot, a little outdoor restaurant. He called it the "fly" restaurant; I soon found out why: flies were everywhere—all over the chairs, all over the tables... Flies aside, Uncle Nuey was right: the fish chu chee we had was amazing. This recipe would be delicious with shrimp or any other type of fish or seafood; just be sure to cut it into small pieces so it can cook evenly under the broiler.

For the red curry sauce
vegetable or canola oil, as needed
½ cup good-quality red curry paste
    (store-bought, or homemade—
    see recipe below)
4 cups coconut milk
2 tablespoons fish sauce
½ tablespoon palm sugar
salt, as needed

For the seafood
olive oil, as needed
2 cups wiped clean and trimmed
    button mushrooms
1 pound dry-packed sea scallops,
    side muscles removed
2 tablespoons minced fresh kaffir
    lime leaves

salt, as needed

To garnish and serve
3 or 4 raw button mushrooms,
    wiped clean, stems trimmed, and
    sliced thinly
½ cup whole fresh cilantro leaves
lime wedges, to serve
hot cooked jasmine rice

First prepare the red curry sauce. Heat a little oil in a medium saucepan set over medium-high heat. When hot, add the curry paste and sauté until aromatic, about 3 minutes. Add the coconut milk and bring to a boil. Reduce the heat and simmer the sauce for about 15 minutes. Add the fish sauce and palm sugar; stir well, then remove from the heat. Season to taste with salt, and set aside. The curry sauce can be made ahead and stored in the fridge in an airtight container for 3 days, or in the freezer for 3 months.

When ready to assemble the dish, preheat the broiler to medium-high.

Heat a little olive oil in a skillet over high heat. When hot, add the 2 cups of mushrooms and sauté until tender, about 3 to 4 minutes. Season to taste with salt.

Arrange the raw scallops and the cooked mushrooms on a heatproof platter. Reheat 2 cups of the red curry sauce in a saucepan over medium heat and stir in the kaffir lime leaves. Spoon the sauce evenly over the scallops and mushrooms, then place the platter under the broiler. Broil until the scallops are just cooked through and the sauce is beginning to brown in spots, about 7 minutes.

Remove from heat and garnish with the sliced raw button mushrooms and cilantro leaves. Serve with lime wedges on the side and with hot jasmine rice.

Red Curry Paste
1½ ounces large dried red chilies,
    soaked in warm water for 10
    minutes then drained
¾ cup plus 2 tablespoons guajillo
    chili paste
3 medium shallots, roughly chopped
20 garlic cloves roughly chopped
1½ cups peeled and roughly
    chopped galangal
6 ounces lemongrass, tender lower
    bulbs only, roughly chopped
⅔ cup fresh kaffir lime leaves
⅔ cup kaffir lime peel
½ cup chopped cilantro root
⅓ (rounded) cup shrimp paste
2 tablespoons whole white
    peppercorns, toasted and ground
2 tablespoons whole coriander
    seeds, toasted and ground
½ teaspoon ground nutmeg

Using a pestle and mortar, pound all the ingredients until you have a smooth paste. Alternatively, use a food processor. The curry paste will keep for 2 weeks refrigerated in an airtight container or 3 months in the freezer.

PLAA MUK TOD KAMIN
(BABY SQUID WITH FRESH TURMERIC AND GARLIC)

SERVES 4

This is a variation on a southern Thai dish that's usually prepared with whole fish. When I was a child, my mother would often substitute baby squid and serve it as a snack.

1 pound baby squid, cleaned
1 tablespoon plus ½ cup olive oil
6–8 large garlic cloves, minced
1 large or 2 medium shallots, minced
2 tablespoons fresh turmeric root, peeled and minced
½ small red onion, very thinly sliced
¾ cup chopped fresh cilantro leaves, stems and root
2 tablespoons fresh lemon juice
salt and freshly ground black pepper, as needed

Place the squid in a large bowl and season with salt and pepper. Add the tablespoon of the olive oil to a skillet set over high heat. When very hot, add the squid to the pan and quickly sear all over, stirring, until just cooked through. Transfer to a serving platter and set aside.

Turn the heat down to medium, then add the garlic, shallot, turmeric, and red onion to the skillet, together with 1 teaspoon of salt and the remaining ½ cup olive oil. Swirl the ingredients in the pan over the heat until the garlic starts to toast and becomes golden brown. Turn off the heat and add the minced cilantro and lemon juice.

Pour the mixture over the squid and serve immediately.

MASSAMAN CURRY WITH WILD BOAR AND GREEN PEPPERCORNS

SERVES 6

If wild boar isn't available, feel free to substitute pork, chicken, or beef—all equally delicious choices! If you make the massaman paste from scratch, feel free to double the recipe and freeze the leftover paste. It will stay fresh for at least 3 months and be at the ready for your next batch of curry.

For the massaman curry sauce
¼ cup olive oil
¾ cup massaman curry paste (store-bought, or homemade—see recipe below)
6 cups coconut milk
2 cups water
⅓ cup tamarind concentrate or paste (preferably Wangderm brand)
¼ cup fish sauce, plus more as needed
⅛ cup (packed) palm sugar

For the boar
3 wild boar foreshanks, each one about 1¼ pounds
olive oil, as needed
3 medium Yukon Gold potatoes, peeled and cut into large dice
2 red onions, cut into large wedges
3 tablespoons green peppercorns, fresh if available, otherwise in brine, rinsed and drained well)
salt and freshly ground black pepper, as needed

To garnish and serve
½ cup redskin peanuts, toasted and crushed
½ cup fresh cilantro leaves
Deep-fried Shallots (see recipe below, page 152)
hot cooked jasmine rice

Make the massaman sauce. Heat the ¼ cup of olive oil in a large saucepan over medium-high heat. Add the curry paste and sauté until fragrant, about 3 minutes. Add the rest of the ingredients and bring to a boil. Taste and add more fish sauce, if needed. Remove from the heat and set aside. The curry sauce can be made ahead and stored in the fridge in an airtight container for 3 days or in the freezer for 3 months.

Season the wild boar shanks all over with salt and pepper. Heat a large heavy-bottomed braising pot over medium-high heat and add enough olive oil to coat the bottom of the pot. Add the shanks to the pot, in batches if necessary, and sear them until browned all over. Transfer to a large bowl or platter and set aside.

Add more oil to the pot, if necessary, then add the diced potatoes. Sear, stirring occasionally, until golden all over. Remove from the pot and transfer to another bowl; set aside. Add the onion wedges to the pot and cook until browned, again adding a little more oil if necessary. Once the onion is caramelized and colored, return the shanks to the pot. Pour the massaman curry sauce over them and bring to a boil.

Turn down the heat and simmer the curry, partially covered, for 2½ hours or until the shanks are tender.

Return the browned potatoes to the pot and simmer until the potatoes are tender, about 15 minutes. Add the green peppercorns, stir well, and turn off the heat. Taste the curry and adjust the salt to taste.

Transfer the curry to a serving dish and garnish with the peanuts, cilantro leaves, and crisp shallots. Serve with jasmine rice.

Massaman Curry Paste
2 ounces dried red chilies, soaked in warm water for 15 minutes and drained
5 or 6 shallots, sliced
36 garlic cloves, peeled
½ cup peeled and roughly chopped galangal
2 cups thinly sliced lemongrass, tender bulbs only
2 cups chopped cilantro root and stems
canola oil, as needed
1 teaspoon salt
1 cup peanuts, roasted
½ cup whole coriander seeds, toasted and ground
3 tablespoons cumin seeds, toasted and ground
1½ teaspoons toasted and ground cloves
1 teaspoon ground nutmeg
1 tablespoon ground turmeric
2 (2½-inch) cinnamon sticks, toasted and ground
seeds, ground, from 2 tablespoons cardamom pods, toasted and split open

➤

Preheat the oven to 350°F. Place the first 6 ingredients in an ovenproof roasting pan or skillet. Add a little oil and toss to mix. Roast until fragrant and dark golden, about 35 minutes. Leave to cool.

Transfer the roasted mixture to the food processor along with the remaining ingredients and process until you have a fine paste. The curry paste will keep for 2 weeks refrigerated in an airtight container or 3 months in the freezer.

Deep-fried Shallots
3 shallots, thinly sliced
2 tablespoons rice flour
2 cups canola oil

Equipment
A deep fryer or a deep saucepan
  and deep-frying thermometer

Sprinkle the rice flour over the shallots and toss to coat. Heat the oil in the deep fryer to 350°F (or use the thermometer to measure the temperature in the saucepan). Carefully add the floured shallots to the hot oil and fry for 10–14 minutes until golden brown. Remove with a slotted spoon and leave to drain on paper towels.

KHAO GUN JIIN
(JASMINE RICE WITH PORK, BLOOD, AND HERBS STEAMED IN BANANA LEAVES)

MAKES 8 PARCELS

Traditionally this recipe is a go-to for using up leftover rice. The blood adds an element of richness to the dish that is perfectly counterbalanced by the fresh herbs; however, if you have difficulty getting hold of fresh pork blood, you can simply omit it.

For the rice, pork, and blood filling
canola or vegetable oil, as needed
½ pound ground pork
¼ cup chopped fresh cilantro leaves, stems and root
2 tablespoons minced garlic
3 cups cooked, cold jasmine rice
½ tablespoon freshly ground black peppercorns
3 tablespoons soy sauce (preferably Golden Mountain brand), plus more as needed
1 teaspoon fish sauce
1 tablespoon minced, peeled ginger
¼ cup chopped fresh cilantro leaves and stems
2 tablespoons minced fresh lemongrass (use the tender bulbs of the stalk)
2 tablespoons minced fresh kaffir lime leaves
½ cup fresh pork blood (available from your local butcher) (optional)
salt, as needed

For the wrapping
4 whole banana leaves, with central stems removed and cut into 8 strips measuring 12 x 7 inches
aluminum foil

To serve
1 cup fresh whole cilantro leaves
1 sweet white onion, thinly sliced
5 tomatoes (a variety of your choice), sliced

Equipment
A steamer rack

Make the filling. Heat a little oil in a large skillet set over medium-high heat. When hot, add the pork and cook, stirring, until it begins to brown. When the pork is almost completely cooked through, stir in the cilantro and garlic and let the pork finish cooking. Season with salt to taste. If the mixture is at all runny, pour it into a colander and drain well, discarding the liquid.

Transfer the mixture to a large bowl along with the remaining ingredients for the filling, except the blood, if using, and mix well. Taste and add more soy sauce, if needed, then stir in the blood.

Now assemble the parcels. Cut a piece of foil a little smaller than a banana leaf and place the leaf on top of it. Scoop a heaped ½ cup of the filling and place it on the center of the leaf, then spread it out a little along the length. Fold the long sides of the leaf over the filling—first the left side, then the right. Now fold over the top and bottom of the leaf to form a parcel. Wrap the foil around the parcel to enclose it completely and hold it together. Repeat with the remaining banana leaf strips until all the filling is used up.

To cook the parcels, pour about 1 inch of water into a wide pot or wok. Set a steamer rack inside this; it should rest just above the water, not touching it. Bring the water to a simmer over medium-high heat, then arrange a few parcels on the rack (you'll need to cook them in batches). Steam for 15 minutes. Open the parcels at the table and serve them with cilantro leaves and slices of raw onion and tomato.

MEDITERRANEAN AND MIDDLE EASTERN

EINAT ADMONY 157

Smoked Eggplant Salad with Pepper and Tomato · Kibbeh with Tzatziki · Braised Short Ribs with Wine, Prunes, and Harissa · Green Shakshuka

RAWIA BISHARA 167

Labaneh · Lentil Salad · Cauliflower Tagine · Bell Peppers Stuffed with Meat and Rice

SARA JENKINS 177

Cardoon Sformato with Salsa Verde · Classic Beef Ragù Lasagna · Ricotta and Herb-filled Ravioli with Burst Cherry Tomato Sauce · Pork Chop with Fennel Pollen, White Beans, and Lacinato Kale

MISSY ROBBINS 189

Grilled Branzino with Calabrian Chili Vinaigrette and Pickled Eggplant · Braised Veal Shanks with Fennel and Sweet Garlic · Risotto with Sunchokes and Bone Marrow · Linguine with Zucchini, Clams, Mint, and Lemon

ZAHRA TANGORRA 197

Long-cooked Broccoli with Stracciatella, Radishes, and Bagna Cauda · Porchetta-style Lamb with Black Sesame Tahini Sauce, Parsley and Meyer Lemon Salad, and Burnt Carrots · Olive Oil-poached Swordfish with Asparagus Pesto and Squid Ink and Cheddar Farro Risotto · Pork Belly with Nectarine Agrodolce and Yogurt

JODY WILLIAMS 207

Winter Walnut Pesto with Toasted Country Bread · Clam and Sorrel Chowder · Rosemary Fried Rabbit and Artichokes · Oxtails Braised in Red Wine and Bitter Chocolate

EINAT ADMONY

No matter what else she set her mind to, Einat Admony couldn't escape her inclination to feed people. At 18, she began her two years of mandatory military service in Israel. As a pilot in the air force, she soon found the pantry and began cooking for all the other pilots. At 20, she traveled from Tel Aviv, where she had grown up, to Germany; there, she set herself up as a street vendor. Even then, while she was living out of an RV, she would prepare meals for friends. When she returned to Israel she considered going into the import-export business, but the venture never got off the ground. Instead, Admony succumbed to the thing that made her the happiest and enrolled in the Tadmor Culinary School in Herzliya. "I might have more talents for some other things, but I love to cook the most."

Admony (whose mini New York culinary empire consists of restaurants Balaboosta, in Nolita, and Bar Bolonat, in the West Village, plus two outlets of Taïm, a falafel fast food concept) would even argue that cooking is ingrained in her DNA. Admony's Iranian-Jewish mother is a fervent and accomplished home cook. To the table already heaving with braised short ribs, fresh-baked challah, and Israeli salads her mother would bring bold Persian dishes enriched with dried fruits, pomegranate, and saffron. That her Aunt Chana's portrait hangs so prominently in Balaboosta is a testament to the inspiration her ample feasts roused. Admony's Israeli-born father never let anyone forget about his Yemenite roots: the varied breads and pungent fenugreek sauce that were staples of his heritage were omnipresent.

Admony has been cooking since she was five. While her sister was in charge of cleaning in preparation for the Shabbat, Admony was in the kitchen. So she found culinary school a breeze (or "useless" if she's being frank). Still, the classical French training she acquired gave her the confidence to apply, and secure, a job at Keren, the pinnacle of haute cuisine in Tel Aviv. After a year, she moved to New York, where she cooked under some of the city's greatest chefs: Bobby Flay, at Bolo; David Bouley, at Danube; and Floyd Cardoz, at Tabla.

In 2005, Admony and her husband, Stefan, opened the first branch of Taïm (which means "tasty" in Hebrew). Hidden on a side street in the West Village, the blink-and-you'll-miss-it spot suffered a tough first year despite the impeccably conceived falafel. Then, out of the blue, a *New York* magazine article on Taïm's take on the "sabich" (a traditional Israeli sandwich of hummus, thin slices of fried eggplant, hard-boiled egg, and salad leaves) changed its fortunes overnight.

Leaving others to serve the crowds at Taïm, Admony set up her first real restaurant, Balaboosta, in 2011. Though it literally means "perfect housewife" in Yiddish, to Admony the name signifies a strong woman: staunch of heart and resolute in her principles. Is it self-referential? Why not? At Balaboosta, Admony cooks what she wants: Middle Eastern-inspired Mediterranean fare. As any strong woman would do, she built upon her already considerable success and, in 2012, unveiled a second, larger Taïm, around the corner from Balaboosta.

At the super slick and sexy Bar Bolonat, which opened in the summer of 2014, Admony has returned to her roots, in a sense. The focus here is squarely on Israeli food but inflected by modern, whimsical touches that are uniquely hers. This means that her Everyday Cauliflower is served with bamba, a much-loved Israeli peanut-flavored puffed corn snack, and drizzled with peanut tahini. It means that her Jerusalem bagels come with a fancy extra-virgin olive oil and house-made za'atar. It also means that you'll never be able to find her Yemenite curry with shrimp anywhere else but in her corner spot on Hudson Street.

Who or what has most influenced your cooking?
My old Aunt Chana, not only because she is an amazing cook but also because she's passionate over food and feeding people. When it comes to food her heart is completely opened up.

Is there one rule of conduct in your kitchen that above all others has to be abided by/that you enforce most strictly?
Tasting food before it goes out.

Is there a dish by another chef or that you've seen in a cookbook/magazine that you wished you had created, and why?
Not really, but ... several times I've had an amazing idea that I thought I'd created and then saw it somewhere else. That's very disappointing.

Of all your travels, which country's cuisine do you love exploring the most?
Thailand.

Is there a secret to making the perfect falafel?
Not really ... avoid fillers like bread or flour; avoid baking soda or baking powder.

SMOKED EGGPLANT SALAD WITH PEPPER AND TOMATO

SERVES 6

Being an Israeli, I make eggplant the cornerstone of many of my vegetable dishes. This salad was inspired by a similar one I first had at my good friend Nina's house—I fell in love with the smokiness of its flavors. I added a few more vegetables and an element of spiciness to my version to create a wonderful accompaniment to almost anything you'd serve at a barbeque or dinner party.

2 medium eggplants (about 1 pound each)
1 tablespoon fresh lemon juice
4 tablespoons blended oil (a mix of 50 percent canola oil and 50 percent olive oil)
5 garlic cloves, thinly sliced
½ medium jalapeño pepper, deseeded and thinly sliced
1 red bell pepper, deseeded and chopped into ½-inch cubes
3 plum tomatoes, chopped into ½-inch cubes
1 tablespoon distilled white vinegar
½ teaspoon honey
2 tablespoons fresh, roughly chopped flat-leaf parsley
½ teaspoon ground cumin
¼ teaspoon sweet Hungarian paprika
¼ teaspoon chili flakes
2 teaspoons kosher salt
freshly ground black pepper, as needed

Using a knife or a skewer, pierce both eggplants a few times all over. Holding the eggplants with long-handled tongs, grill over an open flame on the stove, until completely soft on all sides, from head to toe. Or, if you prefer, place them in a pan and roast them in a 425°F oven for about 45–50 minutes.

Once the eggplants are cool enough to handle, halve them and scoop out the insides into a colander set over the sink, discarding the skin. Leave for 15–20 minutes to allow the bitter juices to drain away. Drizzle the eggplant flesh with a few drops of the lemon juice, then chop into rough 1-inch pieces. Transfer to a bowl and set aside.

Heat 2 tablespoons of the blended oil in a skillet over medium heat. Sauté the garlic until golden brown, then add the jalapeño followed by the bell pepper. Once the pepper starts to soften, after about 5 minutes, add the tomatoes and sauté for another 2 minutes.

Transfer the tomato and bell pepper mixture to the bowl with the eggplant. Let the mixture cool down slightly, then add the vinegar, honey, remaining lemon juice and oil, parsley, cumin, paprika, chili flakes, salt, and a pinch of black pepper, to taste. Stir to combine all the ingredients thoroughly, then transfer to a serving dish.

KIBBEH WITH TZATZIKI

**SERVES 4–5
(MAKES ABOUT 12–14)**

Growing up, my siblings and I loved my mom's kibbeh, but that seemed to make her anxious. Forming the patties of meat-filled bulgur pockets into the massive discs, as she did, was very difficult, and every delicious serving came with a side of nerves. I serve it now with a side of tzatziki, which would never have been allowed in my mom's kosher home.

For the filling

1½ tablespoons blended oil (a mix of 50 percent canola oil and 50 percent olive oil)
1 small onion, finely chopped
½ medium jalapeño pepper, deseeded and minced
¾ pound ground beef
⅓ cup chopped fresh flat-leaf parsley leaves
generous pinch of ground cinnamon
1 teaspoon ground paprika
¼ (rounded) teaspoon ground turmeric
1 teaspoon ground cumin
¼ teaspoon freshly ground black pepper
1 teaspoon salt
1 small bay leaf
1 tablespoon dried currants
1 tablespoon pine nuts

For the dough

½ pound medium-grind (#2) bulgur wheat
½ cup flour
1 teaspoon kosher salt
pinch of freshly ground black pepper
1 teaspoon ground paprika
¼ teaspoon chili flakes
pinch of ground cumin

To cook

canola oil, as needed

To serve

Tzatziki (see recipe below, page 162)

First make the meat filling. Heat the oil in a medium skillet over medium heat. When hot, add the onion and jalapeño and cook down until soft. Add the beef and mix well, then add the parsley, cinnamon, paprika, turmeric, cumin, black pepper, salt, and bay leaf, and cook, stirring occasionally, until the meat is slightly browned and broken down, about 6–8 minutes. Remove the pan from the heat, taste, and adjust the seasoning as needed.

Remove the bay leaf from the meat mixture and discard. Transfer the mixture to a strainer to let some of the fat drain off, being careful not to dry out the meat too much. Put the meat into a bowl, then mix in the currants and pine nuts, and set aside.

To make the dough, first wash the bulgur thoroughly, strain, and place in a mixing bowl.

Heat a medium saucepan filled with water over high heat. After the water boils, pour it over the bulgur until you have around 2 inches of water standing in the bowl. Let the bulgur soak for 40 minutes, then strain again, using your hands to squeeze out the excess moisture.

Place the bulgur in a clean mixing bowl, along with the flour, kosher salt, black pepper, paprika, chili flakes, and cumin. Mix well until the mixture has a doughlike consistency.

To form the kibbeh, shape a 1½-inch ball of dough in your hand. Make a deep indentation and fill it with a spoonful of the meat mixture. Work the dough around the meat so that it is completely encased and you have a small patty. Make sure the dough is as thin as possible without breaking. If the dough is hard to work with, moisten your hands with cold water to stop it from sticking. Repeat with the remaining dough and filling.

Cook the kibbeh. Fill a heavy-based skillet with 1 inch of canola oil and set over medium-high heat. When the oil reaches 375°F when tested with a deep-frying or candy thermometer, work in batches to fry the patties until golden brown and crisp, about 2–3 minutes on each side. Remove from the oil with a slotted spoon and drain on a tray lined with paper towels.

Serve the kibbeh with a generous spoonful of tzatziki for dipping. **➤**

Tzatziki (makes about 2 cups)

1½ cups plain yogurt
2 tablespoons olive oil
2 teaspoons fresh lemon juice
*⅓ cup finely chopped, unpeeled
    cucumber*
½ garlic clove, finely chopped
*1½ tablespoons finely chopped fresh
    mint leaves*
*1 tablespoon chopped cilantro
    leaves (optional)*
¾ teaspoon salt
pinch of freshly ground black pepper
⅛ teaspoon granulated sugar

Combine all the ingredients in a
large bowl and whisk until
thoroughly mixed. Taste and add
more salt if necessary. Keep the
tzatziki chilled until ready to use. It is
best served on the day it is made,
but can be stored in the refrigerator,
covered, for up to 3 days.

BRAISED SHORT RIBS WITH WINE, PRUNES, AND HARISSA

SERVES 4

This is a great dish to impress your dinner party guests without your having to spend hours slaving over the stove. The prep is fairly simple, and the oven does most of the work, giving you that extra time to make sure the house is actually clean this time. Use your fingers with this dish, and be sure to lick them clean afterward!

2 tablespoons canola oil
1 medium Spanish onion, diced
1 clove garlic, thinly sliced
1 leek, thinly sliced (white and light green parts only)
1 large carrot, peeled and cut into ¼-inch-thick slices
1 celery stalk, thinly sliced
5 dried stoned prunes, cut in half
⅛ teaspoon chopped fresh rosemary leaves
⅛ teaspoon chopped fresh thyme leaves
1 tablespoon harissa paste
1 tablespoon honey
1¼ cups red wine
1½ cups chicken stock
½ teaspoon ground cumin
¼ teaspoon ground cinnamon
⅛ teaspoon sweet Hungarian paprika
½ teaspoon ground star anise
1 bay leaf
¼ cup orange juice
2 pounds English-style beef short ribs (3 or 4 [6–7-inch] ribs)
½ tablespoon salt
⅛ teaspoon freshly ground black pepper

Preheat the oven to 350°F.

Heat the oil in a large cooking pot over medium heat. When hot, add, in this order: the onions, garlic, leek, carrot, celery, and prunes. Sauté until softened, about 4–6 minutes. Add the rosemary and thyme, followed by the harissa paste and honey, and mix thoroughly.

Pour the red wine and chicken stock into the pot and bring to a simmer. Combine the cumin, cinnamon, paprika, star anise, and bay leaf in a small bowl, then add the spices to the vegetable mixture all at once. Finally, pour in the orange juice, bring back to a simmer, and cook until the vegetables are very soft and slightly broken down. Remove from the heat.

Season the short ribs all over with the salt and black pepper. Combine the meat and the cooked vegetables, wine, stock, and orange juice mixture in a Dutch oven, making sure some of the vegetables are underneath the ribs and some are over the top. Place the lid on the Dutch oven and cook in the oven for 2½–3 hours, until the meat is very tender and comes easily off the bones.

When the ribs are cooked, skim off as much fat as possible. Alternatively, leave to cool, then refrigerate overnight and spoon off the solidified fat.

When ready to serve, gently reheat the braised beef ribs over medium-low heat (if previously chilled). For a fancy presentation, remove the meat and ribs from the pot and discard the bones. Pass the remaining vegetables and liquid through a strainer, pressing out as much of the liquid as possible. Transfer the liquid to a blender, along with the prune halves (if you can find them) and blend until smooth. Pour the liquid into a medium saucepan and place over medium-high heat. Simmer until the liquid reduces to a sauce consistency. Taste and adjust the seasoning as necessary.

To serve, arrange the meat on plates or on a large platter (slice the meat in half, if desired) and pour the sauce over the top. Serve with regular couscous, Israeli couscous, mashed potatoes, or rice.

If you're not feeling fancy or don't have any extra time, the ribs and vegetables can be served straight from the Dutch oven, ideally over a bed of one of the above accompaniments.

GREEN SHAKSHUKA

SERVES 4

I love shakshuka, a dish of eggs poached in a rich tomato sauce. But in recent years it has been overdone by many places, so I decided to shake up the dish by replacing the tomatoes with tons and tons of healthy greens.

4 tablespoons olive oil, plus a little extra
2 whole leeks, white part diced and green tops very thinly sliced
3 cloves garlic, thinly sliced
1 small to medium jalapeño pepper, deseeded and thinly sliced
1 bunch of Swiss chard (about 5 or 6 stalks), leaves roughly chopped and stalks thinly sliced
½ bunch of Tuscan kale (about ¼ pound), trimmed and roughly chopped
3 cups (about ¼ pound) baby spinach (or regular spinach: 3 cups of roughly chopped trimmed leaves)
1 teaspoon ground caraway
1 teaspoon ground cumin
kosher salt and freshly ground black pepper, as needed
½ cup chicken or vegetable stock or water
1 tablespoon freshly squeezed lemon juice
6–8 medium eggs
5 ounces feta cheese, crumbled into large chunks

To serve
za'atar
1 loaf of crusty bread, thickly sliced

Heat the olive oil in a (12-inch or larger) skillet over high heat. When hot, add the white and green parts of the leeks, followed by the garlic, then the jalapeño pepper, and finally the Swiss chard stalks (only). Sauté until softened, about 6–8 minutes. Next add the kale, spinach, and chard leaves, in batches if necessary, cooking down until the leaves are wilted and soft, about 8–10 minutes. Add the caraway and cumin, and salt and pepper, to taste.

Add the stock (or water) and lemon juice to the skillet. Reduce the heat slightly and simmer the mixture for 5 minutes, then turn the heat down to low.

Depending on how many eggs you are using, create 6 to 8 little wells in the vegetable mixture in the skillet, then carefully break an egg into each well. Cover the skillet and cook until the whites of the eggs are firm and opaque but the yolks are still slightly runny, about 10 minutes.

Remove the skillet from the heat. Sprinkle the crumbled feta over the top, then drizzle a little olive oil over this. Finally garnish with a couple of pinches of za'atar and serve warm, straight from the skillet, accompanied by crusty bread.

RAWIA BISHARA

awia Bishara has come a long way since opening her Brooklyn restaurant Tanoreen in 1998. In those days she was running the front of house, back of house, and everything in between. Furnished with a mere 10 tables, plus a display case of Arabic dishes encapsulating the flavors of the Levant region, it scarcely qualified for the label "restaurant." Still, Bishara's patrons cared little for the décor, or lack of it. Eventually the display case could no longer hold the ever-growing assortment of daily specials so in 2006, Bishara moved her Bay Ridge enterprise to a nearby, larger location with a modern interior. Her daughter Jumana joined her as co-owner and manager leaving Bishara to focus her energies on what she did best: spicing, stirring, and saucing.

Bishara knows how to cook only one way—from the heart—and her heart remains true to the culture of her homeland. Born and raised in Nazareth, northern Israel, she grew up on olives and olive oil from her grandparents' grove, rice and whole grains, like freekeh and cracked wheat, and homegrown eggplant, cucumbers, tomatoes, and okra—fresh during summer and pickled or dried during the colder months.

For the most part, Bishara's cuisine of mezze, hearty stews, stuffed cabbage rolls and artichokes, baked eggplant and lamb casseroles, fried fish, and grilled kabobs features the hallmarks of classic Palestinian home-style cooking. But in some ways, her food stands apart. She is more liberal with her use of spices than most Palestinian cooks—a characteristic of her mother's cooking—enlivening her dishes with a selection of heady spices and herbs like lemony sumac and dried wild thyme, cinnamon, cumin and coriander, and nutmeg. In fact, Tanoreen is really a tribute to her mother, a schoolteacher whose culinary skills Bishara speaks of with the utmost reverence.

With certain dishes that she holds especially dear, like her fish kibbie, patties of chopped fish and onion surrounded by a crust of cracked wheat and finely ground fish, and maftoul, a sort of giant couscous, she refuses to stray from her mother's recipes. With others, she applies a more innovative approach. Her sayadiyya, a fisherman's one-pot meal of shredded fish, caramelized onions, and rice, has been vastly improved, she says, by cooking it more like Spanish paella. Her take on musakhan, a labored preparation of whole roasted spiced chicken, transforms this banquet dish into a flatbread "pizza" in which shredded chicken and slow-cooked onions are piled high and topped with slivered almonds.

Bishara moved to the U.S. in 1974 as a young bride. She brought with her to Bay Ridge a memory bank brimming with her mother's recipes and a few staples from home including jars of pickled cheese in olive oil, packets of za'atar—the iconic Middle Eastern seasoning—and freekeh. For the next 20 years she worked at a number of desk jobs and also headed the Union of Palestinian Women's Association in America. All the while she cooked for family, she cooked for friends, and she cooked for the women she helped. Only once her children were grown did she allow herself to pursue her dream of running a restaurant.

Not only has Tanoreen won impressive reviews from notable publications, including the *New Yorker* and the *New York Times*, it has also secured accolades as diverse as a ranking in *Gourmet* magazine's "11 Best Restaurants Worth your Money" and *New York* magazine's "Best Mezze" award. Seventeen years since opening her restaurant, Bishara has realized her dream, then trumped it again and again and again.

What is the biggest misconception you encounter from misinformed diners about Middle Eastern cuisine?
That Middle Eastern cuisine is all about shish kebob or falafel or hummus, when in fact our kitchen is rich with healthy and delicious recipes. In fact, shish kebob (lamb) is pretty pricey, so a lot of people can't afford to eat it often. There is a world of dishes beyond the 'usual suspects' in Middle Eastern food. Tanoreen, my restaurant, is famous for doing exactly this. I cook there the food that you would eat in an Arab home.

What piece of kitchen equipment can you absolutely not live without?
Three, actually. A chef's knife, a skillet, and a stovetop. With these three pieces you can cook up a storm.

What dish/dishes would make your customers revolt if you removed it from the menu?
Eggplant Napoleon, Baked Med Eggplant, and Lamb Fetti. The first is not a traditional Middle Eastern dish but my own creation, and it has become wildly popular. The Baked Eggplant is a best-seller on Tanoreen's menu, and the Lamb Fetti was put on our daily specials, but now I practically can't take it off since it is requested so often!

LABANEH

SERVES 4–6

This is a staple of the Middle Eastern breakfast—typically served with za'atar and olive oil next to fresh veggies and olives. It has so few ingredients and is so easy to make that there is no excuse not to have it in your refrigerator! My daughter uses it as a condiment instead of mayo.

1½ (32-ounce) tubs of low-fat plain yogurt (6 cups in total), or homemade yogurt (see note)
1 tablespoon salt
1 pinch sour salt (powdered citric acid) (optional; see suppliers, page 286)

To store
olive oil

Combine the yogurt, regular salt, and sour salt together in a large bowl and mix until smooth. If you have cheesecloth, line a second large bowl with a large square piece of it so the cheesecloth hangs over the edge. Pour the yogurt mixture into the cheesecloth, then bring up the corners and tie securely. Using kitchen string, hang the bundle over a sink or large bowl for 18–24 hours to drain.

Alternatively, line a large strainer with 2 sheets of 2-ply, heavy-duty paper towels. Pour the yogurt into the lined strainer. Fold the corners of the paper towel over to cover and/or place another piece of paper towel over the top of the yogurt mixture.

Place the strainer on top of a bowl and leave the yogurt to drain off the excess water for 24 hours.

Transfer the labaneh into a container with a lid and top with olive oil to cover the surface; seal the container and refrigerate. It will last for approximately 10–12 days. Labaneh is best eaten with pita bread drizzled with olive oil along with chopped tomatoes and cucumbers.

Note
Homemade yogurt will yield the best results. Also, in either case, you can use regular yogurt instead of low-fat.

LENTIL SALAD

SERVES 8

This is a super-simple, fresh recipe that you can make for a quick lunch or as a side dish. The protein-rich lentils, herbs, and vegetables make it very healthful. I happen to love cilantro, but if you don't, simply omit it. Don't be afraid to substitute your own favorite ingredients to customize the dish to your own taste.

For the salad

1½ cups small brown lentils, rinsed
1 fennel bulb, trimmed and diced
3 tablespoons chopped fresh dill
3 tablespoons chopped fresh flat-
    leaf parsley leaves
½ cup chopped fresh cilantro leaves
½ cup finely diced fresh hot peppers
    of your choice, deseeded if
    desired
½ cup finely diced red onion
½ cup finely diced pitted olives of
    your choice
1 tablespoon ground cumin

For the dressing

1 teaspoon salt, plus more as
    needed
6 tablespoons olive oil
juice of 1–2 medium lemons, as
    needed
3 cloves garlic, minced

To garnish

20–25 cherry tomatoes, halved

Place the lentils in a medium saucepan and cover with water. Bring to a boil and cook for approximately 15–20 minutes or until tender; strain and leave to cool.

In a large bowl mix together the lentils with the fennel, herbs, peppers, onion, olives, and cumin. In another bowl combine all the dressing ingredients, using the juice of 1 lemon to begin with, and whisk to emulsify.

Add the dressing to the salad and toss. Taste, and adjust salt and lemon juice as needed. Transfer the salad to a serving bowl or platter and garnish with the cherry tomatoes.

CAULIFLOWER TAGINE

SERVES 4–6

Cauliflower tagine is extremely rich and hearty. It is a dish that I like to serve in this vegetarian version, but it can easily be made with meat. My preference is to use beef, although lamb or chicken could easily be substituted. A recipe for the meat variation is given below.

For the cauliflower

2 medium heads of cauliflower, trimmed and broken into florets
4 tablespoons olive oil
5 medium shallots, finely sliced
salt, as needed

For the tahini sauce

2 cups tahini
1 cup fresh lemon juice
1 cup water
2 tablespoons hot pepper paste (optional)
4 tablespoons pomegranate molasses
½ (packed) cup chopped cilantro
2 tablespoons crushed garlic
1 tablespoon salt, plus more as needed
1 teaspoon ground cumin
1 teaspoon freshly ground black pepper
1 teaspoon ground coriander
½ teaspoon ground allspice
vegetable oil, for frying

Bring a large pot of salted water to a boil. Add the cauliflower florets, bring back to a boil, and cook for about 5 minutes, or until tender, then strain and set aside. Heat the olive oil in a small skillet over medium-high heat and add the shallots. Sauté until golden brown, about 4–6 minutes, then remove from the heat and set aside.

Put all of the tahini sauce ingredients into a blender and process until smooth. Taste, and add more salt, if needed. Set aside.

Traditionally the cauliflower in this dish is fried. Fill a large, medium-depth skillet with 1½ inches of vegetable oil. Add the cauliflower florets in batches and fry until golden brown. Transfer to a plate or tray lined with paper towel and leave to drain. Alternatively, brush the florets with vegetable or olive oil and bake in a 500°F oven until golden brown, about 20 minutes.

Preheat (or lower) the oven to 400°F.

Place the cooked cauliflower in a deep roasting pan. Pour the tahini sauce over the cauliflower, then evenly distribute the cooked shallots over the top. Using a large spoon, gently fold the ingredients over once or twice to combine. Cover the pan with aluminum foil and bake for 40 minutes. Uncover and bake for another 5 minutes to brown the top.

Serve with Arabic bread or traditional Arabic rice with toasted vermicelli noodles (see below for recipe, page 173).

Variation: Cauliflower and Beef Tagine

2 pounds trimmed beef chuck, cut into 1½-inch cubes
⅓ teaspoon ground nutmeg
1 tablespoon ground allspice
salt, as needed
3 tablespoons olive oil
4 cups water

Place the meat in a bowl and add the nutmeg, allspice, and a generous amount of salt. Combine with your hands, rubbing the spices into the beef. In a medium pot, heat the olive oil over medium-high heat. When hot, add the meat and sear until browned all over, stirring every now and then—about 5 minutes. Slowly add the water, bring to a boil, then reduce the heat and simmer until tender, about 1 hour. The beef can be boiled 1 day in advance and refrigerated until ready to use in the tagine.

To make the tagine, strain the beef, reserving the cooking liquid. Reduce the liquid in a small saucepan over medium-high heat to about ½ cup. Follow the main recipe above, adding the cooked beef and the reduced beef cooking liquid to the roasting pan with the cauliflower and tahini sauce. Continue as directed in the main recipe.

Arabic Rice and Toasted Vermicelli Pilaf (serves 8–10)

When in doubt, serve any entrée with this mix of rice and broken pasta strands. When my daughter, Jumana, was a young girl, she made it her main course whenever she didn't want what I was serving. Centuries ago, this pilaf was made exclusively with bulgur or smoked wheat, but when rice was introduced to the Arab world, it became a popular substitute. Egyptian rice kernels are small, round and broken; this is the only rice to use to make the authentic version of this dish. Chinese and Carolina white rice are the next best options. If you have gluten sensitivities, eliminate the vermicelli altogether along with 1 cup of the water, then add another ½ cup of rice.

⅔ cup extra-virgin olive oil
¼ cup ghee or butter (or ½ stick butter)
1 pound vermicelli
4 cups Egyptian rice (alternatively you can use Chinese or Carolina rice)
8–9 cups boiling water
1 tablespoon sea salt, or to taste

Combine the oil and ghee in a medium pot and place over high heat until hot. Add the vermicelli and stir until golden brown, 7–10 minutes. Add the rice and stir until opaque, 3–5 minutes. Pour in the boiling water and salt, reduce the heat to low, cover and simmer until the rice is fluffy, about 12 minutes, stirring once halfway through. Off the heat, stir once more, cover, and let stand 5 minutes. Serve warm.

Recipe originally published in *Olives, Lemons & Za'atar* (Kyle Books; 2014)

BELL PEPPERS STUFFED WITH MEAT AND RICE

SERVES 6

I am giving two options for the sauce on this dish. If it is summer and tomatoes are in season and wonderfully ripe, go the fresh tomato route. Otherwise, you can use good-quality canned, crushed tomatoes.

6 large bell peppers, any color
½ cup vegetable oil
2 shallots, diced
1 small poblano pepper, diced
1½ tablespoons ground allspice
1 tablespoon Tanoreen Spices (see suppliers, page 286) or ¼ tablespoon ground cumin, ¼ tablespoon ground coriander, and a pinch of ground cinnamon
1 teaspoon freshly ground black pepper
½ teaspoon ground nutmeg
2–2¼ pounds deboned and well-trimmed leg of lamb cut into ½-inch cubes
2 tablespoons chopped fresh dill
½ cup chopped fresh cilantro
1½ tablespoons salt
4 tablespoons tomato paste
1½ cups Egyptian (short-grain) rice or Carolina rice
3–4 pounds large ripe tomatoes, peeled and puréed, OR 1 (28-ounce) can crushed tomatoes

Cut around the stem of each bell pepper to form a "lid" for the stuffed pepper. Pull out the stems and set aside, then remove and discard the seeds and cores from the inside of the peppers.

In a medium skillet, heat the vegetable oil over medium-high heat. Sauté the shallots and poblano pepper until tender, about 2–3 minutes. Add all the ground spices and continue to sauté until fragrant, about 1 minute. Add the chopped meat and stir. Cook until the meat turns brown and there are no traces of pink, about 5–7 minutes. Sprinkle in the dill, cilantro, and 1 tablespoon of salt.

Next add the tomato paste; stir and turn off the heat. Add the rice to the meat mixture and stir to combine. Use a spoon to stuff each pepper with the meat and rice mixture until it is about three-quarters full, making sure to leave room at the top for the rice to expand. Cap each pepper with the reserved stem.

Arrange the peppers snugly in a Dutch oven or heavy ovenproof casserole with a tight-fitting lid. The stuffed peppers can be cooked on the cooktop or in the oven. If baking, preheat the oven to 400°F.

If using the fresh tomato pureé, combine it with the remaining ½ tablespoon of salt and pour the mixture over and around the peppers. Alternatively, combine the crushed canned tomatoes with 4 cups of water and the remaining salt, and pour this over and around them.

If cooking the peppers on the cooktop, place the pot over high heat and bring the sauce to a boil. Lower the heat to a simmer, cover, and cook for about 50 minutes to 1 hour or until the rice is cooked through. If using the oven, cover and bake for about 1 hour 15 minutes to 1 hour 45 minutes or until the rice is cooked through.

To serve, lift out the peppers from the pot, leaving behind the sauce, then arrange them in a large, shallow serving bowl. Carefully slice the peppers down the middle and ladle the sauce onto the stuffing.

SARA JENKINS

She may not have a trace of Italian blood coursing through her veins, but chef Sara Jenkins knows the food of Italy better than many of its natives. The owner of Porchetta, a diminutive joint in the East Village dedicated to the typical central Italian street food it is named for, and of nearby Porsena, among Manhattan's top pasta restuarants, has earned her bragging rights.

Jenkins acquired her knowledge of Italy's food firsthand. She lived in Rome between the ages of 10 and 15, when her father, a foreign correspondent, was posted there. Her family has owned an ancient farmhouse near the Tuscan town of Cortona since 1971, returning every fall to harvest the fruit of 150 olive trees and produce their own green-gold oil. Jenkins speaks fluent Italian and has used this gift to elicit precious recipes from her Tuscan neighbor, Mita. It is Mita's pasta dough that Jenkins relies on at Porsena for her lasagna, tagliolini, and ravioli, and Mita's gnocchi with ragu that soothes diners when the colder weather hits.

When Jenkins returned to the States to attend boarding school in Maine, she began cooking to re-create the flavors she missed from Italy, but it was only later that her interest transmuted into a career. First, she attended the Rhode Island School of Photography and tried to make her way as a photographer. On the side, she took on kitchen jobs. Enthused more by her part-time endeavors than her photography, she studied cookbooks and turned up for work brimming with ideas for new dishes. Finally yielding to the inevitable, she quit photography.

The neophyte cook scored a job in Todd English's pizza-and-pasta-focused eatery, Figs, in Boston. Two years on, having risen to the rank of executive chef, Jenkins headed back to Tuscany, where she stayed for three years. First, she assisted with the culinary program at a winery, then she cooked at a restaurant in Florence where there was no deviating from the classic Florentine fare, with its emphasis on steak and beans.

In 1999, she landed in New York City and made the East Village her professional stamping ground—first as the chef of the regional Tuscan eatery I Coppi, then at Il Buco, followed by Patio Dining. Next came a brief migration to the West Village with 50 Carmine before Jenkins took time off to have her son and write her first cookbook.

With the realization that 18-hour days in someone else's kitchen were incompatible with her new role as a mother came the impetus to start her own business. In 2008 Jenkins teamed up with her cousin Matt Lindemulder and set about translating porchetta to accommodate New Yorkers' palates and the strictures of the health department. In place of the whole pig roasted with guts and all, Jenkins settled on pork loins wrapped in pork bellies then seasoned with an aromatic mixture of wild fennel pollen, sage, thyme, rosemary, and garlic. After slow roasting in her specially programmed Electrolux oven, the sliced pork is served hot—instead of at room temperature, as it is in Italy. The result? Her transformed porchetta was an instant hit.

Success triggered itchy feet, and Jenkins yearned to helm a proper restaurant where she could serve "solid Italian bones." So in November 2010 she opened Porsena. With an interior that recalls a Roman trattoria, it offers a much wider-ranging menu: Jenkins draws her inspiration from anywhere in Italy that excites her, also even venturing occasionally into southern France and the Middle East. And why not? After you have mastered one cuisine, as she has, the natural progression is to take liberties with it. Still, the essence remains firmly Italian. As Mario Batali said of Jenkins, "She's one of the few chefs in America who understands Italy, and how Italians eat."

What's in your fridge at home?
Condiments, Middle Eastern pickles, three different kinds of hot sauce, tahini sauce, unsweetened cranberry juice, apples, kale, leftover cooked rice, lemons, limes, rosé wine.

If there was one person, chef/artist/writer/anyone, that you could collaborate with, whether it's on a pop-up restaurant, writing a book, creating a dish together—whatever you like—who would it be and what would you do?
I'd like to do a dinner with Federico Fellini, a massive bacchanalian feast for all the characters in his movies, set on the beach where *I Vitelloni* was filmed.

What moment—good or bad—in your professional career will you never forget?
Coming to New York and getting two stars in the *New York Times* three months later.

Is there one rule of conduct in your kitchen that, above all others, has to be abided by/that you enforce most strictly?
Show up and be present.

Aside from Italy, what country's cuisine do you most love to explore, in or out of your restaurant kitchen?
Vietnamese.

CARDOON SFORMATO WITH SALSA VERDE

SERVES 6

A sformato is a classic Italian appetizer or side dish. Essentially a savory custard, it's easily varied to incorporate whatever vegetables are in season. I use cardoons here; they have a haunting, ephemeral artichoke flavor that makes for a very delicate and subtle opening to a meal.

For the sformato
juice of 1 lemon
1¼ pounds cardoons (about 7 to 8 stalks)
2 tablespoons unsalted butter
1 Spanish onion, peeled and minced
pinch of salt, plus more as needed
3 cups heavy cream
9 large egg yolks
1 cup fresh ricotta cheese
freshly ground black pepper, as needed

For the salsa verde
⅓ cup salt-packed capers
3 garlic cloves, peeled and smashed
1 cup roughly chopped flat-leaf parsley
2 anchovy fillets
finely grated zest of 1 lemon
½ teaspoon fine sea salt
½ cup extra-virgin olive oil, plus more as needed
2 tablespoons red wine vinegar

Equipment
6 (8-fluid-ounce) ramekins

Half-fill a large bowl with cold water and add the lemon juice. Trim the cardoons and remove the stringy bits from them using a vegetable peeler. Drop the cleaned cardoons into the acidic water to prevent them from darkening. Bring a large pot of salted water to a boil and add the drained cardoons. Blanch until soft and tender, about 10 minutes. Drain well, and set aside.

Preheat the oven to 275°F.

Melt the butter in a skillet set over medium heat and sauté the minced onion in the butter, along with a pinch of salt, very gently and slowly. After about 5 minutes add 1 cup of water to let the onion really soften and sweeten, then let it cook gently until all the water has evaporated and the onion mixture is like a pap, about 10–15 minutes.

Transfer the onion and cardoons to a food processor and purée until smooth. Spoon the mixture out into a bowl and whisk in the cream, egg yolks, and ricotta. Season with salt and pepper. Divide the mixture between the ramekins and place the ramekins in a roasting pan. Slowly pour hot water into the side of the pan until it reaches halfway up the ramekins (make sure to avoid pouring any water into them). Cover the pan with aluminum foil and bake for about 50–60 minutes or until the sformato is just set in the middle.

While the sformato is cooking, make the salsa verde. Soak the capers in a bowl of cold water for 10 minutes, then rinse well, changing the water 2 or 3 times. Drain and transfer to a food processor, along with the garlic, parsley, anchovy fillets, lemon zest, and salt. Process until the mixture is finely chopped. With the machine running, slowly add ½ cup olive oil and the vinegar. If the sauce is too thick, add the remaining olive oil as necessary.

Serve the sformato warm or at room temperature, along with the salsa verde.

CLASSIC BEEF RAGÙ LASAGNA

SERVES 8

Traditional Tuscan lasagna is a little different from the American version. It's about lightness and as much about the layers of pasta as the filling between them. This was my neighbor Mita Antolini's classic Sunday lunch; she would slip it into the wood oven after the week's bread was baked in the morning. I like to see exactly how many layers I can get in before I come up over the top of the pan.

The ragù is something of a labor of love and takes more than 3 hours to cook from start to finish. This recipe yields enough to make 3 lasagnas, so you don't have to start completely from scratch every time. Simply divide the ragù into 3 batches and freeze 2 of them; they will keep for up to 6 months.

For the Tuscan ragù

2 carrots, peeled and cut into 1-inch pieces
2 celery stalks, cut into 1-inch pieces
2 garlic cloves, peeled and left whole
1 leek, halved, thoroughly cleaned and roughly chopped
1 medium onion, peeled and quartered
1 sprig of fresh rosemary (optional)
¼ cup extra-virgin olive oil
1 tablespoon concentrated tomato paste
4½ pounds ground beef
1 (35-ounce) can whole peeled plum tomatoes and their juices, preferably San Marzano variety
fine sea salt, as needed

For the besciamella (béchamel) sauce

6 cups whole milk
2 stalks celery, cut into 4 pieces
1 medium onion, quartered (skin on)
1 leek, cut in half lengthwise, washed well and chopped
1 carrot, cut into 4 pieces
⅓ bunch of fresh flat-leaf parsley
5 sprigs of fresh sage
4 bay leaves
2 garlic cloves, peeled and kept whole
½ teaspoon whole black peppercorns
7 tablespoons unsalted butter
¾ cup all-purpose flour
pinch of fine sea salt
¼ teaspoon freshly grated nutmeg
1 cup freshly grated Parmigiano-Reggiano cheese

To assemble the lasagna

fresh pasta dough: twice the quantity for the Ricotta and Herb-filled Ravioli (2 pounds) (see recipe, page 183)
all-purpose flour, for dusting
3 cups Tuscan ragù
5 cups besciamella sauce
3¼ cups freshly grated Parmigiano-Reggiano cheese
1 tablespoon unsalted butter, cut into small pieces
freshly ground black pepper, as needed

Equipment

A pasta machine (optional)
A deep glass or ceramic baking dish, 9 x 13 inches—preferably terracotta, as this imparts a lovely earthy flavor

Start by making the ragù. In the bowl of a food processor, pulse the carrots, celery, garlic, leek, onion, and rosemary, if using, until finely minced.

Heat the oil in a large Dutch oven or heavy-bottomed saucepan over high heat. Add the chopped vegetable mixture and a pinch of sea salt. Cook, stirring once or twice, until the vegetables begin to soften, about 1–2 minutes. Add 1 cup of water and the tomato paste, stirring to dissolve the paste. Bring to a boil and cook, stirring frequently, until the liquid is mostly evaporated, about 7 minutes. Add the ground beef, stirring with a spoon to break up the chunks into small bits and incorporate them into the vegetable mixture. Keep stirring constantly for about 10 minutes—you want to be sure to break up the meat as much as possible to achieve a nice texture and avoid clumps.

Add a little more salt, reduce the heat to low, and simmer the ragù, partially covered, for 40 minutes. While the meat is cooking, pass the tomatoes and their juices through a food mill or a strainer, or purée them in a food processor. Set the puréed tomatoes aside.

Add ½ cup of water to the pan, stir, and cook for 10 more minutes. Now stir in the puréed tomatoes and continue to simmer gently, partially covered, until the ragù is thick and flavorful, about 2 more hours. **>**

Meanwhile, make the besciamella sauce. Place the milk, celery, onion, leek, carrot, parsley, sage, bay leaves, garlic, and peppercorns in a large saucepan; set this over medium heat and bring to a gentle simmer to scald the milk. Once small bubbles form around the surface of the milk, remove from the heat and leave to steep for 1 hour. Strain the infused milk into a bowl or pitcher, discarding the solids.

Melt the butter in a clean, heavy-bottomed saucepan over medium heat. Add the flour and, using a wooden spoon, stir rapidly to incorporate and create a roux. Cook, stirring constantly, for 3 minutes. Add the milk, ½ cup at a time, stirring well and making sure to scrape the corners of the pan, to fully incorporate it before the next addition. Add the salt and nutmeg, and cook, stirring occasionally, for 5 minutes. Add the cheese, and cook, stirring, for 2 more minutes. Reduce the heat to low and continue to cook gently, stirring occasionally, until the sauce is redolent with the flavor of the aromatics and there is no trace of flour flavor, about another 5–10 minutes. Taste and adjust the seasoning. Remove from the heat and place a piece of plastic wrap directly on the surface of the sauce to prevent a skin from forming. Set aside.

When the ragù is ready, season with salt to taste. Remove from the heat and set aside, at room temperature if preparing the lasagna immediately. Otherwise, cool, and refrigerate or freeze until ready to use.

Next, make the pasta dough, if not previously made.

If using a pasta machine to roll out the pasta, divide the dough into 9 equal pieces and pass these repeatedly through the machine using increasingly thin settings, starting with the widest setting. Fold a piece of dough in half crosswise, and pass it through the machine several times at this setting, folding it over, stretching it, and shaping it each time until you have a regular, rectangular shape.

Now, roll the dough through the second-widest setting. Repeat, adjusting the setting each time to create a thinner and thinner sheet until the strip of pasta is about 1⁄16 inch thick and 3 inches wide. Dredge the dough in flour between each new thickness. Trim the ends of the strip and cut it into 2 shorter strips, each 12 x 3 inches. Place the pasta sheets flat on a clean towel (or tablecloth) and cover with another towel. Repeat with the remaining 8 pieces of dough. You should end up with 18 cut strips, 3 for each layer of the lasagna.

If rolling by hand; divide the dough into 6 equal portions. Keeping the rest of the dough covered, lightly dust one piece with flour and use a rolling pin to roll it out on a lightly floured surface to about 8½ x 12½ inches. Using a sharp knife, trim to a 8- x 12-inch rectangle, discarding the scraps. Lay the pasta sheet flat on a clean towel (or tablecloth) and cover with a second towel. Repeat with the remaining 5 pieces,

covering each with a clean towel as you go.

Preheat the oven to 400°F.

Bring a large saucepan of well-salted water to a boil. Fill a large mixing bowl with ice and water and set aside. Add 1 hand-rolled lasagna sheet or 2 (smaller) machine-rolled sheets to a boiling water. Cover and cook the pasta for 1 minute. Transfer the cooked sheet or sheets to the ice water bath for 30 seconds, then remove with a slotted spoon and lay flat on a dish towel. Repeat with the remaining sheets.

To assemble the lasagna, first spread about ⅓ cup of the besciamella sauce and ¼ cup ragù over the bottom of the baking dish, mixing the two sauces together.

Follow this with a layer of pasta to cover. Now top with about ⅔ cup besciamella and ½ cup ragù, spreading them together evenly over the pasta. Next sprinkle with ½ cup of cheese and a good grinding of pepper. Top with a layer of pasta. Continue adding these quantities of sauce, cheese, and pasta until the last layer of pasta is in the dish. There should be 6 layers of pasta in total.

Finally top with the remaining 1⅓ cup besciamella, ¼ cup ragù, and ¾ cup cheese. Trim the edges just a bit, if needed, so there's no overhang.

Dot the top of the lasagna with the butter and bake in the center of the oven until piping hot inside and golden brown and bubbly on top, about 45 minutes. (If not baking immediately and the lasagna has been chilled in the fridge, be sure to bring it up to room temperature before putting in the oven.) Let it rest at least 10 minutes before cutting.

RICOTTA AND HERB-FILLED RAVIOLI WITH BURST CHERRY TOMATO SAUCE

SERVES 6–8

Entranced by an amazing array of wild and cultivated herbs outside my kitchen door in Tuscany, I started making the classic ricotta filling for ravioli with a mixture of herbs instead of the usual blanched spinach. The trick is to load up on milder varieties like basil and parsley and show restraint with the stronger mint and tarragon. During winter I serve these ravioli with brown butter and sage, but they are really at their best with a summer sauce of bright cherry tomatoes wilted in a hot pan.

For the pasta dough

2½ cups all-purpose flour, plus more as needed for kneading and rolling out
3 large eggs
3 tablespoons water
1 tablespoon extra-virgin olive oil

For the ravioli filling

1½ cups fresh sheep's or cow's milk ricotta
½ cup chopped mixed fresh herbs such as flat-leaf parsley, basil, chives, marjoram, thyme, tarragon, mint, and wild fennel pollen
1 large egg
¼ cup freshly grated Grana Padano cheese
salt and freshly ground black pepper, as needed

To assemble the ravioli

egg wash made with 1 beaten egg thinned down with a little water
semolina flour, as needed

For the cherry tomato sauce

⅓ cup extra-virgin olive oil
3 pints mixed heirloom cherry tomatoes or grape tomatoes
2 large garlic cloves, peeled and smashed
¾ cup thinly sliced fresh basil leaves
salt and freshly ground black pepper, as needed
freshly grated Parmigiano-Reggiano cheese, as needed

Equipment

A pasta machine
A piping bag
A pasta cutter

First make the pasta dough. Mound the flour in a large mixing bowl; make a well in the center and add the eggs and water into it. Using a fork, gently break up the eggs and slowly incorporate flour from the inside rim of the well. Continue doing this until all the liquid is absorbed (about half of the flour will be incorporated). Using your hands, knead the dough in the bowl, drawing in the rest of the flour until it forms a uniform mass.

Transfer the dough to a board lightly dusted with flour and knead for another 8 minutes. Drizzle the oil over the top, then knead for 4–5 more minutes to incorporate it into the dough, adding a little more flour if necessary. Wrap the dough tightly in plastic, then leave to rest for 15 minutes at room temperature or up to 3 hours in the refrigerator.

Meanwhile, make the filling. Pass the ricotta through a food mill or a strainer, or briefly blitz in a food processor. Transfer to a medium bowl and add the herbs, eggs, and cheese. Mix to combine thoroughly, seasoning with salt and pepper to taste. Spoon the filling into a piping bag and place in the refrigerator until ready to use.

Remove the dough from the refrigerator, if chilled, and leave for a few minutes to warm up to room temperature. Divide the dough into 6 equal-sized pieces on a lightly floured surface. Keeping the rest of the dough covered under a kitchen towel, roll the first piece through the pasta machine repeatedly to achieve the desired thinness, flouring as necessary. First fold the sheet crosswise and set the machine to its widest setting. Pass the dough through the rollers several times—folding over, stretching, and shaping it each time until you have a regular rectangular shape. Now adjust the machine to the second-widest setting and repeat. Continue in this way, adjusting the machine to create a thinner and thinner sheet, until you reach the second-thinnest setting, making sure to dredge the dough in flour each time before rolling it. You should end up with a sheet thin enough—about ½-inch—so that you can just see your hand through it and between 3½ and 4 inches wide. Place the dough on a well-floured surface and cover with a kitchen towel to stop it from drying out. Roll out the other pieces of dough in the same way.

To fill the ravioli, first lightly brush a pasta sheet along its whole length but only from the center to one side ➤

edge, with the egg wash. Pipe out the ravioli filling in 1– 1½-teaspoon mounds at intervals over the egg-washed part of the pasta sheet, leaving at least ½ inch between each mound.

Fold over the dry, un-brushed half of the pasta sheet to cover the filling and press to seal around the ricotta mounds. Use a pasta cutter to cut out the ravioli into square parcels. Transfer the ravioli to a tray or rimmed baking sheet sprinkled with semolina flour. Repeat with the remaining filling and pasta sheets.

Refrigerate the ravioli while you prepare the cooking water and make the sauce.

Bring a large pot of well-salted water to a boil.

Select a skillet large enough to hold all the tomatoes for the sauce in a single layer. Set it on high heat and add the olive oil, tomatoes, and garlic; cook, stirring occasionally. As the tomatoes brown they will burst and collapse in on themselves. Sprinkle half the basil over them and add salt to taste. Continue to cook until the collapsed tomatoes start to become jammy. Remove from the heat and keep hot under a lid or in a warm oven.

Cook the ravioli in a boiling water and scoop them out, using a slotted spoon, as they float to the top, after 2 or 3 minutes, shaking off the excess water. Toss with the burst cherry tomato sauce, remaining basil, and grated Parmigiano-Reggiano cheese, to taste. Serve immediately.

PORK CHOP WITH FENNEL POLLEN, WHITE BEANS, AND LACINATO KALE

SERVES 4

There are few more iconic dishes in Tuscan cuisine than a pork chop served with slow-cooked white beans and lacinato kale. It's a perfect combination that simply doesn't need to be modified. The creamy butteriness of the beans, the sweet pork, and the slightly bitter kale brightened with garlic and chili all come together to form a perfect mouthful.

1 cup dried cannellini or other
  white beans, rinsed then soaked
  in water overnight with 2 cloves
  peeled garlic, 1 sprig of sage, and
  a bay leaf.
4 thick-cut, bone-in pork chops,
  ideally from a heritage breed
2 bunches of lacinato kale (about 10
  ounces per bunch)
6 tablespoons extra-virgin olive oil
1½ tablespoons wild fennel pollen; if
  not available use ground toasted
  fennel seeds
3 cloves garlic, smashed
1 small dried chili such as arbol or
  pequin, lightly crushed
salt and freshly ground black
  pepper, as needed

Put the beans, their soaking liquid, and the garlic, sage, and bay leaf in a large pot, making sure the liquid covers the beans. Set the pot on the stove and bring to a simmer, then lower the heat and cook very slowly at a low simmer until the beans are tender. They will take 45 minutes or more to cook, depending on the age of the beans. Once cooked, drain, discard the garlic and herbs, and season to taste with salt. Keep warm while you prepare the pork and the kale.

Score the rim of fat on the edge of the pork chops and season all over with salt and pepper. Set aside to rest at room temperature. Preheat the oven to 350°F.

Bring a large pot of heavily salted water to a boil. Strip the lacinato kale leaves of their stems and cut into ribbons 1–1½ inches wide. Blanch them in a boiling water for about 3 minutes, then drain and reserve.

To cook the pork chops, heat 4 tablespoons of the olive oil in a large cast-iron skillet over high heat. When very hot, add the pork chops and sear them on both sides until well browned, about 4–5 minutes on the first side and 2–3 minutes on the second. (Cook in batches, if necessary.) Transfer to a roasting pan or baking sheet and sprinkle them evenly with the fennel pollen or toasted fennel seeds. When all the pork chops are seared, pop them in the oven to cook them through, about 7–10 minutes, depending on the thickness of the chops.

Meanwhile, pour the excess fat out of the skillet, but don't wash it. Set it over a medium-low flame and add the remaining 2 tablespoons of olive oil. Add the smashed cloves of garlic and cook gently until golden. Add the crushed chili, followed by the reserved lacinato kale ribbons. Toss to combine, then season with salt and pepper to taste. Remove from the heat.

To serve, divide the beans between 4 plates. Lay the pork chops over the beans and top with the kale.

MISSY ROBBINS

It was her shrewd letter-writing skills that set Missy Robbins on the path to becoming an acclaimed Michelin-starred chef. As a senior at Washington's Georgetown University, majoring in art history, she wrote to Charlie Trotter after a memorable meal at his eponymous Chicago restaurant. Her enthusiasm for his craft and her impassioned pleas to train in his kitchen won her an impromptu phone interview. On his advice, Robbins racked up what kitchen experience she could at Washington's 1789 restaurant while at the same time working on her degree. Trotter kept his word, and she also took some time off to stage (intern) for him in Chicago.

After graduation, she returned full-time to 1789, earning $7 an hour. A year on, in 1994, Robbins, who grew up in Connecticut, moved to Manhattan to attend Peter Kump's New York Cooking School (now the Institute of Culinary Education). Stints at Arcadia and at March, where she worked under Wayne Nish, followed before Robbins landed her first sous-chef role at The Lobster Club. While there, Robbins decided to study Italian cuisine. With the blessing and help of her chef and mentor, Anne Rosenzweig ("She yelled a lot but she treated me like her daughter"), Robbins embarked on a culinary tour of northern Italy. She worked in small, storied restaurants in Emilia-Romagna, Tuscany, and Friuli, where the pasta was hand rolled by women who were as much revered cooks as they were mothers and wives.

Her next move saw her change gears dramatically when she became the sous-chef at Manhattan's Soho Grand Hotel. To her mastery of pasta doughs she added the savvy to navigate a profit and loss statement and manage a large team—skills that proved vital when, in 2003, she joined Tony Mantuano's four-starred Spiaggia as Executive Chef. It was under his stewardship that she developed her philosophy: a sophisticated yet pared-down approach to Italian cuisine that honors the ingredients above all. And it was under her stewardship that the restaurant was twice nominated by the James Beard Foundation for its Outstanding Restaurant award.

In 2008, Robbins returned to New York to head A Voce and its spin-off A Voce Columbus, her biggest role yet. Five years later, having earned Michelin stars at both establishments for her thoughtful execution of modern Italian fare, she departed with three goals in mind. She sought to travel—an aspiration she fulfilled with month-long trips to Asia and Italy. She wanted to restore a frame battered by years of hard graft; so she took up pilates. And she set time aside to plan her next move.

While evaluating her options, Robbins kept her knives sharp by cooking at festivals and in pop-ups and by collaborating with other chefs. She consulted for Laura Maniec's wine bar Corkbuzz in Manhattan's Chelsea Market, where Robbins executed Italian-influenced small plates that the duo devised.

In February 2015, Robbins announced her next adventure. Partnering up with Matt Kliegman of The Smile and Black Seed, she's opening an Italian restaurant called Lilia in a former auto-body garage in Williamsburg, Brooklyn.

With a focus on pasta, fish, and vegetables, her food will capture that magical spot between fine dining and rustic simplicity, proselytizing her style of updating traditional, regional Italian dishes while remaining respectfully truthful to their origins.

Robbins' careful, studied approach in this upcoming project is no different from her astute mapping of her past career moves, and will no doubt yield her as much success.

What dish that you've created are you most proud of?
I don't know if there is just one, but I am most proud of all the work I have done with pasta. It is a true craft to learn and I am continually trying to improve.

Is there a food that no matter how hard you've tried to like it, you just can't stand?
Canned tuna fish. Just the smell makes me ill.

What's your favorite cuisine to enjoy on a night off?
Anything spicy and usually something Asian.

It's your final meal; where are you, what are you eating, who are you eating it with, and what are you washing it all down with?
I am with old friends and family, eating pizza, preferably from Sally's, in New Haven, and drinking lots of bubbly.

What's your gastronomic guilty pleasure?
Häagen-Dazs!

If you could change one thing in your career, or if you could do one thing all over again, what would it be, and how would it be different?
I probably would have spent a few years doing pastry to be better rounded.

What piece of kitchen equipment couldn't you live without?
My pasta roller.

GRILLED BRANZINO WITH CALABRIAN CHILI VINAIGRETTE AND PICKLED EGGPLANT

SERVES 4

Branzino is one of my favorite fish, and it goes especially well with summer ingredients. This dish is bursting with flavor, from heat to acid to earthiness. The vinaigrette and the pickled eggplant can be prepared in advance, making the dish perfect for spur-of-the-moment entertaining. They are also very versatile and can be used to complement other fish, meat, and vegetables.

For the vinaigrette
½ cup dried whole cherry tomatoes, finely chopped
zest and juice of 1 orange
zest and juice of 1 lemon
2 tablespoons crushed Calabrian chilies (can be found at Italian specialty stores)
⅓ cup olive oil
salt, as needed

For the pickled eggplant
3 cups red wine vinegar
1 cup water
¾ cup granulated sugar
2 tablespoons salt, plus more as needed
3 garlic cloves, smashed
2 shallots, thinly sliced
1 teaspoon chili flakes
1 teaspoon fennel seeds
1 teaspoon whole black peppercorns
1 teaspoon coriander seeds
2 Japanese eggplants (halved crosswise if very long) and sliced ⅛-inch thick lengthwise, ideally on a mandoline
2 tablespoons olive oil

For the branzino
4 fillets of branzino (Mediterranean sea bass)
1 tablespoon olive oil
1 lemon, halved
¼ cup small to medium fresh basil leaves, to garnish
salt, as needed

First make the vinaigrette. Combine the tomatoes, citrus zests, and chili flakes in a bowl and mix. Add the citrus juices and olive oil. There should be a nice balance between heat and citrus. If there is too much heat (the chilies will vary), add more zest and juice and a touch more olive oil; alternatively, for more punch add more chili flakes. Season with salt to taste. Set aside. The vinaigrette will keep in a covered container in the refrigerator for up to 7 days.

Pickle the eggplant. To make the pickling liquid, combine all the ingredients in a small saucepan, except for the eggplant and the olive oil. Bring to a boil, then remove from the heat and let sit for 30 minutes for the spices to infuse.

Meanwhile, bring a large pot of water to a boil; salt to taste. Fill a bowl with ice and cold water and set aside. Place the eggplant strips in a boiling water and blanch for 5–10 seconds. They should be partially cooked but not falling apart. Shock the eggplant quickly in the ice bath, then drain well and pat dry. Place the eggplant in a bowl, then strain the pickling liquid directly over it through a fine sieve. Discard the solids and let the eggplant marinate

in the liquid. After 20 minutes remove 1 slice of eggplant from the pickling liquid, pat dry, and taste it. If it is not pickled enough, leave it for longer, testing every 10 minutes.

When the eggplant strips are ready, remove them from the pickling liquid, pat dry, then season with the 2 tablespoons of olive oil and salt, to taste. Set aside.

When ready to serve, heat a grill to medium-high heat (if you don't have a grill, you can use a grill pan on your stove). Season each fish fillet on both sides with salt, then brush the skin-side of each with a little olive oil. Gently place the fish, skin-side down, on the hot grill and cook for 3–4 minutes, then rotate 45 degrees to achieve nice crisscross grill marks and so as not to burn the skin. Cook for another 2 minutes until the skin is nice and crisp and the flesh is opaque. (The fish should not be flipped to the flesh side.) Transfer from the grill to a platter, and squeeze some lemon juice over each fillet.

Divide the pickled eggplant among 4 plates and arrange the fish on top. Dress each plate with about 2 tablespoons of the vinaigrette then garnish with the basil leaves. Serve immediately.

BRAISED VEAL SHANKS WITH FENNEL AND SWEET GARLIC

SERVES 6–8

There is nothing better on a cold fall or winter night than digging into a braised meat dish. This is a nice light version, enlivened by the fennel and chilies. Serving the shanks whole makes a fantastic presentation as well.

2 whole veal shanks
¼ cup salt
1 tablespoon ground fennel seed
½ to 1 tablespoon ground chili flakes, depending on how much heat you like
¼ cup plus 2 tablespoons olive oil, kept separately
3 carrots, cut into ¼-inch dice
2 onions, cut into ¼-inch dice
2 fennel bulbs, cut into ¼-inch dice
1 head of celery, cut into ¼ inch dice
1 head of garlic, with the cloves peeled and kept whole
½ bottle of white wine
3 quarts chicken or veal stock
1 (28-ounce) can San Marzano tomatoes, strained and crushed by hand
1 ounce thyme sprigs
2 fresh bay leaves

To garnish
1 tablespoon fennel pollen
¼ cup fennel fronds
extra-virgin olive oil

Generously season the veal shanks all over with the salt, ground fennel seed, and chili flakes. Place on a tray, cover, and let sit overnight in the refrigerator.

Preheat the oven to 300°F.

When ready to cook the shanks, remove from the fridge and pat completely dry with paper towels. Allow to come up to room temperature, if possible. Heat a large heavy-bottomed skillet or Dutch oven over high heat. When hot, pour in the ¼ cup of olive oil, then carefully place the veal shanks—one at a time—in the pan and brown on all sides. Remove from the pan and set aside.

Add the remaining olive oil to the same pan, then add the carrots, onions, fennel, celery, and garlic. Gently sauté for 3–5 minutes over low heat until the vegetables are coated in the oil and begin to caramelize. Pour in the wine to deglaze the pan, scraping the bottom of the pan with a wooden spoon to release any stuck-on bits. Let the wine reduce until there's almost no liquid left.

Place the shanks in a deep, heavy-bottomed roasting pan and spoon the cooked vegetable mixture over them. Add the stock, then the crushed tomatoes, thyme, and bay leaves.

Tightly cover the pan with several layers of foil and place in the oven. Cook for about 4–5 hours until the veal is tender and pulling away from

the bone, but not mushy. If the stock does not cover the shanks, turn them halfway through the cooking time.

When the veal is cooked, remove the shanks from the pan and transfer to a serving platter. Using a slotted spoon, transfer the vegetables to a bowl or other container, then strain the liquid through a fine sieve into a saucepan and bring it to a boil over medium-high heat. Reduce by half until it has a bit of body, then transfer the vegetables to the saucepan and heat through.

To serve, pour the sauce with the vegetables over the shanks. Garnish with the fennel fronds, fennel pollen, and extra-virgin olive oil.

RISOTTO WITH SUNCHOKES AND BONE MARROW

SERVES 4–6

This is an elegant and somewhat lighter version of a conventional risotto. The sunchoke purée in the recipe adds flavor and richness without the addition of excessive fat, and the minimal amount of bone marrow contributes depth (a little goes a long way). This really exemplifies Italian cooking at its best.

1 marrow bone, split
zest of 1 lemon, finely grated
5 tablespoons olive oil
3 cipolline onions, peeled
5 medium sunchokes, peeled and
    chopped into large pieces
2 cups milk
1 garlic clove
1 sprig of thyme
3 tablespoons butter
1 large Spanish onion, finely diced
2 cups carnaroli risotto rice
2 cups white wine
3 quarts hot chicken stock
½ cup freshly grated Parmigiano-
    Reggiano, plus more as needed
salt and freshly ground black
    pepper, as needed

Equipment
A microplane grater (optional)

First soak the marrow for several hours in cold water until it is free of any blood and impurities, changing the water several times.

Place the soaked bones in a pot just large enough to hold them and cover with cold water. Place over medium heat and bring the water to a boil. Meanwhile prepare a large bowl with ice and cold water. Remove the bones from the pot as soon as the water boils and transfer them to the ice bath.

When the bones are cool, scoop out the marrow, using a spoon, into a bowl. Using a pastry scraper or a spatula, push the marrow through a fine sieve into a small bowl. Chill the marrow in the freezer until it is firm enough to mold into shape, about 30 minutes.

Season the chilled marrow to taste with salt and pepper and add the lemon zest. Using a piece of parchment or wax paper, roll the chilled marrow into a log about 1 inch thick. Place back in the freezer until solid.

Prepare the cipolline onion garnish. Pour 2 tablespoons of the olive oil into a skillet and place over medium heat. When hot, add the cipolline onions to the pan and slowly cook, about 3–5 minutes on each side, until just tender, but not too soft, and slightly golden in color. Transfer to a chopping board. Once cool enough to handle, slice each onion into quarters, then separate each piece into individual petal-like slivers. Set aside.

Make the sunchoke purée. Place the peeled sunchokes in a small saucepan and cover with the milk. Add the garlic clove and thyme, then place the pan over medium heat. Bring to a simmer then reduce the heat to medium-low and slowly cook the sunchokes in the milk until they are soft, about 25–35 minutes.

When cooked, lift the sunchokes from the milk (leaving behind the garlic and the thyme) and blitz in a blender with just enough of the cooking milk to create a silky purée. Transfer to a bowl and set aside.

Cook the risotto. In a wide, heavy-bottomed pot set over low heat, place 2 tablespoons of the butter and the remaining 3 tablespoons of olive oil. Once the butter is melted, add the diced Spanish onion and cook slowly until the onion is tender and translucent. Add the rice and stir to coat well in the oil and butter. Turn up the heat, then add the white wine and bring to a simmer. Stir the rice and onions until the wine reduces almost completely. Add the hot stock, 2 cups at a time, while continuously stirring and waiting for each addition to be absorbed before adding the next. Continue this process until the rice is cooked through but still al dente, approximately 20 minutes. (You may not need to use all the stock.)

Remove the risotto from the heat and stir in the remaining tablespoon of butter plus ½ cup of the sunchoke purée and the Parmigiano-Reggiano. Taste and add more cheese and/or purée, as desired. Divide the risotto between 4 plates, grate the frozen marrow over the top (ideally with a microplane grater), and garnish with the petals of cipolline onion. Serve immediately.

LINGUINE WITH ZUCCHINI, CLAMS, MINT, AND LEMON

SERVES 4

I grew up in a kosher home, so my love affair with clam pasta started later in life. The flavors of this version are vibrant, light, familiar, yet dynamic all at the same time. The zucchini add unique texture and also a healthful touch.

3 dozen littleneck clams
½ cup plus 2 tablespoons olive oil, kept separately
5 garlic cloves, smashed, plus 2 cloves finely chopped, kept separately
1 bottle of dry white wine
6 sprigs of fresh thyme
1 tablespoon chili flakes
4 tablespoons bread crumbs made from day-old bread ground in a food processor or spice grinder
½ stick unsalted butter
1-pound package dried linguine
3 medium zucchini, shredded into long strips on a mandoline to resemble linguine
juice of 1 lemon
salt, as needed

To garnish
3 sprigs of fresh mint, leaves only
zest of 1 lemon, finely shredded

First prepare the clams. Check to make sure that they are all closed, discarding any that are open and that don't close up when gently tapped. Heat a large pot over medium-high heat. Add the ½ cup of olive oil and smashed garlic and gently sauté the garlic just until you smell its perfume. Add the clams to the pot, followed by the white wine, then the thyme and ½ tablespoon of the chili flakes.

Bring the liquid to a boil, then reduce to a simmer and cover the pot. Leave the clams to steam in the liquid, shaking the pot occasionally. As the clams open up, after about 4–7 minutes, immediately remove them from the pan and transfer to a bowl or dish. The clams will cook at different rates, so be sure to check every now and then to avoid overcooking them. Once all the clams are cooked (discard any that don't open) remove the pot from the heat and strain the liquid through a fine sieve into a bowl. Set aside.

When the clams are cool enough to handle, remove the meat from the shells and set aside, discarding the shells. Chop half the clams, leaving the rest whole, to provide textural and visual contrast, and transfer to a bowl. Pour over enough of the reserved clam cooking liquid to cover the clam meat and set aside.

Cook the bread crumbs. Heat a small skillet with the remaining 2 tablespoons of olive oil over medium heat. When hot, add the bread crumbs to the pan and toast, stirring continuously, until golden brown and crisp. Set aside.

When ready to assemble the dish, heat a large pot of water over high heat and bring to a boil. Heavily salt the water; it should taste like the ocean.

Meanwhile, heat a large skillet over low heat. Add 3 tablespoons of the butter to the pan with the chopped garlic, and sweat, stirring, for about 30 seconds until you can smell the aroma of the cooking garlic. Add 2 cups of the reserved clam liquid to the pan, bring to a boil, and let bubble until reduced by about two-thirds.

When the pot of water is rapidly boiling, drop in the pasta and cook for about 7–8 minutes until al dente. While the pasta is cooking add the chopped and whole clams to the pan of garlic and reduced clam liquid, and gently warm the meat through. Stir in the remaining ½ tablespoon of chili flakes.

Drain the pasta when ready, reserving about ½ cup of the cooking water. Add the pasta to the pan with the clams. Next add the shredded zucchini and toss everything together over medium heat so the zucchini wilts. Add ¼ cup of the reserved pasta water and cook until the pasta absorbs most of the sauce.

Add the remaining tablespoon of butter to the pasta and continue to toss. The butter will add a touch of richness and sheen to the dish. If the pasta tightens up you can add a little more clam liquid or pasta cooking water to loosen it.

Just before serving, add the lemon juice to the pasta and toss again. Divide between 4 bowls and garnish with the mint leaves, lemon zest, and toasted bread crumbs.

ZAHRA TANGORRA

When Zahra Tangorra opened Brucie, an atypical Italian red sauce joint with a modern retro vibe, she flouted every rule in the book. As both chef and owner, she had never cooked professionally, never hired staff, never built out a restaurant space, and certainly never filled out a purchase order form. Still, at 26, armed with an instinct for creating soul-satisfying food, Tangorra hit upon a magic formula that has since made Brucie one of the most beloved neighborhood eating places in Brooklyn's Cobble Hill.

Tangorra grew up on the North Shore of Long Island with parents who once ran a catering business called the Lovin' Oven. Her mother's family came from the former Yugoslavia, but it was Tangorra's paternal Italian heritage that influenced family mealtimes. Memories of baking bread with her father, learning to cook without recipes from her mother, and seeing Grandpa perched on a stool at the stove, stirring the marinara, all inform Tangorra's intuitive approach in the kitchen.

However it was only by accident—literally—that she became a restaurateur. With a background in fashion, she started out as a display artist for Urban Outfitters and then for Brooklyn Industries. In 2006 she left New York City to join a hip-hop artist friend on tour. The bus they traveled in careered off a 40-foot cliff near San Diego, and Tangorra suffered terrible injuries to her right hand. The settlement from the accident offered Tangorra, already an ardent home cook who plied friends with large, family-style meals, the rare opportunity to pursue her passion.

After much soul-searching she resolved one day—while cooking her first batch of made-from-scratch ravioli—to open a small deli-style eatery. In 2010 she found the space on Court Street and ploughed into it the $150,000 she had nearly died for. Using skills accrued from her former design days, she put up the wallpaper, built the light fixtures, and even installed the moldings and wainscoting herself. Next, she hired a sous-chef, a cook, and three servers and got to work figuring out how to run a food business and feed diners every evening.

Brucie has changed enormously since Tangorra first conceived it. What was initially intended to be an Italian market with a few daily menu items promptly evolved into a bona fide restaurant. "I was expecting that people would get up from their seats and order at the cash register. Now we sell $140 steaks!" Though her food has never been prosaic (the secret of her meatballs, the only perennial item on Brucie's ever-changing menu, is lemon zest), her cooking over the last four years has become bolder and more experimental. Harissa enlivens her risotto with squash blossoms; beets are teamed with sesame, mustard seeds, pistachios, and soppressata; and whole pigs' heads are braised in Negroni.

Then there is her tireless push for authenticity. She makes her own stracciatella cheese, goat's milk ricotta, bread, pickles, and fresh pasta in-house, as well as delicacies more advanced chefs wouldn't touch, such as buttery monkfish liver torchon. Undaunted even by whole-animal butchery, Tangorra happily breaks down carcasses of pigs; she learned how from a YouTube video because she didn't have the time to take a class. Try telling her now that she isn't a real chef!

What's your favorite season to cook during?
Summer into fall. Sweet potatoes and tomatoes ... ahhhh!

What kitchen pet peeve is bound to get you really riled up?
Sloppy stations, towels lying around.

What's sexier: salad or dessert? (And why?)
Well, a salad is more difficult to eat off of someone ...

What dish that you've created are you most proud of?
Arancini filled with egg yolk in broth.

Is there an ingredient that you detest, but have to cook?
I eat everything except frog, but I would never allow a frog anywhere near me!

What do you love to see when you look around a packed house of diners?
Smiling faces. Genuine heartfelt joy. People laughing and drinking good wine.

What do you hate to see when you look around a packed house of diners?
People standing in their own way of a good time.

Women chefs are better than men chefs at?
Bearing children. Having fabulous hair and nails. Perhaps cooking without a recipe.

What has been your most memorable moment professionally?
Having April Bloomfield tell me that she loved my house-made burrata.

LONG-COOKED BROCCOLI WITH STRACCIATELLA, RADISHES, AND BAGNA CAUDA

SERVES 4–6

At Brucie we make as much as we possibly can in-house, from bread and yogurt to butter and pasta. One of our most popular house-made products is stracciatella, a stringy, creamy cousin of mozzarella. Sometimes we pair it with pasta; at other times it makes a perfect partner for roasted stone fruit and salted caramel for dessert. But my favorite way to eat it is with sharp and salty bagna cauda (a Piedmontese "hot dip") and a variety of raw and cooked seasonal veggies, like this flavorful oven-braised broccoli.

For the long-cooked broccoli

1 large head of broccoli (about 1¼ pounds) cut into large chunks, stems and all
4 small cloves garlic, peeled and mashed
1 small red onion, thinly sliced
¾ cup chicken stock or water
¾ cup white wine
1 tablespoon fresh lemon juice
salt and freshly ground black pepper, as needed

For the bagna cauda

2 sticks organic butter
1 tablespoon thinly sliced garlic
2 (2-ounce) jars best-quality flat anchovy fillets, chopped, with oil reserved
1½ tablespoons fresh lemon juice
2 tablespoons water

1 pound stracciatella or burrata cheese, torn into large pieces
1 bunch (6–8 ounces) of breakfast radishes, cleaned and trimmed
¼ cup fresh flat-leaf parsley leaves
good-quality extra-virgin olive oil, as needed
freshly cracked black pepper, as needed

Prepare the broccoli. Preheat the oven to 375°F. Combine all the ingredients in a large baking dish or roasting pan, season well with salt and pepper, then cover with foil. Bake for 55–60 minutes or until the broccoli stems are tender. Remove the foil, then continue to bake uncovered for about 10 minutes or until the liquid is syrupy and has reduced by at least two-thirds of the original quantity.

Meanwhile make the bagna cauda. Combine the butter and garlic in a sauté pan or in a small saucepan set over medium heat until the butter is melted and just starts to brown. Add the anchovies and their oil, the lemon juice, and the water. Cook, whisking, until the anchovies melt and the sauce is emulsified.

To serve, arrange the broccoli on the bottom of a large, shallow serving bowl. Top with pieces of stracciatella or burrata, then scatter the radishes over and drizzle with the warm bagna cauda. Toss the parsley leaves over the top and finish with a generous pour of extra-virgin olive oil and a few grinds of cracked black pepper.

PORCHETTA-STYLE LAMB WITH BLACK SESAME TAHINI SAUCE, PARSLEY AND MEYER LEMON SALAD, AND BURNT CARROTS

SERVES 8

In the great outdoor markets of Tuscany, porchetta is a staple. Whole pigs, mostly deboned and stuffed with herbs and garlic, rolled and slow roasted, are a real spectacle. With this recipe, I have taken the classic porchetta flavors and cooking methods, and made them my own by using lamb, and pairing it with Middle Eastern flavors. This dish is pretty much the essence of what we do at Brucie: taking familiar and traditional Italian recipes and putting a spin on them.

For the lamb
1 (6–8-pound) leg of lamb, deboned and butterflied—your butcher will do this for you
Maldon sea salt and freshly ground black pepper, as needed
3–6 (6-inch) sprigs of fresh rosemary sprigs
extra-virgin olive oil, as needed

For the ground lamb stuffing
1 pound ground lamb
1 cup fresh bread crumbs
5 garlic cloves, well crushed
½ tablespoon fennel seeds
1½ tablespoons fresh rosemary leaves, finely minced
1 tablespoon shredded fresh sage leaves
1 teaspoon ground cumin
¼ teaspoon crushed red pepper flakes
½ teaspoon salt

For the black sesame tahini sauce
1 cup tahini
½ cup extra-virgin olive oil
¼ cup red wine vinegar
¼ cup water
2 tablespoons fresh lemon juice
2 tablespoons honey
2 cloves garlic, finely minced
1½ teaspoons salt
2 tablespoons black sesame seeds

For the burnt carrots
12 medium whole carrots, with skins left on
extra-virgin olive oil, as needed
generous pinch of ground cinnamon
salt, as needed

For the parsley salad
1 Meyer lemon, peeled and segmented
3 tablespoons good-quality extra-virgin olive oil
2 bunches (about 4–6 ounces) of flat-leaf parsley, leaves only, washed
1 bunch (about 5–6) of scallions, sliced thinly (tops as well as bulbs)
½ red onion, sliced thinly in half moons
2 tablespoons coarsely chopped fresh dill
¼ cup shelled, crushed pistachios
salt and freshly ground black pepper, as needed
Crisp Lemon Chips (see recipe below, page 201)

To finish
a generous drizzle of extra-virgin olive oil
a few pinches of Maldon sea salt
a squeeze of fresh lemon juice

Remove the leg of lamb from the refrigerator and allow to come up to room temperature.

Preheat the oven to 500°F.

Place all the ingredients for the ground lamb stuffing in a large bowl and mix until combined, being careful not to overmix.

Lay the lamb, skin-side down, on a large chopping board or other flat surface and season liberally with the Maldon salt and black pepper.

Spread the ground lamb and herb mixture filling evenly over the central portion of the butterflied lamb, leaving a margin of about ½ inch around the edges. Starting from the longer side of the lamb, roll it up tightly. You may need to cut off some excess lamb from the ends of the rolled piece and use it to patch exposed stuffing by tucking it into place where there are gaps. Using kitchen twine, tie up the rolled meat at 3-inch intervals. With the seam side down, tuck the rosemary sprigs under the twine, in a row, down the length of the middle of the joint.

Place a roasting rack in a roasting pan. Arrange the meat on the rack and sprinkle over a healthy amount of sea salt and pepper and drizzle liberally with extra-virgin olive oil.

Place the lamb in the oven for 15 minutes, then turn the heat down to 300°F and roast it for about 3–3½ hours (covering with foil if the top becomes too dark) until a thermometer inserted into the ground lamb stuffing of the thickest part of the roll reads 160°F.

While the lamb is cooking, make the tahini sauce. Combine all the ingredients in a bowl and whisk until an emulsified sauce forms. Cover with plastic wrap and set aside.

When the meat is cooked, remove the twine and discard it, along with the rosemary sprigs. Leave the lamb to rest and firm up for 30–40 minutes; if sliced too soon, it will fall apart.

Turn the oven up to 450°F.

Arrange the carrots on a rimmed sheet tray and drizzle liberally with the olive oil. Sprinkle the cinnamon evenly over the top and season with plenty of salt. Roast the carrots for 20–25 minutes or until they are tender.

Using tongs, char the carrots over the open flame of a stove-top burner, or over a grill or fireplace, until blackened in most places. Although the skin of the carrots will have burnt, the insides will remain sweet and succulent, making for a really interesting flavor.

Just before serving assemble the parsley salad. Combine all the ingredients in a large bowl, seasoning with salt and pepper to taste. Crunch up the lemon chips, using your hands, add to the salad, and toss well.

To serve, carve the meat into slices and arrange these on a large serving platter or tray. Artfully arrange the parsley salad over the lamb, then place the burnt carrots to one side (or in a separate serving bowl). Dress the carrots with extra-virgin olive oil, some sea salt, and a squirt of fresh lemon juice. Drizzle the whole tray or platter with the tahini sauce. Serve with harissa, Greek yogurt, pickles, and fresh pita bread on the side, if desired.

Crisp Lemon Chips
2 Meyer lemons, sliced very thinly using a mandoline
1 tablespoon extra-virgin olive oil
salt, as needed

Preheat the oven to 500°F.

Arrange the lemon slices on a sheet tray lined with parchment paper, drizzle with the olive oil and sprinkle with salt. Roast in the oven for about 10 minutes or until they are crunchy (like potato chips!), and caramelized but not burnt. Remove from the oven and leave to cool. Store in an airtight container until ready to use.

OLIVE OIL-POACHED SWORDFISH WITH ASPARAGUS PESTO AND SQUID INK AND CHEDDAR FARRO RISOTTO

SERVES 4–6

I spent a few weeks in Sicily last year and fell in love with the landscape, the wine, the people, and especially the cuisine, with its abundant seafood. The Sicilians seemed to eat swordfish, or spada, in many different preparations for virtually every meal. I often had it for lunch poached in saffron brodo and also carpaccio style, simply adorned with local capers, lime, ricotta salata, and of course a dousing of peppery new harvest olive oil. Needless to say, I came back with a real passion for using swordfish in my own cooking. Here I poach it in extra-virgin olive oil and herbs, imbuing it with an unctuous texture and a clean, elegant flavor, and pair it with a play on a Sicilian-style risotto.

For the asparagus pesto
½ bunch of asparagus (about ½ pound), trimmed
2 tablespoons plus 1 cup good-quality extra-virgin olive oil, kept separately
¼ cup fresh mint leaves
¼ cup fresh flat-leaf parsley leaves
¼ cup fresh dill
4 cloves garlic, peeled
½ cup freshly grated pecorino romano
1 tablespoon freshly grated lemon zest
½ cup shelled walnuts
salt and freshly ground black pepper, as needed

For the olive oil-poached swordfish
2–3 pounds swordfish loin, cut into ½-pound steaks
salt, as needed
4 cups extra-virgin olive oil, good quality but not "finishing" or best quality
4 cups white wine
6–8 sprigs of fresh thyme
3–5 (6-inch) sprigs of fresh rosemary
3–5 sprigs of fresh oregano
pinch of crushed chili flakes
1 teaspoon freshly grated lemon zest
1 head of garlic, cut in half horizontally
1 medium red onion, thinly sliced

For the squid ink and Cheddar farro risotto
2 cups farro
2 cups cleaned, trimmed, and thinly sliced leeks
2 tablespoons thinly sliced garlic
1 small bulb or ½ large bulb of fennel (about 12 ounces) trimmed and finely diced
6 sprigs of fresh thyme
¼ cup bacon fat or extra-virgin olive oil
3 tablespoons squid ink (available from Italian specialty markets)
2 cups homemade fish or chicken stock
1 cup finely grated Cabot Clothbound Cheddar, or other very good-quality English-style Cheddar
2 tablespoons butter
salt, to taste
1 bunch of chives, finely chopped

To finish
Sicilian extra-virgin olive oil
Maldon sea salt
fresh lemon juice

Make the asparagus pesto. Preheat the oven to 450°F. Arrange the asparagus on a rimmed sheet tray, drizzle the 2 tablespoons of olive oil over it, and sprinkle with sea salt. Roast for 7 minutes. Remove the asparagus from the oven, leave to cool for at least a few minutes, then roughly chop.

Turn the oven down to 300°F.

Place all the ingredients for the pesto in the bowl of a food processor, and process until everything is just combined and not too smooth. Season to taste with salt and pepper. Transfer to a bowl, cover with plastic wrap, and set aside.

Season the swordfish steaks generously all over, then place them in a large baking dish. Pour the oil and wine over them, and evenly spread all the other ingredients on top and in between the steaks. Cook uncovered for 30 minutes.

While the fish is in the oven, make the risotto. Cook the farro in boiling, salted water according to the package instructions. Strain, transfer to a large bowl, and set aside.

In a large saucepan over medium heat, combine the leeks, garlic, fennel, thyme, and bacon fat or olive oil. Sauté, stirring occasionally, until the vegetables are translucent and ➤

just beginning to brown, about 8 minutes. Add the cooked farro to the pan, then stir in the squid ink and ½ cup of stock. Keep stirring until most of the liquid has been absorbed, then continue adding the stock ½ cup at a time, making sure the previous addition has been absorbed before adding more, until the farro is tender, about 15 minutes. Turn off the heat, add the Cheddar and butter, and season with salt, to taste. Finally stir in the chives.

Serve immediately. Spoon the risotto onto a large platter. Lift the fish steaks out of the oil and arrange over the farro, then drizzle the pesto over them. Add a few healthy glugs of good-quality Sicilian extra-virgin olive oil, a pinch or two of Maldon sea salt, and a squeeze of fresh lemon juice.

PORK BELLY WITH NECTARINE AGRODOLCE AND YOGURT

SERVES 6–8

Although we're constantly creating new dishes at Brucie, there are some combinations that tug at our heartstrings so hard that we just keep coming back to them. One such combo is crisp, fatty pork belly paired with a sweet and sour agrodolce and perfectly contrasted with cool and creamy Greek yogurt. Here I use nectarines for the agrodolce, which is ideal during the summer months when stone fruit are at their best. At any other time of the year, substitute different seasonal fruit; think apples in the fall or strawberries in spring or early summer.

For the pork
2 pounds pastured and antibiotic- and hormone-free pork belly
salt, as needed
2 teaspoons vegetable oil
1 large white onion, sliced
2 heads garlic, cut in half horizontally (with skins left on)
1 cinnamon stick
2 fresh bay leaves
½ cup granulated sugar
½ cup distilled white vinegar
2 cups vegetable or canola oil, for deep-frying

For the agrodolce
3 ripe nectarines, stoned and cut into large chunks (with skins left on)
¼ cup red wine vinegar
⅓ cup granulated sugar
¼ cup water
1 teaspoon salt

For the yogurt sauce
½ cup Greek yogurt
½ teaspoon minced garlic
1 tablespoon fresh lemon juice
salt, as needed

To finish
1 or 2 thinly sliced scallions
A few pinches of Maldon sea salt
A generous drizzle of extra-virgin olive oil

Preheat the oven to 375°F.

Salt the pork belly liberally all over. Set a large skillet over high heat and add the vegetable oil. When hot, place the pork, fat-side down, in the pan, and sear until deep golden brown, about 4 minutes. Turn down the heat to medium, carefully flip over the meat, and sear for 4 minutes on the other side.

Transfer the pork to a roasting pan and add the onion, garlic, cinnamon stick, and bay leaves. Combine the sugar and the vinegar in a small bowl and stir until the sugar is mostly dissolved. Pour this over the pork. Cover the pan tightly with foil and roast for 2 hours, or until the meat is tender. Remove and leave to cool.

Place the pork in the fridge and leave it to chill for at least 1 hour, so that it's easy to carve without falling apart, then cut into roughly 2-inch cubes.

Combine all the ingredients for the agrodolce in a medium saucepan. Bring to a simmer and cook over medium heat for 10 minutes, stirring every few minutes, until the fruit is tender and broken down but still a little chunky. Remove from the heat and set aside to cool.

To finish the pork, heat the 2 cups of vegetable or canola oil over medium-high heat in a deep sauté pan or medium saucepan until the oil reaches 360°F on a deep-frying thermometer. Carefully add the pork belly pieces to the hot oil and fry for about 3 minutes until dark brown and crisp on the outside and hot in the center, turning with tongs as necessary. Transfer the pork to a plate lined with paper towels.

Make the yogurt sauce. Combine the first 3 ingredients in a bowl and mix well. Season to taste with salt.

To assemble the dish, use a brush to paint the yogurt decoratively on the bottom of a large, shallow serving bowl, then arrange the pork on top. Spoon the agrodolce over the meat and around the dish, then sprinkle the thinly sliced scallions and Maldon sea salt on top. Finish with a healthy drizzle of extra-virgin olive oil.

JODY WILLIAMS

Chef Jody Williams doesn't believe in rules. Buvette Gastrothèque, in the West Village, is a study in the unconventional. Firstly, the very word "gastrothèque" is nonsense. Williams coined the term because no descriptor fitted her idea of Buvette, which she opened in 2011. It occupies that nebulous space between neighborhood wine bar, charming bistro, and old-world European café (albeit an extremely diminutive version), with viennoiseries served on footed silver trays and smartly dressed wait staff in crisp white shirts, ties, and pressed aprons. It is, as Williams says, "what you want it to be." If you want to eat lunch at 4:00 p.m., so be it. If you want to wander in for a Negroni at 1:00 a.m., a bartender welcomes your order and invites you to stay for another. If you want something substantial enough to carry you through the evening but not so hefty as to render you immobile, Williams' first-rate coq au vin or cassoulet, served in petite earthenware dishes and individual cast iron pots, will fit the bill.

With no formal training, Williams, a native of northern California, picked up all she knows about cooking on the job. Her six months as a banqueting steward at what is now the Four Seasons Hotel in San Francisco was no easy introduction to the industry. "You had to clean up stock pots with a shovel. It was tough; you learned to cry in the walk-in [refrigerator] box." Hardened from that experience, she tried her luck in New York. When the stock market crash of the late 1980s shuttered restaurants across the city, and Williams was fired from Thomas Keller's Rakel, she packed her bags and left for Europe.

For three years she worked at Caffè Arti e Mestieri, in Reggio Emilia. When she had absorbed all that she could from that archetypal northern Italian kitchen (where there were no food processors and the bread and pasta were made by hand), she moved to Rome. Another three years on, and with a résumé bolstered by positions at the famous Hassler Hotel, Harry's Bar, and the Michelin-starred Da Patrizia e Roberto del Pianeta Terra, Williams returned to the U.S., by way of a brief detour to Japan.

In her cookbook *Buvette: The Pleasure of Good Food*, Williams likens the restaurant industry she encountered back in New York City to the "Wild West." Not one to be discouraged, she embraced it with a swagger and took jobs as the chef at various establishments—Il Buco, Gusto, Morandi, Gottino (where she was once also a co-owner), and Giorgione—before she could brandish enough experience to go it alone.

Thwarting restaurant industry convention with her gastrothèque has worked wonders for Williams. Glowing reviews and a near-permanent line of locals and tourists waiting their turn to enjoy her Gallic-inspired menu spurred a second location in Paris in 2013 and a third (opening soon) in Tokyo.

With such success, it's no wonder Williams has again subverted the rules with her latest venture, an Italian "gastroteca." Refuting the old adage "Too many cooks...," Via Carota, which opened its doors in the West Village in February 2015, has not one but two chefs. As for the universal caution never to mix business with pleasure, that too remained unheeded. Helmed by Williams and her business and domestic partner, Rita Sodi, of the nearby Tuscan restaurant I Sodi, Via Carota is the quietly seductive older sister to the coquettish Buvette—both alluring, both unmistakably Williams.

Of all your travels, which country's cuisine did you enjoy exploring the most, and why?
Japan was exotic. Italy was comforting.

What is your idea of the perfect comfort food?
Every season has its comforts. In August it may be simply a wedge of watermelon, in January maybe a bowl of lentils. Cheese omelets, too, I find comforting.

If you had one piece of advice to pass on to an aspiring cook, what would it be?
Go to the source. Do not adulterate the truth or culture of the cuisine.

What's your most prized possession in the kitchen, and would you share it with anyone?
Victorian maple syrup pitcher—yes, share. Twenty-year-old Sabtier paring knife would not share.

What is your biggest pet peeve when you go out to dine?
Mean people and dumb food.

Is there one rule of conduct in your kitchen that, above all others, has to be abided by/that you enforce most strictly?
Work clean; be polite; no cursing.

If there were one pressing issue in the restaurant industry that you could address/solve today, what would it be?
Sustainable farming/fishing/animal husbandry.

WINTER WALNUT PESTO WITH TOASTED COUNTRY BREAD

SERVES 4; MAKES 1 CUP

Perfect for cold-weather entertaining, this make-ahead, unctuous walnut pesto can be slathered onto slabs of grilled country bread for a casual appetizer. Alternatively, substitute crisp slivers of crostini to make canapés for a cocktail party.

1 cup shelled walnuts
¼ cup freshly grated Parmesan cheese
3 sprigs of fresh thyme
¼ teaspoon salt, plus more as needed
splash of sherry vinegar
1 small garlic clove, crushed
½ cup extra-virgin olive oil
2 tablespoons minced golden raisins

To serve
4 slices of country bread or about 30 crostini

Combine the walnuts, Parmesan, thyme, salt, vinegar, and garlic in a food processor and pulse until well mixed but still coarse. Stir in the olive oil and golden raisins. If not using immediately, transfer to a container, cover, and keep refrigerated until ready to use (it will keep for 2 or 3 days).

To serve, bring the pesto up to room temperature, if chilled. Preheat a grill, a grill pan over the stove, or the broiler. Toast the country bread, then spread liberally with the pesto while still warm. Alternatively, spread a heaped teaspoon of the pesto on crostini for bite-size canapés. Serve immediately.

CLAM AND SORREL CHOWDER

SERVES 4

An unexpected and fresh approach to clam chowder. The natural flavors of the clams take center stage in this cream-less soup. Don't skimp on the sorrel; tangy and herbaceous, it's the ideal foil to the brininess of the shellfish.

Extra-virgin olive oil, as needed
1 cup chopped leeks (avoid the dark green leaves)
1 cup chopped onion
1 stalk celery, chopped
1 pound small potatoes such as Yukon Golds, peeled and cut into ½-inch cubes
2 pounds littleneck clams (about 20–24 clams), washed and scrubbed
1 bay leaf
1½ teaspoons kosher salt, plus more as needed
2 cups boiling water
1 cup roughly chopped, rinsed, and dried fresh sorrel leaves
6 fresh basil leaves
¼ cup fresh flat-leaf parsley leaves
1 garlic clove, peeled and kept whole

To serve
4 slices of toasted country bread

Set a large, heavy-bottomed pot with a lid, such as a Dutch oven, over medium heat and pour in about 3 tablespoons of olive oil.

Add the leeks, onions, and celery and cook until the vegetables are translucent and soft, about 4–6 minutes. Add the potatoes to the pot and continue to cook for another 5 minutes, stirring occasionally.

Discard any raw clams that are open and don't close when they are tapped. Add the closed clams, bay leaf, salt, and boiling water to the pot. Cover and let simmer for about 5–10 minutes until the potatoes are tender. Transfer the clams to a bowl as they open up. Remove any clams that have not opened up and discard them.

Meanwhile, using a pestle and mortar, grind the sorrel, basil, parsley, and garlic to a paste with 2 tablespoons of olive oil. Alternatively, use a food processor to pulse to a purée. Set aside.

Stir the garlic and sorrel pesto into the pot with the potatoes, vegetables, and broth and continue cooking for an extra minute. Return the clams to the pot, then taste and adjust the seasoning. Remove from the heat.

To serve, first season the toasted country bread with a little salt and olive oil, then place in 4 soup plates. Next, divide the clams evenly over the bread and spoon the vegetables and broth over them. Drizzle generously with olive oil. (If you prefer, the clam meat can be removed from the shells and returned to the broth before plating.)

ROSEMARY FRIED RABBIT AND ARTICHOKES

SERVES 4

Like fried chicken, but better. Rosemary- and garlic-infused rabbit pieces are simply tossed in cornstarch then deep fried until they take on a shatteringly crunchy outer crust while staying juicy and tender on the inside.

1 fresh rabbit including the liver and kidneys, about 2 pounds, cut into 10–12 pieces
1 cup all-purpose flour
1 cup cornstarch
6 cups vegetable oil
6 young artichokes
kosher salt, as needed

For the garlic rosemary brine
1 head of garlic, unpeeled, cut in half horizontally
3 sprigs of fresh rosemary
½ cup kosher salt
1 tablespoon sugar
8 cups hand-hot water

To serve
1 lemon, cut into wedges

Equipment
Brown paper for draining and serving

To section the rabbit yourself, begin by removing the shoulders and splitting each into 2 pieces. Next, take off the legs and divide them into 3 pieces by separating the lower leg from the thigh and then dividing the thigh in 2. Remove and discard the rib cage and chop the back into 2 pieces. Finally divide the saddle and flaps horizontally into 3 or 4 pieces. Rinse off the rabbit pieces.

Make the brine by combining the split garlic head, rosemary, salt, sugar, and hot water into a large container that will fit into your refrigerator. Stir to dissolve the sugar and salt. Taste for seasoning; the brine should be strong but easy enough to swallow. Dilute with more hot water if it's too salty. Add the rabbit to the container; cover and let it sit for 14–16 hours in the refrigerator.

When ready to cook, combine the flour and cornstarch in a large bowl and set aside. Fill a large, deep, heavy-bottomed pot with 3 inches of vegetable oil and heat to 375°F.

Meanwhile, prepare the artichokes by trimming away the dark green leaves in the outer layers with a paring knife, then spooning out the bristly choke. Cut the artichokes in half or into quarters, if large. Let rest on a plate with a sprinkling of the flour mixture until ready to fry. (For this recipe there's no need to rub the artichokes with lemon juice.)

Drain the rabbit, reserving the garlic and rosemary, then rinse under cold running water and pat dry. Dredge the rabbit pieces in the flour and cornstarch mixture, making sure to coat each piece completely. Place the floured rabbit on a platter or tray and set aside.

Carefully add the flour-dusted artichoke to the hot oil, in 2 batches, and fry until fork tender, about 6–8 minutes. When cooked, transfer to brown paper to drain off the excess oil.

Next, fry the rabbit together with the garlic and rosemary in batches, without crowding the pot, until golden and cooked through, about 10–12 minutes. Remove from the oil and drain on the brown paper.

Season the fried artichokes and rabbit with a sprinkling of kosher salt and serve over fresh pieces of brown paper with lemon wedges.

OXTAILS BRAISED IN RED WINE AND BITTER CHOCOLATE

SERVES 3–4

Riffing off a classic Roman oxtail stew, coda alla vaccinara, with its characteristic sweet and sour note, the inclusion of bittersweet chocolate imbues this melt-in-the-mouth meaty braise with rich complexity, a hint of sweetness, and a silky, seductive consistency.

2½–3 pounds trimmed oxtails, cut into 2-inch rounds
extra-virgin olive oil, as needed
1 medium onion, roughly chopped
1 medium carrot, roughly chopped
1 medium leek, roughly chopped
2 cups dry red wine
2 cups chicken or veal stock
2 cups water
3 ounces bittersweet chocolate
1 bay leaf
3 crushed juniper berries
2 sprigs of fresh rosemary
peel of half an orange
coarse salt and freshly ground black pepper, as needed

Preheat the oven to 350°F.

Season the oxtails generously with salt and pepper and set aside. Add 1–2 tablespoons olive oil to a heavy-bottomed casserole with a tight-fitting lid and place over medium heat. When hot, add the oxtails and sear until browned all over. Transfer the oxtails to a plate.

Pour off and discard the fat from the pot. Add 2 more tablespoons of olive oil to the casserole and return to the heat. Add the chopped vegetables and cook, stirring occasionally, until tender, about 7–9 minutes. Pour in the red wine, bring to a boil, and simmer until reduced by at least half. Next, add the chicken or veal stock and water to the casserole, together with the chocolate, bay leaf, juniper berries, rosemary, and orange peel. Bring to a boil, then reduce the heat to a simmer and return the oxtail to the pot. Cover the casserole and place in the oven. Cook for about 2 hours, or until the meat is falling off the bones.

Remove the casserole from the oven and skim off the fat from the surface. If the cooking liquid is too thin, remove the oxtails from the pan and transfer to a plate. Bring the cooking liquid up to a boil and lower to a simmer, then reduce until the liquid thickens to a sauce consistency. Taste and adjust the seasoning as needed. Serve the oxtail with the sauce over soft polenta or potato purée.

FANY GERSON 219

Lime Chili Doughnut Holes · Mexican-inspired Rugelach · Mango-Passion Fruit Napoleons · Meyer Lemon Paletas with Verbena-steeped Berries

GHAYA OLIVEIRA 229

Moelleux Provençals (Almond-Pistachio Moelleux, Lemon Chiboust, and Wild Strawberries) · Almond Mousseux with Chocolate Crémeux, Lemon-Praliné Sauce, and Citrus Confit Ice Cream · Apricot Vacherin with Verbena-White Chocolate Chantilly and Honey Mishmish Sauce · Poire aux Marrons (Licorice-poached Pear with Chestnut Cream Vermicelli and Licorice Ice Cream)

KATHERINE THOMPSON 243

Coconut Semifreddo with Almond-Coconut Cake, Bittersweet Chocolate Sauce, and Toasted Coconut · Chocolate Crostata · Frutti di Bosco Tiramisù · Cranberry-Pumpkin Budino with Apple Vinegar Caramel and Spiced Pecans

CHRISTINA TOSI 257

Birthday Cake Truffles · Cereal Milk Panna Cotta · Blueberry Bagel Bombs · Peaches and Cream Cookies

JENNIFER YEE 267

Jasmine Tea and Apricot Mousse Cake · Milk Chocolate Pots de Crème with Chai Tea Foam and Cacao Nib Crumb · Butterscotch Coffee Éclairs · Raspberry Pistachio Macaron Tartlets

FANY GERSON

"**I**n Mexico, we say people are jealous, but really we mean they are protective," explains pastry chef Fany Gerson, when recalling her difficulty in cajoling the locals to share their recipes. Despite her own Hispanic heritage (having been born and raised in Mexico City), this doyenne of Mexican sweets does not share this trait and is happy to impart her own knowledge of Latin confectionery.

Now based in New York City, Gerson has two published cookbooks under her belt. *My Sweet Mexico* (nominated for a James Beard Award) is a comprehensive survey of the traditional candies, pastries, breads, desserts, and sweet beverages of her homeland, while *Paletas* digs deep into the subject of Mexican ice pops.

Gerson's entrée into chefdom was something of an accident. After high school, she traveled to New York City to check out the School of Visual Arts, where she had secured a partial scholarship. She heard about the Culinary Institute of America during her trip and visited the campus on the one free day she had. "As I pulled into the C.I.A. in a taxi, I knew that this was where I belonged. I told my parents that this was my art, and it's the only art that uses the five senses."

After completing the full culinary degree program at the C.I.A. (having rejected art school in its favor), a 20-year-old Gerson spent a year cooking in San Sebástian, Spain. Then, back in New York City, she made the switch from the savory side of the kitchen to the sweet at Megas, working with contemporary Basque cuisine. In 2012 she moved to Eleven Madison Park, where she stayed for two years. Then it was on to Rosa Mexicano to reinvent its Latin-oriented pastry program.

The year she spent traveling throughout Mexico doing research for *My Sweet Mexico* proved so inspiring that when Gerson returned to New York in 2010 she started her own business. A dream she had about ice cream determined the genre of Mexican sweets she would focus on. Her pragmatism farther honed her plans: she opted to sell paletas since they required less specialist equipment than ice cream. Calling her venture La Newyorkina, Gerson provides refreshing, flavorful ices concocted from a palette of exotic ingredients like chili, horchata, and hibiscus, combined with rich Mexican chocolate and tropical and local fruits. Throughout the summer her branded pushcarts are fixtures on the High Line Park and at fairs such as the Hester Street Fair in Manhattan's Lower East Side.

The quiet winter months provided Gerson with an opportunity to try her hand at something altogether different. An entrepreneur she had worked for previously at Choice Market, a gourmet bakery and café in Brooklyn, was opening a doughnut shop in Bedford-Stuyvesant and needed a pastry chef to develop its menu. At Dough, Gerson plays with unusual flavor combinations that pay homage to her roots but also celebrate ingredients found outside the Latin tradition. In 2014, Dough opened its second outlet in Manhattan's Flatiron district.

Over the last five years, La Newyorkina's product line has evolved to include specialty Mexican cookies and traditional confectionary such as puffed amaranth chocolatey morsels and coconut lime candies, as well as American treats inspired by flavors Gerson grew up with—for example, her Goat's Milk Caramel Brownies. An online store is currently a placeholder for a bricks and mortar one while Gerson scours the city for the sweet spot for her ... well, sweets.

Who or what has most influenced your cooking?
Mexico. The markets, the flavors of my childhood, the energy, the colors, the culture ...

It's your final meal; where are you, what are you eating, and what are you washing it all down with?
I am at a street market in Oaxaca eating a fresh blue corn tortilla quesadilla with quesillo, squash blossoms, epazote, and raw tomatillo sauce with avocado. Washing it down with fresh tamarind agua fresca but would finish it off with a mezcal.

If you weren't a chef, you'd be ...
Career-wise, I'd be doing something else creative like graphic design or architecture or be a teacher—in my dreams, a singer. Either way, I feel I'd be sleeping more for sure!

Which chef or food figure, famous or not-so-famous, do you most admire, and why?
The list is long, but I have to mention the *mayoras*. These are women who run many kitchens in Mexico, and they are an inspiration. They have kept traditions alive, and many cook indigenous dishes that are incredibly delicious and amazing.

What's your gastronomic guilty pleasure?
A classic hot fudge sundae with lots of hot fudge and whipped cream, but hold the cherry on top.

LIME CHILI DOUGHNUT HOLES

MAKES 4 DOZEN

These small, spicy doughnuts are like little bites of clouds, and it is hard to stop eating them. In Mexico, we love our chilies—not simply for their heat but also for the different layers of flavors they provide. Here, the guajillo chili adds some fruity notes, which complement the lime very well, and the arbol chili adds spice.

For the doughnuts
½ cup milk
2 teaspoons plus ⅓ cup granulated sugar, kept separately
½ tablespoon active dry yeast
2½ cups all-purpose flour, plus more as needed
½ teaspoon arbol chili powder (you can substitute cayenne pepper)
¼ teaspoon salt
1 teaspoon freshly grated lime zest
¼ cup water
1 large egg, at room temperature
½ stick butter, cut into cubes, at room temperature
2½ quarts vegetable oil, for frying

For the lime chili topping
1 cup granulated sugar
1½ tablespoons grated lime zest
1 teaspoon arbol chili powder
2 teaspoons guajillo chili powder
½ teaspoon salt

Warm the milk in a small saucepan until it feels slightly warm but not hot (if it's too hot it will kill the yeast). Pour the milk into a small bowl and stir in the 2 teaspoons sugar and the yeast, using a fork. Set aside for about 10 minutes until the mixture bubbles slightly.

In the bowl of a stand mixer fitted with the hook attachment, combine the flour, the remaining ⅓ cup sugar, the arbol chili powder, the salt, and the lime zest.

In a small bowl whisk the water and the eggs together; set aside.

Add the yeast mixture to the flour mixture on slow speed, then, still mixing, gradually add the egg mixture. Increase the speed to medium once most of the egg is absorbed into the dry mixture, then add the butter, a few pieces at a time.

Once all the butter has been added, continue to knead on medium speed until the dough feels elastic and pulls away from the sides of the bowl. This will take about 15–20 minutes depending on your mixer (resist the urge to add more flour if the mixture seems too sticky).

Place the dough in a large, greased bowl and sprinkle a bit of flour over the top. Cover tightly with plastic wrap and refrigerate overnight.

Take out the dough and let it sit for about 20 minutes or until it comes to room temperature. Meanwhile, line a couple of baking sheets with parchment paper and spray lightly with cooking spray.

Next prepare the lime chili topping by mixing all the ingredients in a medium bowl with a whisk. Set aside.

When the dough is at room temperature, roll it out on a lightly floured surface to ¼-inch thickness. Cut out rounds using a 1½-inch-diameter cutter and place the dough rounds on the prepared baking sheets, spaced about 1 inch apart. Cover the trays lightly with plastic wrap, clean towels, or cheesecloth and leave the dough to rise in a warm place for 30 minutes.

When you're ready to cook the doughnut holes, fill a large heavy-bottomed pot with the vegetable oil and place over medium-high heat. (If you prefer, use a deep fryer.) Place a wire rack over a baking sheet and set aside.

When the oil registers 375°F on a candy or deep-frying thermometer, carefully drop the doughnut holes into the hot oil, in batches. Fry, moving them around with a slotted spoon and flipping them as needed, until golden brown all over and cooked through, about 1–1½ minutes. Transfer the cooked doughnut holes to the wire rack. Allow the oil to return to 375°F in between batches.

Once the holes are cool enough to handle but still warm, toss them in the bowl with the topping mixture. Scoop them out with a slotted spoon to remove the excess sugar. Although they can be made in advance, to enjoy them at their best you should serve them immediately while still warm.

MEXICAN-INSPIRED RUGELACH

MAKES 2–2½ DOZEN

Rugelach is one of my all-time favorite cookies. My grandmother baked them during the many Jewish holidays, but I suspect she hid some from me because I simply couldn't stop eating them! The three different versions here represent the different aspects of my heritage—my Mexican and Jewish roots—in a delicious cookie that I hope no one hides from you.

For the dough (adequate for one version)
2 cups all-purpose flour
½ teaspoon kosher salt
2 sticks unsalted butter, cut into
    small cubes, chilled
¼ pound cream cheese, cut into
    small cubes, chilled
2 tablespoons sour cream
½ teaspoon pure vanilla extract
1 egg yolk
confectioners' sugar, as needed, to
    roll out the cookies
your chosen filling (see recipes
    below and page 224)

For the cherry-chipotle topping
1 large egg yolk
¼ cup granulated sugar

For the pineapple-coconut topping
1 large egg yolk
¼ cup granulated sugar
¼ cup shredded unsweetened
    coconut

For the Mexican chocolate topping
1 large egg yolk
¼ cup turbinado sugar (sometimes
    called raw sugar)
1 tablespoon ground cinnamon,
    preferably Mexican

Equipment
A 10- x 15-inch baking sheet

To make the dough, first combine the flour and salt in the bowl of a food processor and pulse a few times to mix. Scatter the cubes of butter and cream cheese over the flour, then pulse a few more times until the mixture resembles coarse crumbs.

In a small bowl, whisk together the sour cream, vanilla, and egg yolk. Pour this over the butter and flour mixture. Run the processor continuously until the dough begins to clump together. Turn out onto a clean surface.

Knead the dough lightly to form a ball, then divide into 3 portions. Flatten each one into a 1- to 2-inch-thick rectangle. Wrap in plastic wrap and refrigerate for at least 2 hours. The dough will keep, refrigerated, for up to 3 days; if frozen, for up to 2 months.

When ready to bake, preheat the oven to 350°F. Line the baking sheet with parchment paper and grease it lightly with oil or cooking spray. Set aside.

Dust a clean surface with some sifted confectioners' sugar. Unwrap one portion of the dough and roll it out into a rectangle about ⅛- to ¼-inch thick. Spread one-third of your chosen filling over the dough, using an offset spatula or the back of a spoon, being sure to leave a border about ¼-inch wide around the edges. Then, starting with one long side, roll up the dough to make

a tight cylinder. Flatten it a bit, then wrap the cylinder in plastic wrap and place in the freezer for about 10–15 minutes to firm up. Repeat with the remaining 2 portions of dough.

Slice the dough cylinders into 1¼-inch pieces, and place each piece seam side down on the prepared baking sheet.

For the topping, whisk the egg yolk in a small bowl and brush this over the tops of the cookies. Then sprinkle the ingredient(s) appropriate to your chosen filling on top.

Bake the cookies for about 20–25 minutes, or until golden and crisp, rotating the sheet pan 180° halfway through cooking. Let the rugelach cool for a few minutes on the pan, then transfer them to a wire rack to cool completely before serving.

Cherry-Chipotle Filling
1¼ cups dried tart cherries
1 or 2 dried, stemmed chipotle
    chilies, depending on how spicy
    the chilies are and also on your
    taste
¼ cup granulated sugar
¼ cup brown sugar
½ cup water
¼ teaspoon kosher salt

Combine the cherries, chipotle chilies, both types of sugar, water, and salt in a medium saucepan and bring to a boil over medium-high heat. Reduce the heat and simmer until the mixture looks a little syrupy, about 5–7 minutes. Remove the pan from the heat and allow to cool. Remove the cooked chilies and **>**

about 5–7 minutes. Remove the pan from the heat and allow to cool. Remove the cooked chilies and set aside. Transfer the mixture to a food processor and purée it. Add one of the cooked chilies and process. Taste, then add the other chili if desired.

Pineapple-Coconut Filling
½ of a medium pineapple, skin
   removed
½ cup water
½ cup granulated sugar
juice and zest of 1 lime
¼ teaspoon salt
½ cup unsweetened shredded
   coconut

Grate or very finely chop the pineapple; you should have at least 1 cup. Place the pineapple and water in a small saucepan, bring to a simmer, and cook over medium-low heat until the pineapple is soft, about 5–10 minutes, stirring occasionally. Add the sugar and lime juice and continue to simmer until the mixture is thick and jammy and almost all the liquid has evaporated, about 35–45 more minutes. Remove from the heat, stir in the lime zest and salt, transfer to a bowl, and leave the mixture to cool. Add the shredded coconut and mix well so everything is evenly incorporated.

This filling is also delicious with finely chopped jalapeño or serrano chilies. Use about 1–1½ tablespoons and add them along with the lime zest.

Mexican Chocolate Filling
⅓ cup pecans, lightly toasted
6 ounces Mexican chocolate (see
   suppliers, page 286)
¾ teaspoon pure vanilla extract
¾ tablespoon unsalted butter
¼ teaspoon kosher salt

Grind the pecans until fine in a food processor and set aside. Place the chocolate in the top of a double boiler, add the vanilla and butter, and stir until the ingredients are completely combined and melted. The mixture will be grainy because of the way Mexican chocolate is made, but this is nothing to worry about. Stir in the pecans and salt and set aside to cool.

MANGO-PASSION FRUIT NAPOLEONS

SERVES 6

You know how some people always order the chocolate dessert, no matter what it is? Well I always get any fruit dessert that has a strong tart or acidic component, like this one. The phyllo crisps add a lovely crunch to the fruity cream, and the fresh chopped mangoes add an additional layer of flavor and texture.

For the phyllo crisps
½ cup shelled, raw pistachios
⅓ cup granulated sugar
½ tablespoon lime zest
3 (17- x 12-inch) phyllo dough
  sheets
½ stick unsalted butter, melted and
  cooled

For the filling
2 medium mangoes, peeled, stoned,
  and cut into small dice
1 tablespoon chopped fresh mint
  leaves
1 cup chilled heavy cream
1 cup Passion Fruit Curd (see recipe
  below)

Make the phyllo crisps. Preheat the oven to 350°F. Finely grind ⅓ cup of the pistachios with the sugar and lime zest in a food processor. Set aside.

Finely chop the remaining pistachios and reserve for later.

Place the phyllo sheets on a clean work surface and cover with a sheet of plastic wrap, followed by lightly dampened paper towel. Take one phyllo sheet from the stack, place on a cutting board (cover the rest of the sheets), and brush with some of the melted butter. Sprinkle the phyllo sheet evenly with half of the ground nut mixture, then top with another sheet of phyllo. Brush the second sheet of phyllo with some butter and sprinkle with the remaining ground nut mixture. Now top with the last phyllo sheet, pressing down gently, then brush with the remaining butter. Chill for 10 minutes in the refrigerator.

Cut the chilled phyllo stack into evenly sized rectangles about 2 x 3½ inches in size; you'll need a total of 18 pieces for each serving. (Alternatively, you can cut the stack into squares and then diagonally slice each square to make triangles.)

Transfer the cut phyllo pieces to a baking sheet lined with parchment paper. Bake until golden, about 5–7 minutes. Cool the phyllo crisps on a wire rack and set aside.

Now make the filling. Combine the mango with the mint and set aside. Beat the cream in a bowl with a handheld electric mixer until it thickens and holds soft peaks, and then gently fold the whipped cream into the passion fruit curd until evenly combined.

To assemble the dessert, place a phyllo crisp on each plate. Top each crisp with 1 heaped tablespoon of the passion fruit cream, followed by some of the chopped mango. Layer over another phyllo crisp, top with more passion fruit curd and more mango, and finish with a phyllo crisp. Sprinkle the reserved chopped pistachio nuts over the napoleons and serve immediately.

Passion Fruit Curd (makes 2 cups)

If you have difficulty finding pure passion fruit purée, you can substitute fresh lemon or lime juice, or a combination of both. The curd can be made ahead of time, and any left over makes a delicious accompaniment to fresh berries or a spread for breads.

1 tablespoon plus 2 teaspoons finely
  grated fresh lemon zest
1 cup pure passion fruit purée
1⅓ cups granulated sugar
4 large eggs
½ teaspoon salt
1¾ sticks unsalted butter, cut into
  tablespoon-size pieces

Combine the lemon zest, passion fruit purée, sugar, eggs, and salt in a medium, heavy-based saucepan and set over medium-low heat. Whisk constantly until the curd is thick and small bubbles rise to the surface. Remove from the heat, whisk in the butter all at once, then immediately strain the curd through a fine sieve into a bowl. Place plastic wrap directly on the surface of the curd and chill.

The curd will keep in an airtight container in the refrigerator for up to 2 weeks or in the freezer for up to 1 month.

MEYER LEMON PALETAS WITH VERBENA-STEEPED BERRIES

MAKES 6

When my good friend Bryan (one of the owners of the Big Gay Ice Cream Shop) and I were in L.A. for an event, we went to the amazing farmers' market in Santa Monica to look for fresh fruit to inspire us. We were enamored with our surroundings and came up with this flavor combination to use in my paletas, or Mexican ice pops, while we walked around. It is one of my absolute favorites, and now anytime I see lemon verbena I think of Bryan, and it inevitably makes me smile!

1¼ cups water
½ cup plus 2 tablespoons
    granulated sugar, kept separately
4 sprigs of fresh lemon verbena
½ cup red raspberries
½ cup black raspberries
⅔ cup fresh Meyer lemon juice
¼ teaspoon salt

Equipment
6 ice pop molds

Place the water and the ½ cup sugar, along with 2 sprigs of lemon verbena, in a small saucepan. Heat the mixture, stirring frequently, until the sugar is fully dissolved. Remove the pan from the heat and allow the mixture to cool. Transfer to a pitcher, cover, and refrigerate until ready to use.

Meanwhile remove the lemon verbena leaves from the stems of the remaining sprigs. Place the red raspberries in one bowl and the black raspberries in another, and divide the lemon verbena leaves and the remaining 2 tablespoons of sugar equally between the bowls. Mix gently and leave to sit for 15 minutes to allow the natural juices to come out of the fruit.

Strain the chilled syrup, discarding the verbena, then combine the syrup with the Meyer lemon juice and salt and pour into a pitcher or a measuring cup with a spout.

Pour the berries and their juices into 6 ice pop molds, combining the two kinds of raspberries in each mold, and pour the Meyer lemon syrup on top, leaving about ½ inch at the top of the molds so the paletas have room to expand.

Place the paletas in the freezer and allow to freeze completely—about 4–6 hours, depending on your freezer.

To unmold the paletas, fill a container deeper than the length of the paletas with warm water. Submerge each mold completely for 10–20 seconds and then pull it out of the water and gently unmold it before moving on to the next. Store the paletas in individual bags in the freezer until ready to serve.

GHAYA OLIVEIRA

hat life can unexpectedly throw you a curveball is a familiar cliché. For Ghaya Oliveira, however, it was a fact of her life.

Born and raised in Tunisia, Oliveira graduated with a degree in economics from a local university. After a prompt job offer with an investment bank in Tunis, a future in finance seemed set.

Except it wasn't. When Oliveira's sister, who was living in New York, fell ill, Oliveira moved to be with her. Unfortunately Oliveira's qualifications as a stock trader were not recognized in the U.S., and she had neither the finances nor the time to study afresh. Also a highly accomplished ballerina, Oliveira next tried to carve an alternative career out of dance. But there, too, her training was deemed inadequate.

Still, she had to make a living, and so she took on a job as a dishwasher in a restaurant. "I knew I could rise up in this business; there was strategy in my decision. Chefs who are stars started at the bottom." She initiated her ascent by moving to Placido Domingo's restaurant, Domingo, and taking on her first commis role in pastry—a move inspired, she admits, by pragmatism not passion.

But the passion came soon enough. When Domingo closed unexpectedly, a colleague gave Oliveira the business card of one of the managers at Café Boulud, prompting her entrée into Daniel Boulud's formidable restaurant empire. In 2001, she joined as the rookie of the pastry crew. Her first two weeks presented so many challenges that she nearly quit. But she found an ally in her chef, an old-school taskmaster, with whom she was able to converse in French. She learned quickly; nonetheless, with every new skill acquired there were a dozen to grasp. So she would stay hours past her shift to perfect these—pulled sugar one evening, chocolate work the next... In this way, a newfound passion was ignited, and with it a single-minded determination that propelled her forward until Oliveira came to run the pastry kitchen.

In 2007, Oliveira left Café Boulud to become the opening executive pastry chef of Bar Boulud, a Lyonnais-style bistro, relinquishing elegant plated desserts in favor of playful takes on typical French tarts and coupes glacées. Five years later, when the Mediterranean-inspired Boulud Sud opened next door, Oliveira took over the desserts there too. Recalling the Tunisian sweets of her childhood, Oliveira transformed those luscious custards, fried pastries, honeyed baklava, and decadent halva into restaurant-style compositions. Mining her deep understanding of aromatic spices and Mediterranean staples to invigorate her creations, her inventiveness earned her a 2012 and 2015 James Beard nomination in the Outstanding Pastry Chef category.

"Ghaya is a success story I never tire of telling," noted Daniel Boulud when announcing that Oliveira would helm the pastry department of his flagship restaurant, Daniel, in 2013. Classic desserts articulated in surprising ways is Oliveira's signature style at the Michelin-starred eatery with coherence centered in contradictions—creaminess must be met with crunchiness, acidity is countered with sweetness. There must be balance even in the aesthetics, and so her plates are painstakingly composed.

From washing dishes to winning one of the most coveted executive pastry chef roles in New York City's gastro-scape—Oliveira's tale has few equals in her profession. Yet she has no intention of sitting on her laurels. "I always say it because it's the truth: I'm never satisfied."

What dessert from your childhood is most memorable?
My mother's custard.

Is there one dessert or pastry technique that is your ultimate nemesis?
Working with sugar. I burnt myself pretty bad one day when I was taking lessons from my chef. I got really traumatized.

For pure old-fashioned indulgence, what is your favorite treat—sweet or savory?
Mille-feuille!!!

What piece of equipment or machine that hasn't been invented yet would you love to see designed?
A self-sanitizing kitchen!!!

Which hole-in-the-wall, or off-the-beaten track eatery in New York City would you recommend for the ultimate cheap eat?
Korean Barbecue—they're open 24/7!!!

What kitchen mishap or mistake will your colleagues never let you forget?
Yes, of course: my burnt toast in the oven. I will always be reminded of that. I love to eat toasted bread, no matter what kind, but I always forget it in the oven.

MOELLEUX PROVENÇALS
(ALMOND-PISTACHIO MOELLEUX, LEMON CHIBOUST, AND WILD STRAWBERRIES)

SERVES 8

I've always loved the delicate floral and fruity flavors of Provence, such as orange blossom, Cavaillon melon, and strawberries. So when I created this dessert I harmonized these flavors with another complementary one from my childhood: almond-flavored candies called calissons. Here homemade calissons are combined with an ice cream echoing those same flavors; a tender, moist cake; lightly cooked strawberries; and a lemon chiboust, a citrusy mousse-like variation of a traditional French pastry cream lightened with whipped cream.

For the pâte calisson
1¼ cups tightly packed almond paste
⅓ cup loosely packed almond flour
3 tablespoons melon purée (see suppliers, page 286)
3 tablespoons orange marmalade

For the royal icing
¾ cup confectioners' sugar
½ large egg white
2 tablespoons fresh lemon juice

For the wild strawberries
4 cups wild strawberries, hulled and cleaned

For the calisson ice cream
¾ cup packed almond paste
⅓ cup plus 1 teaspoon milk
⅔ cups melon purée
1½ teaspoons honey
1¾ cups water
3 tablespoons granulated sugar
zest of 1 orange

For the lemon chiboust
1 sheet gelatin (140 bloom/bronze strength (see suppliers, page 286)
¼ cup plus 2 tablespoons lemon juice
3 tablespoons granulated sugar
2 tablespoons cornstarch
¼ cup lightly beaten egg yolks
½ cup egg whites
¼ cup plus 3½ tablespoons granulated sugar (kept separately from the amount given above)
¼ cup crème fraîche

For the almond-pistachio cake
1 cup plus 3 tablespoons granulated sugar
2⅔ cups loosely packed almond flour
1 tablespoon cornstarch
4 large eggs
2 sticks unsalted butter
2¼ teaspoons orange blossom water (see suppliers, page 286)
3 tablespoons whole Sicilian pistachios
1½ tablespoons finely chopped candied lemon strips (see suppliers, page 286)

To decorate
candied pistachios (see suppliers, page 286)
fresh cantaloupe melon, cut into small cubes
micro peonies (see suppliers, page 286)

Equipment
An instant-read thermometer
An ice cream maker
A tray of 16 (1½-inch-diameter) silicone dome molds (see suppliers, page 286)
A ring cutter with diameter of 1–1½ inches
A half sheet pan

Make the pâte calisson. Place all of the ingredients in a food processor and process until just combined. Roll out the paste thinly between two sheets of parchment paper, to about ⅓-inch thickness. Cover and set aside while you make the royal icing.

For the royal icing, first place the confectioners' sugar in the bowl of a stand mixer fitted with a wire whisk. On medium speed, slowly add the egg white and whip until the mixture is thick and shiny. Add the lemon juice and continue to whip until fully incorporated into the icing. If the icing is too thick you may need to add more egg white; if too thin, add more sugar. Transfer to a small bowl.

Using an offset spatula, spread a thin layer of the royal icing onto the top of the rolled pâte calisson. Before the icing sets, cut the calisson into small squares or diamond shapes and separate right away. Leave to set completely, then store in an airtight container.

Prepare the wild strawberries. Place half the strawberries in a heatproof bowl and cover with plastic wrap; reserve the rest. Set the bowl over a small saucepan of gently simmering water set over low heat, and cook for 3 hours. Pass the strawberries and their juice through a fine-meshed sieve into a bowl. Discard the solids and keep the juice.

Place the remaining pint of strawberries in a saucepan with the strawberry juice and set over low heat. Simmer gently until the fruit is tender. Using a slotted spoon, remove the strawberries from the pan and transfer to a bowl. Turn up the heat and continue to cook the juice for a few more minutes until a syrupy texture is obtained. Strain and reserve the cooked strawberries and the juice separately; the juice will be the sauce for the plated dessert.

Now make the calisson ice cream. Slowly blend the almond paste with the milk in a large bowl, then add the melon purée, honey, and water and mix well. Transfer this mixture to a saucepan and heat gently until it reaches 104°F on an instant-read thermometer. Remove from the heat and whisk in the sugar and orange zest. Return the saucepan to the stove and heat to 180°F. Strain the mixture into a container, cover, and chill in the refrigerator overnight. Churn the mixture in your ice cream maker according to the manufacturer's instructions, then transfer to an airtight container and place in the freezer until firm, around 4–6 hours.

Make the lemon chiboust. Soak the gelatin sheet in a bowl of cold water until softened, about 10 minutes, then squeeze out the excess liquid. Place the lemon juice in a small saucepan and bring to a boil. Meanwhile, combine the 3 tablespoons of sugar with the cornstarch and the egg yolks in another small saucepan. Pour the

hot lemon juice over the yolk mixture and whisk gently to combine. Place the pan on low heat and bring the egg yolk and lemon mixture to a simmer. Continue to cook gently, stirring all the time, until the mixture is shiny and smooth, about 1–2 minutes. Remove from the heat and add the softened gelatin; stir until dissolved. Transfer the mixture to a large bowl, cover with plastic wrap directly on the surface, and leave to cool.

Meanwhile, place the egg whites in the bowl of a stand mixer fitted with the wire whisk and whisk on medium-high speed until medium peaks form. While the egg whites are being whisked, place the remaining quantity of sugar in a saucepan with a little water. Heat over medium heat until the sugar dissolves completely, then bring to a boil and let bubble until the sugar syrup reaches 250°F on an instant-read thermometer. When ready, pour the syrup onto the whites in a thin, steady stream while continuing to whip on high speed. Keep whipping until the meringue mixture is cool.

Remove the plastic wrap from the lemon mixture and carefully fold the meringue into it, then finish by folding in the crème fraîche. Spoon the lemon chiboust mixture into 16 silicone molds and freeze for 4–6 hours or until completely frozen. Keep in the freezer until ready to serve.

Now make the almond-pistachio cake. Preheat the oven to 350°F.

Grease and line a half sheet pan with parchment paper. Set aside. Place the sugar, almond flour, and cornstarch in a food processor. Process, adding the eggs one at a time, until the mixture is smooth. Melt the butter in a small saucepan and bring to a boil. As soon as it starts to boil, remove from the heat and slowly stream it into the mixture in the food processor with the motor running on medium speed; process until the butter is fully incorporated. Transfer the mixture to a large bowl and fold in the remaining ingredients. Pour the mixture into the prepared sheet pan. Bake for 6 minutes then rotate the pan 180° and bake for another 8–10 minutes or until golden and cooked through. Remove from the oven and leave to cool completely.

Assemble the dessert. First unmold the lemon chiboust domes and let them defrost at room temperature for about an hour. Using the ring cutter, cut out 16 discs from the almond-pistachio cake. On large, round plates, line up 2 cake discs and 2 lemon chiboust domes, alternating, down the center of each plate. Arrange the cooked strawberries around the cake and lemon chiboust, spooning some of the sauce around the plate. Next, place 2 pieces of calisson on each plate, then garnish with the cubes of melon, the candied pistachios, and the micro peonies. Finally, sit a small scoop, or quenelle, of the calisson ice cream on top of each of the two cake discs. Serve immediately.

ALMOND MOUSSEUX WITH CHOCOLATE CRÉMEUX, LEMON-PRALINÉ SAUCE, AND CITRUS CONFIT ICE CREAM

SERVES 8

I am a big fan of homemade praline: nut-based pastes that can be made with caramelized almonds, walnuts, hazelnuts, pistachios, or any other nut of your choice. I added a citrus element to brighten the rich and luxurious paste that features prominently in this dessert.

For the citrus confit ice cream
2¾ cups milk
¼ cup heavy cream
3 tablespoons finely chopped candied lemon strips (see suppliers, page 286)
½ cup plus 1 tablespoon granulated sugar
3 tablespoons plus 1 teaspoon dextrose (see suppliers, page 286) or light corn syrup
4 tablespoons milk powder

For the almond mousseux
5 sheets gelatin (140 bloom/bronze strength: (see suppliers, page 286)
1 cup milk
1 cup plus 1½ cups heavy cream, kept separately
⅔ (tightly packed) cup almond paste

For the chocolate crémeux
1 (8.82oz) Valrhona Caraibe 66% (cocoa) Baking Bar or other good-quality dark chocolate, chopped
1¼ cups heavy cream
1¼ cups milk
½ cup egg yolks (from 6 or 7 large eggs)
¼ cup plus 1 teaspoon sugar

For the almond-hazelnut crumble
½ (rounded) cup granulated sugar
½ cup plus 3 tablespoons loosely packed almond flour
½ cup plus 3 tablespoons loosely packed hazelnut flour
¾ cup plus 2 tablespoons all-purpose flour
1 stick butter, cold and cubed
6 ounces bittersweet chocolate, melted and cooled, for enrobing

For the flourless chocolate sponge
5¾ ounces extra-dark chocolate
2¾ tablespoons unsalted butter, cubed
2 tablespoons egg yolks (from 2 medium eggs)
1 cup egg whites (from 5 or 6 eggs)
¼ cup granulated sugar

For the citrus-praliné spread
¾ cup plus 2 tablespoons heavy cream
grated zest of ½ orange
grated zest of ½ lemon
1 cup Valrhona Hazelnut Praline (see suppliers, page 286), or other hazelnut praline paste

For the lemon-praliné sauce
½ cup plus 2 tablespoons heavy cream
zest of ½ lemon
½ cup plus 2 tablespoons Valrhona Praline à l'Ancienne (see suppliers, page 286), or Cacao Barry Hazelnut/Almond Praline Paste (see suppliers, page 286)
½ cup Valrhona Hazelnut Praline (see suppliers, page 286), or other hazelnut praline paste
2 tablespoons fresh lemon juice

To decorate
chocolate décor (optional: see recipe below, page 235)

Equipment
An ice cream maker
An instant-read thermometer
A 1½-inch-high half sheet pan frame, or extender (see suppliers, page 286)
A piping bag fitted with a small plain nozzle
A pair of disposable latex gloves

Note
You will need to make the components of this dessert, apart from the chocolate décor, the day before serving it.

First make the citrus confit ice cream. In a saucepan, warm the milk, cream, and candied lemon strips. When the mixture begins to steam, remove from the heat, transfer to a blender, and process until smooth. Combine the sugar, dextrose (or corn syrup), and milk powder in a bowl. Whisk in a little of the milk mixture, making sure there are no lumps. Transfer to the blender, together with the rest of the milk mixture, and blend until smooth and evenly incorporated. Place the mixture in a bowl and refrigerate for a few hours or overnight. Churn the chilled mixture in your ice cream maker according to the manufacturer's instructions. Transfer to an airtight container and place in the freezer until firm, around 4–6 hours.

➤

Next make the almond mousseux. Soak the gelatin sheets in a bowl of cold water until softened, about 10 minutes, then squeeze out the excess liquid. Meanwhile, in a saucepan over medium heat, bring the 1 cup of milk and 1 cup of cream to a simmer. Remove from the heat, then blend in the almond paste until smooth. Add the softened gelatin and stir until dissolved. Transfer to a bowl and place this in a separate, larger bowl filled with ice and water.

In another bowl, whip the 1½ cups of heavy cream to medium peaks. When the dairy, gelatin, and almond mixture is cold, gently fold in the whipped cream, in small amounts, until fully incorporated. Cover and chill until ready to use.

For the chocolate crémeux, first place the chopped chocolate in a large bowl; set aside. In a saucepan, bring the cream and milk to a boil, then immediately remove from the heat. Meanwhile whisk together the egg yolks and sugar in a medium bowl. Pour a little of the hot liquid onto the yolks and whisk quickly to combine. Repeat again, whisking a little more of the hot dairy mixture into the yolks, then pour the warm egg yolk and dairy mixture back into the pan with the remaining cream mixture. Stirring all the time with a rubber spatula, cook the custard over very low heat until it thickens and reaches 170°–175°F on an instant-read thermometer. Immediately remove from the heat and pour the chopped chocolate over, whisking to melt the chocolate and incorporate it fully into the custard. Cover with a piece of plastic wrap placed directly on the surface of the custard. Set aside and leave to cool, then chill until ready to use.

Next make the almond-hazelnut crumble. Preheat the oven to 360°F. Combine the dry ingredients in the bowl of a stand mixer fitted with the paddle attachment. With the motor running at medium speed, slowly add the cold cubes of butter. Continue to mix until the dough is just combined. Place the dough between 2 sheets of parchment paper and use a rolling pin to roll it out to a sheet about ⅓-inch thick. Transfer to a greased baking tray and place the dough in the freezer for about 1 hour or until frozen. Cut the frozen dough into ⅓-inch cubes. Return the cubes to the baking tray, making sure to separate them completely and leave a little space between them. Place the tray in the freezer and chill until firm.

Bake the dough cubes for 6–8 minutes, rotate the tray 180°, then cook for another 6–8 minutes or until golden. Remove from the oven and leave to cool completely.

Once cool, the crumble needs to be enrobed with the melted chocolate. Place a small amount of chocolate into a gloved hand and gently roll a few pieces of the cooled crumble, making sure to cover the cubes completely with chocolate. Place the enrobed cubes on a baking tray lined with parchment paper and leave to set. Repeat until all the cubes have been coated.

Make the chocolate flourless sponge. Preheat the oven to 450°F. In a saucepan, over medium-low heat, melt the chocolate and butter together, stirring to combine. Remove from the heat and leave to cool briefly. Add the egg yolks and fold into the chocolate mixture until fully combined. Set aside while you make the meringue.

Place the egg whites in the bowl of a stand mixer fitted with the whisk attachment, making sure the bowl is completely free from any grease. Beat on medium speed until the egg whites are foamy and forming soft, floppy peaks, then slowly add the sugar and continue whipping on high speed until stiff and glossy peaks form. Carefully fold the meringue into the chocolate and egg yolk mixture.

Transfer the batter to half-sheet tray greased and lined with parchment paper, spreading the mixture evenly with a spatula. Bake for 4–5 minutes, then rotate the tray 180° and bake for another 4–5 minutes until tender and cooked through. Remove from the oven and leave to cool.

For the citrus-praliné spread, pour the cream into a medium saucepan, along with the citrus zests, and bring it to a boil. Remove from the heat and leave to infuse for 30 minutes, then strain; discard the zests. Place the hazelnut praline in a bowl and pour the infused cream over it, whisking to incorporate. Set aside and leave to cool, then cover with plastic wrap.

For the lemon-praliné sauce, pour the cream into a medium saucepan, along with the lemon zest, and bring it to a boil. Place both types of praline in a bowl, then strain the lemon cream over the praline, discarding the zest. Whisk the praline and cream mixture to create an emulsion. Add the lemon juice and blend, using a hand or electric whisk, until you have a smooth sauce. Cover with plastic wrap and set aside.

Assemble the dessert. Place the frame in the half sheet pan with the cooled chocolate sponge. Inside the frame, thinly spread the citrus-praliné to an even layer ⅟₁₆–⅛ inch thick, directly over the biscuit (you may not need to use all of it). Loosely arrange some of the almond hazelnut crumble over the top, then pour over or spoon in a 1-inch-thick layer of the almond mousseux. Freeze for 6 hours or overnight.

To portion, cut the frozen layered cake into equal-size long rectangular bars, about 5 inches long and 1 inch wide, or as you desire. Leave to defrost completely.

When ready to serve, spoon the chocolate crémeux into a piping bag fitted with a small plain nozzle and pipe 4 dots, each the size of a quarter, on top of the cake rectangles at regular intervals. Arrange the pieces of chocolate décor, if using, in between the chocolate crémeux dots. Carefully transfer each cake rectangle onto the center of a large round plate, then dot the plates with the lemon-praliné sauce. With a fork or a rolling pin, roughly crush the remaining hazelnut crumble and make a small pile of it on each plate. Set a small scoop, or quenelle, of the citrus confit ice cream on top of the crushed crumble. Serve immediately.

Chocolate Décor
4 ounces of bittersweet chocolate

Equipment
A marble slab or tabletop (optional)
An acetate sheet (see suppliers, page 286)

Fill one-third of a large saucepan with water and bring to a simmer. Place the chocolate in a heatproof bowl and set over the simmering water, stirring occasionally, until the chocolate has fully melted and reaches 113°F on an instant-read thermometer. Remove the bowl from the heat. If you have a marble tabletop or a large slab of marble at room temperature, the chocolate can be poured onto it and slowly folded onto itself, using 2 metal spatulas, until it cools to 84°F. Otherwise, you can leave the melted chocolate in the bowl and slowly stir it until the temperature comes down to 84°F. The chocolate is now tempered. Spread it thinly onto a sheet of acetate, wait until almost set, then cut into your desired shapes, using a small, sharp knife. Leave the chocolate décor to cool and set completely.

APRICOT VACHERIN WITH VERBENA-WHITE CHOCOLATE CHANTILLY AND HONEY MISHMISH SAUCE

SERVES 8

The Apricot Vacherin was the very first dessert I created as Executive Pastry Chef at Restaurant Daniel, and as such it holds a special place in my heart. I arrived at the restaurant in late summer, when sun-drenched apricots are at their sweetest. Mishmish, present in two components of the dessert, is a spice blend; the name means "apricot" in Arabic. It served as my introduction of spices to the dessert menu at Daniel.

For the apricot verbena sorbet
1½ cups loosely packed dried lemon verbena leaves
½ cup plus 2 tablespoons cold water
½ cup plus 2 tablespoons granulated sugar
⅓ cup glucose powder (see suppliers, page 286)
1½ cups apricot purée (see suppliers, page 286)
1 teaspoon fresh lemon juice

For the meringue
1 cup granulated sugar
½ cup egg whites (from 2 or 3 large eggs)

For the apricot gel
1¾ cups plus 2 tablespoons apricot purée
3 tablespoons liquid glucose (see suppliers, page 286)
1¼ teaspoons pectin NH (see suppliers, page 286)

For the opaline mishmish tuile
1 pound 3 ounces pouring fondant (see suppliers, page 286)
1 cup liquid glucose
2 tablespoons unsalted butter
Mishmish spice blend, as needed (see suppliers, page 286)

For the honey mishmish sauce
1¾ cups honey
1⅓ cups plus 2 tablespoons water
2 teaspoons mishmish spice blend (see suppliers, page 286)

For the verbena-white chocolate Chantilly
8 (loosely packed) cups dried lemon verbena leaves (see suppliers, page 286)
1¼ cups heavy cream
1 tablespoon liquid glucose (see suppliers, page 286)
3 tablespoons light corn syrup
½ pound Valrhona Opalys 33% White Chocolate or other good-quality white chocolate, well chopped
2 cups heavy cream, kept separately from quantity above

To decorate
fresh apricots, sliced

Equipment
An ice cream maker
A piping bag with a ½-inch pastry tip and a sultan tip (see suppliers, page 286)
A Flexipan Mold sheet with at least 24 cavities about ⅔–¾ inch in diameter (see suppliers, page 286)
An instant-read thermometer

Note
Begin preparing the dessert the day before needed (the sorbet-filled meringues can be made up to 1 week ahead of time).

First make the apricot verbena sorbet. Soak the verbena in the cold water overnight to infuse. Strain, and bring the water to a simmer in a saucepan. Whisk in the sugar and glucose and bring to a boil. Strain the mixture and transfer to the refrigerator overnight to chill. When the mixture is cold, whisk in the purée and lemon juice, then transfer to the ice cream maker. Churn according to the manufacturer's instructions. Transfer the sorbet to a container and freeze for 4–6 hours. Keep frozen until ready to use.

Now make the meringue. Preheat the oven to 250°F. Place a medium-size pan of water on the stove and bring to a simmer. Place the sugar and egg whites in a heatproof bowl and set this over the pan, making sure the water doesn't touch the base of the bowl. Whisk until the sugar is completely dissolved. Transfer the mixture to the bowl of a stand mixer fitted with the whisk attachment and whip on high speed until the meringue is completely cool and forms stiff peaks.

Using the piping bag, pipe the meringue into 1-inch-diameter rounds on a baking tray lined with a silicone mat. (You will need 3 meringue rounds per serving, plus a few extra in case of breakages.) Place the baking tray in the oven and reduce the temperature to ➤

195°F. After 45–50 minutes, check the meringue; if the exterior of the shells is dry, remove them from the oven and hollow out their insides from the bottom with a spoon. Return the meringue shells to the oven and bake for another 30–40 minutes or until they are completely dry. Remove from the oven and leave to cool completely. Store in an airtight container until ready to serve.

Alternatively, fill the meringues with the sorbet as described below for assembling the dessert; the filled meringues will keep in the freezer for up to 1 week.

For the apricot gel, place the purée and glucose in a small saucepan and heat gently. Stir in the pectin, then bring to a boil, and simmer for 2 minutes. Remove from the heat and pour the mixture into the tray of domed molds; you will need 24 domes of gel (3 per serving). Freeze, then unmold and store in a container in the freezer until ready to serve.

Make the opaline mishmish tuile. Preheat the oven to 360°F. Combine the first 3 ingredients in a saucepan. Set over medium-high heat and bring to a boil, then cook until the mixture reaches 360°F on an instant-read thermometer. Pour the mixture onto a silicone mat and leave it to cool completely. Once cool and solidified, break it up into pieces then use a rolling pin to crush until a fine powder forms. (Alternatively, you can grind it in a coffee grinder.) Spread the powder mixture into

triangle shapes on a baking tray lined with a silicone mat, making them roughly 4 inches along the bottom edge and 3 inches on the sloping sides. (The recipe will make more than the 8 you need, which allows for some breakage.) Sprinkle some of the mishmish spice powder over them, then bake for about 1–2 minutes, until the opaline begins to melt. Remove from the oven and leave to cool before carefully peeling off the silicone mat.

For the honey mishmish sauce, combine all the ingredients in a small saucepan and bring to a boil. Cook until reduced and thickened to a syrupy consistency. Remove from the heat and leave to cool.

Make the verbena-white chocolate Chantilly. Place the dried lemon verbena leaves in a bowl and pour the 1¼ cups cream over them. Leave to infuse for 1 hour. Strain the infused cream and discard the solids. In a saucepan, heat the infused cream with the glucose and corn syrup and bring to a simmer. Place the white chocolate in a large bowl and pour the hot cream over. Whisk until the chocolate melts and is incorporated evenly into the cream. Leave to cool to room temperature.

When almost ready to serve, pour the 2 cups of cream into the white chocolate ganache and blend, using a handheld electric beater or a stand mixer, until medium-stiff peaks form. Be careful not to over-whip or the mixture will become grainy. Use immediately.

Assemble the dessert. Fill a piping bag fitted with a small round tip with the apricot verbena sorbet, and carefully fill the hollowed-out meringues with the sorbet. Place 3 of the sorbet-filled meringues on each serving plate in a triangle formation. Fill a piping bag fitted with a sultan pastry tip with the verbena-white chocolate Chantilly and pipe the cream over each meringue to cover. Top the center of each sorbet-filled meringue with a dome of the apricot gel, then place the opaline mishmish tuile over the triangle of meringues. Finally, decorate the plate with freshly sliced apricots and drizzle with the honey mishmish sauce.

POIRE AUX MARRONS
(LICORICE-POACHED PEAR WITH CHESTNUT CREAM VERMICELLI AND LICORICE ICE CREAM)

SERVES 4

Creating a dessert around a single, whole fruit is, to me, the best way to respect the fruit and its flavors. This particular dessert features a succulent licorice-poached pear accompanied by a smooth chestnut cream and complemented by licorice ice cream.

For the licorice ice cream
2¾ cups whole milk
½ (tightly packed) cup milk powder
7 tablespoons unsalted butter, chopped
¼ cup plus 1 tablespoon egg yolks (from about 4 large eggs)
⅓ cup plus 2 tablespoons granulated sugar
1 tablespoon licorice paste, or 3 to 6 tablespoons anise extract, depending on the strength of the particular brand of extract you are using (see suppliers, page 286)

For the poached pears
3 cups water
1 cup plus 3 tablespoons granulated sugar
2 (6-inch) licorice root sticks, each one broken in half (see suppliers, page 286)
4 Comice pears

For the meringue
1 cup granulated sugar
½ cup egg whites (from 2 or 3 large eggs)

For the chestnut vermicelli
½ (tightly packed) cup sweetened chestnut paste (see suppliers, page 286)
⅔ (loosely packed) cup unsweetened chestnut purée (see suppliers, page 286)
2 tablespoons simple syrup (made from boiling together equal parts of sugar and water)

Equipment
An instant-read thermometer
An ice cream maker
2 disposable piping bags
A half sheet tray
A silicone mat

Make the licorice ice cream. Place the milk in a large saucepan over medium heat. When the milk reaches 105°F on an instant-read thermometer, whisk in the milk powder and butter and bring the mixture to a boil. In another small bowl, whisk together the egg yolks and the sugar. Pour a small amount of the hot milk over the egg and sugar mixture whisking constantly. When completely combined, pour a little more of the hot milk into the egg mixture, still whisking. Now pour the hot egg and dairy mixture back into the pan with the rest of the hot milk. Cook, stirring constantly, over low heat, until the mixture reaches 184°F, then immediately remove from the heat.

If using the anise extract, strain the cooked mixture into a bowl, then add the extract in small increments, stirring it in and tasting it after each addition until you achieve the desired strength. If using the licorice

paste, place this in the bowl and strain the mixture into the bowl, whisking to combine. Cover and chill in the refrigerator overnight. Transfer the chilled mixture to an ice cream maker. Churn according to the manufacturer's instructions, then spoon into a container and freeze for 4–6 hours. Keep frozen until ready to use.

Poach the pears. Begin by making the licorice syrup. Combine all the ingredients in a small saucepan and bring to a boil, stirring until the sugar has dissolved. Simmer for 2 minutes, then remove from the heat and leave to steep until cool, at least 1 hour. Discard the licorice root sticks.

Peel the pears and remove the cores, but keep the stems intact. Place the pears in a bowl of ice water. In a medium saucepan, bring the reserved licorice syrup to a simmer. Place the pears in the syrup and cook until tender. They are ready once a knife goes through the flesh with no resistance, after 15–20 minutes depending on the ripeness of the pears. Remove the pan from the heat, leave to cool for 20 minutes, then refrigerate until chilled.

Make the meringue. Preheat the oven to 175°F. On the stove top, bring a saucepan of water to a simmer. Place the sugar and egg whites in a heatproof bowl and place this over the water, making sure the water doesn't touch the base of the bowl. Whisk until the sugar is completely dissolved.

Transfer the egg white mixture to the bowl of a stand mixer fitted with the whisk attachment and whip on high speed until the meringue is cool and stands in stiff peaks. Fill a piping bag with the meringue and cut a small hole at the tip of the bag about ⅛ inch in diameter. Pipe tiny dots of meringue onto a half sheet tray lined with a silicone mat. Dry completely in the oven for about 2 hours. When completely dry and cooled, store the meringue dots in an airtight container.

Make the chestnut vermicelli. Place the chestnut paste in the bowl of a stand mixer fitted with a paddle attachment and mix until smooth. Add the purée, mix to combine, then add the simple syrup and mix again until thoroughly incorporated. Cover and set aside.

Assemble the dessert. Place a poached pear off-center on each serving plate. Fill a piping bag with the chestnut vermicelli paste mixture and cut a small hole in the bottom. Decorate the pears with a spiral of the paste, working from the middle of each pear up to the tip. Dress the plate with the meringue dots, as you desire. Finally make a small pile of the dots across from the pear, and top with a scoop, or quenelle, of licorice ice cream.

KATHERINE THOMPSON

From the age of 12, when she was obsessed with watching Julia Child on television, Katherine Thompson, now the executive pastry chef at dell'anima, L'Artusi, and L'Apicio, baked at any opportunity. Her high school yearbook predicted her destiny, citing "pastry chef" as her future career. Despite the early indicators, though, hers was not a direct route to the sweet side of the kitchen. After attending the College of William & Mary, in Virginia, the Maryland-born chef moved to Seattle to work first for an online start-up then for a technology company. Three years of sitting at a desk by day and studying her cookbooks in the evening prompted her to enroll in the full program at the Culinary Institute of America.

On leaving school she strategized how she could cook professionally but avoid the usual trajectory of starting as a cook on the line. "It's not that I don't have respect for line cooks, because they are amazing people; honestly it just scared me." So she became a food runner at Per Se, delivering plates from the kitchen to customers. "I would obsessively learn how certain items were cooked. Even though I wasn't in the kitchen, I was trying to teach myself new techniques." Missing that direct connection with food, she became the private event chef at Italian Wine Merchants; from there, she moved to the pastry section of Del Posto. After seven months of intense training in pastry fundamentals, Thompson left to run the private events at the New York Wine Company in TriBeCa. Around this time she started dating her future husband, Gabriel, another chef. When some friends were opening dell'anima, in the West Village, and looking for an executive chef, Thompson recommended her beau.

While working at her day job, now as a pastry sous-chef at Brasserie 44, Thompson moonlighted as the front-of-house manager at dell'anima. Somewhere in between these two roles, she would whip up a daily dessert for dell'anima, since the nascent restaurant could not afford an actual pastry chef then. A few months later, in 2008, having decided that working alongside her new love, as well as living with him, wouldn't necessarily lead to disaster, Thompson joined dell'anima as a bona fide employee.

Though her role was official, her work space was anything but: Thompson prepped in the basement on top of the chest freezer. "A lot of happy accidents happened on the freezer!" Thompson recalls a dry batch of almond cake, not servable as it was, but with caramel sauce, almond brittle, and sea salt gelato she had on hand, Thompson rustled together a glorified sundae. It remains the restaurant's best-selling dessert.

In 2008, when the same team opened L'Artusi, a few blocks south, Thompson began producing desserts for both restaurants. The criteria were simple: they had to be technique heavy in their making but easy for dessert platers to assemble when orders came in. She had hit on a winning formula. More Italian-inspired than authentically Italian, her desserts were either American favorites/French classics with Italian flavorings and ingredients or Italian dishes given an American twist. For example, at her third restaurant, L'Apicio, which opened in the East Village in 2014, Thompson features a Banana Tiramisù, with peanut butter mousse, vanilla wafers, and caramelized bananas, and a Chocolate Hazelnut Ice Cream Cake with salted caramel gelato and a praline hazelnut crunch.

As for the romantic disaster she feared, it's still averted: Thompson and Gabriel remain blissfully married with two children in tow!

Which dessert that you created are you most proud of?
I'm proud of the coconut semifreddo with almond cake and chocolate sauce. I used to hate, hate, hate coconut. I thought it was disgusting. Then I turned 30 and fell in love with it. I wanted to create coconut desserts left and right. This semifreddo is like a hyped-up Almond Joy.

What's the best thing about being a pastry chef?
Making food look beautiful! There is something so rewarding about creating a dessert that not only tastes delicious but looks beautiful too. Whether piping frosting or cutting out perfect garnishes, I am attracted to the technical skill and precision behind creating desserts that look gorgeous.

What's the worst thing about being a pastry chef?
Calories! It is impossible for me to resist warm cookies out of the oven and freshly spun ice cream.

What's the tastiest savory dish that you cook?
My husband suggested my warm roasted mushroom salad with almonds and red wine vinaigrette. I love eating salads on a daily basis. They are quick and easy to make. Throw a fried egg on top, and it is the perfect meal.

COCONUT SEMIFREDDO WITH ALMOND-COCONUT CAKE, BITTERSWEET CHOCOLATE SAUCE, AND TOASTED COCONUT

SERVES 8

For most of my life, I thought coconut was disgusting. I would obnoxiously break open chocolate truffles to make sure there was no coconut in the center. Then when I turned 30, my taste buds suddenly shifted and my hatred of coconut turned into an intense love affair. All I wanted to do was eat all things coconut. When we opened L'Artusi restaurant, my number-one goal was to satisfy my coconut craving and showcase this ingredient in a decadent, luscious dessert.

For the coconut semifreddo
1¼ cups heavy cream
2 tablespoons plus ½ cup cold water, kept separately
1½ teaspoons powdered gelatin
4 large egg yolks, at room temperature
1 large egg, at room temperature
¼ teaspoon kosher salt
½ cup plus 2 tablespoons granulated sugar
2 tablespoons plus 2 teaspoons light corn syrup
1 cup coconut purée or cream of coconut (see note)

To assemble
¾ cup unsweetened coconut chips
1 quantity Almond-Coconut Cake (see recipe below, page 246)
½ cup coconut rum or light rum
1 quantity Bittersweet Chocolate Sauce (see recipe below, page 247)

Equipment
A 9- x 5- x 3-inch loaf pan

Note
At the restaurant, we make the semifreddo with coconut purée, rather than cream of coconut. It is a great product that can also be used for ice creams and sorbets and can be ordered through specialist websites. However, equally smooth and delicious results can be achieved with the more readily available cream of coconut. Some of the components of this dessert can be made well in advance. Read all the recipes first to decide on your order of preparation. Make the semifreddo the day before you plan to serve it (or several days in advance, if you like).

Lightly grease the loaf pan with a coating of nonstick spray. Cut a piece of parchment paper into an 8½- x 16-inch rectangle. Lay the parchment paper in the pan so that the excess hangs over the long sides. Press the paper into the corners of the pan so that it is flat against the bottom and sides.

In a medium-size bowl, whip the heavy cream with a wire whisk until the cream holds medium-stiff peaks. Place the whipped cream in the refrigerator while preparing the rest of the semifreddo ingredients.

Place the 2 tablespoons of cold water in a small bowl and sprinkle the gelatin over it. Set aside the water-gelatin mixture at room temperature so that the gelatin absorbs the liquid. If there are any clumps of unabsorbed gelatin, break them up with a fork.

Using a stand mixer with a wire whisk attachment, whip the egg yolks, egg, and salt at medium speed until the mixture is pale yellow and holds thick ribbons, about 20–30 minutes.

Meanwhile, prepare the sugar syrup. Place the ½ cup cold water, sugar, and corn syrup in a 2-quart saucepan. Over medium-low heat, cook the syrup until a candy thermometer reaches 240°F. This should take about 20 minutes.

Adjust the speed on the stand mixer to medium-low, and slowly pour the hot sugar syrup into the side of the mixer bowl. Immediately add the softened gelatin. Gradually increase the speed to medium-high. Whip the mixture until the bottom of the bowl is cool, about 5 minutes. Turn off the machine and touch the egg mixture with your fingers. It should be at room temperature. (Do not over-whip; if the mixture gets too cold, the gelatin will seize and the mixture will appear grainy.) If the mixture feels warm, continue beating for another minute or so.

Remove the bowl from the mixer. Add the coconut purée or cream of coconut and, using a wire whisk, whip until smooth. Still using the whisk, carefully fold the chilled whipped cream into the egg and coconut mixture. If clumps of cream remain, gently whisk together with a few turns until the mixture is homogenous. Refrain from overmixing. ➤

Immediately pour the mixture into the prepared loaf pan. Leave the parchment paper hanging over the sides and wrap the entire loaf pan with plastic wrap. Place in the freezer and chill overnight or for at least 8 hours.

When ready to unmold the semifreddo, line 2 sheet trays with parchment paper. If your kitchen is warm, you may want first to chill the sheet trays for a few minutes to help keep the semifreddo from melting. Remove the semifreddo from the freezer and discard the plastic wrap. Slide a paring knife along the length of the short sides to loosen the mixture. Turn the pan upside down onto one of the parchment-lined sheet trays. Pull down on one of the overhanging edges of parchment paper with one hand while gently lifting that side of the pan upwards with the other hand to partly dislodge the semifreddo. Repeat with the other edge of parchment paper on the opposite side of the pan and let the semifreddo slide out onto the tray.

Peel off the parchment paper from the semifreddo and discard. Run a large, sharp knife under hot water and dry with a towel. Use the warm knife to trim all 4 edges of the semifreddo loaf so that the sides are vertical, not sloped, and the semifreddo is roughly 8 x 4 inches. Be sure to wash and dry the knife in between each slice; this will ensure clean edges.

Next, slice the semifreddo in half lengthwise. Then cut the two long rectangles into 4 equal pieces each, so that you have 8 slabs of semifreddo, each around 2 x 2 inches. Use an offset spatula to transfer the semifreddo slabs to the other lined tray, leaving some space between each piece. Immediately transfer the tray to the freezer, uncovered, to firm up for 1 day or so.

Toast the coconut chips. Preheat the oven to 325°F. Spread the chips on a rimmed sheet tray and bake until lightly toasted, 5–7 minutes. Leave to cool completely. The flakes can be stored in an airtight container in a cool, dry place for up to 2 weeks.

Just before serving—or several hours in advance, if you prefer—trim the edges of the almond cake, then cut it into 8 pieces, each 2 x 2 inches. Brush each piece generously with about 1 tablespoon of rum, making sure to moisten the sides. If not serving immediately, wrap the pieces with plastic wrap and leave at room temperature.

To serve, gently warm the chocolate sauce in a small saucepan over low heat or in a microwave. The sauce should feel warm but not hot.

Place a rum-soaked piece of cake on each serving plate. Remove the semifreddo from the freezer and use an offset spatula to place a slab on each cake slice, lining up the edges as well as you can. Pour 1 tablespoon of

chocolate sauce (or more if desired) over each serving, letting it run down the sides, but without covering the cake and semifreddo completely.

Alternatively, if you are concerned about the warm chocolate possibly melting the semifreddo, simply reverse the presentation and spoon the chocolate sauce onto the plate first; then place the cake and semifreddo on top of the sauce.

Decorate each block generously with toasted coconut. Serve immediately.

Almond-Coconut Cake (makes a 9- x 13-inch cake)
1 cup unbleached all-purpose flour
1½ teaspoons baking powder
1 teaspoon kosher salt
½ cup sweetened coconut flakes
¾ cup almond flour
3 large eggs, at room temperature
¾ cup granulated sugar
5 tablespoons unsalted butter, melted
¼ cup excellent-quality, fruity, extra-virgin olive oil
½ teaspoon vanilla extract
¼ teaspoon almond extract
½ cup whole milk, at room temperature

Preheat the oven to 360°F.

Lightly coat a 9- x 13-inch rimmed sheet tray or cake pan with nonstick cooking spray. Line the bottom with parchment paper then spray the parchment with nonstick spray. Set aside.

In a medium-size bowl, sift together the all-purpose flour, baking powder, and salt. Finely chop the coconut flakes in a mini food processor or by hand with a large knife. Add the chopped coconut and the almond flour to the sifted ingredients. Set aside.

Whisk together the eggs and sugar in a large bowl. Add the melted butter and olive oil and whisk until smooth. Add the vanilla extract, almond extract, and milk and whisk together. Next add the combined dry ingredients and whisk until the dry mixture is just incorporated and there are no lumps in the batter. Refrain from overmixing.

Transfer the batter to the prepared pan. Use an offset spatula to spread it out evenly. Tap the pan on the counter twice to release any air bubbles. Bake the cake for 25–30 minutes or until a wooden skewer comes out clean when inserted into the center, the sides have come away from the pan, and the cake is a light golden color. Remove from the oven and leave to cool to room temperature before turning out the cake.

The cake can be baked a day in advance, enclosed in plastic wrap, and stored at room temperature.

Bittersweet Chocolate Sauce (makes 1¾ cups)

¾ cup heavy cream
3½ tablespoons light corn syrup
3 tablespoons unsalted butter
pinch of kosher salt
6 ounces chopped bittersweet chocolate, such as Valrhona 70%

Place the heavy cream, corn syrup, butter, and salt in a 2-quart saucepan. Over medium heat, bring this mixture to a boil. Turn the heat to low, add the chocolate, and whisk until the chocolate melts and the mixture is smooth. Remove from the heat and transfer to a heatproof container. Cool the sauce to room temperature, cover, and store refrigerated until ready to serve (or up to 2 weeks).

To serve, gently re-warm, stirring occasionally, in a small saucepan over low heat or in the microwave.

CHOCOLATE CROSTATA

MAKES ONE 9½–INCH TART, ABOUT 10 SERVINGS

This crostata (Italian for "tart") is a cocoa lover's dream. A dark chocolate crust is filled with creamy, pudding-like chocolate custard. Spiked with coffee liqueur, this is a richer, sexier version of your mom's chocolate cream pie. One small slice will satisfy anyone's chocolate cravings.

For the chocolate crust
7 tablespoons unsalted butter, at room temperature
⅝ cup sifted confectioners' sugar
1 large egg yolk
1 cup unbleached all-purpose flour, plus extra for rolling
4½ tablespoons cocoa powder
¼ teaspoon kosher salt

For the chocolate filling
2 tablespoons cold water
1 envelope (2¼ teaspoons) powdered gelatin
1 cup heavy cream
¾ cup whole milk
4 tablespoons plus 1½ teaspoons granulated sugar
¼ teaspoon kosher salt
6 ounces chopped bittersweet chocolate, such as Valrhona 70%
2 tablespoons coffee liqueur, such as Kahlua
¾ teaspoon vanilla extract

To serve
1 quantity Mascarpone Mousse (See Frutti di Bosco Tiramisù, page 251)

Equipment
A 9½-inch tart pan
A piping bag with medium to large nozzle

Make the chocolate crust. Place the butter and confectioners' sugar in the bowl of a stand mixer fitted with the paddle attachment. Cream together, on medium speed, until thoroughly combined and light and creamy, about 1–2 minutes. Add the egg yolk and continue to beat until combined, scraping down the sides of the bowl. Next add the flour, cocoa powder, and salt. Mix on low speed until the dry ingredients are just absorbed to form a dough. Do not overmix. Turn out onto a clean surface and form into a disc. Wrap the dough in plastic wrap and chill for 1–2 hours until slightly firm.

Preheat the oven to 350°F and insert 2 racks. Line a sheet tray with parchment paper.

Dust a work surface and rolling pin with flour and roll out the dough until it is ⅛-inch thick. Roll the dough loosely around the floured rolling pin, then unroll it onto the tart pan. Gently ease the dough into the bottom and sides of the pan. If there are any holes in the tart shell, patch them with pieces of dough torn from the rough edges. Trim off any remaining excess dough by running the rolling pin over the edges of the pan. Place these dough trimmings on the parchment-lined sheet tray.

Next line the tart shell with a generous piece of parchment and fill with pie weights or dried beans. Place the sheet tray with the dough scraps on the lower rack in the oven and the tart shell on the upper rack.

Bake the dough scraps for 12 minutes; remove from the oven and let cool. Bake the tart shell for 15 minutes. Remove the parchment paper and pie weights from the shell, then return the tart shell to the oven and continue baking for an additional 15 minutes, until the bottom is firm and dry to the touch. Leave to cool on a rack until the pastry cools to room temperature, about 40 minutes to 1 hour.

Break off a small piece of a cooled scrap—it should break easily. If the dough seems too soft, return the scraps to the oven for another 3–5 minutes. Once the scraps are cooked sufficiently, break them by hand into crumbs of roughly varied sizes. Transfer to an airtight container and store at room temperature until ready to serve the tart.

Now make the chocolate filling. Place the cold water in a very small bowl. Sprinkle the gelatin onto the water. If there are any undissolved clumps of gelatin, use a fork to break them up. Let the soaking gelatin sit at room temperature while preparing the rest of the ingredients for the filling.

Place the heavy cream, milk, sugar, and salt in a small saucepan. Bring to a simmer over medium heat. Reduce the heat to low, then add the soaked (or "bloomed") gelatin to the dairy mixture and whisk to combine. Next add the chocolate to the pan and whisk until completely melted and incorporated. Remove the chocolate mixture from the heat and whisk in the coffee liqueur and vanilla extract. Pour the filling into the cooled tart shell.

Chill uncovered in the refrigerator for several hours or overnight until the filling has set completely.

To serve, place a slice of the chilled tart on a plate, then pipe a generous amount of mascarpone mousse on top and sprinkle with the tart shell crumbs.

FRUTTI DI BOSCO TIRAMISÙ

SERVES 8

At L'Artusi restaurant, we avoid the standard tiramisù and instead create seasonal interpretations. Using variants of traditional components, such as mascarpone mousse and ladyfinger-like sponge cake, we also like to incorporate more unusual ingredients, such as pumpkin in the fall and rhubarb in the spring. This version takes advantage of all of the "fruits of the forest" that are ripe in summertime. We like to serve tiramisù in highball glasses, which showcase the various layers, but the same components can be assembled in a large bowl and served as a rustic scoop to each guest for an equally delicious dessert.

For the frutti di bosco mousse
3 cups mixed berries (raspberries, blackberries, blueberries, strawberries, pitted cherries, etc.)
1 tablespoon cold water
1 teaspoon powdered gelatin
2 large egg whites
6 tablespoons granulated sugar
pinch of kosher salt
½ cup crème fraîche

For the soaking liquid
3 tablespoons raspberry or red currant jam
2 tablespoons water
3 tablespoons raspberry liqueur, such as Chambord

Sponge Cake (see recipe below, page 252)
Mascarpone Mousse (see recipe below, page 253)

To decorate
10 amaretti cookies, crushed by hand into crumbs of varying size
confectioners' sugar (optional)

Equipment
8 highball glasses (each one about 1 cup capacity)
A round cookie cutter, same diameter as the highball glasses
A disposable piping bag (optional)

Set aside half of the berries to use as a decoration. For the frutti di bosco mousse, place the remaining half of the berries in a mini food processor or blender and purée until smooth. Pass the purée through a strainer to remove seeds and skins. Transfer it to a small bowl and set aside at room temperature.

Place the cold water in a very small bowl. Sprinkle the powdered gelatin on the water. If there are any undissolved lumps of gelatin, use a fork to loosen them. Set aside.

Fill a medium saucepan with 1–2 inches of water. Bring the water to a boil over high heat, then reduce the heat so that the water is just under a simmer. Place the egg whites, sugar, and salt in a medium-size bowl, place the bowl over the hot water, and gently whisk the egg whites and sugar together to dissolve the sugar.

Stirring occasionally, cook the egg whites over the bain-marie until they seem warm to the touch (about 120°F). Remove the bowl from the heat. Using a handheld electric mixer, beat the warm egg whites at medium-high speed until the mixture is cool and the whites form medium-stiff peaks. Set aside.

Place the crème fraîche in a small bowl and whisk by hand or with the handheld electric mixer until it holds medium-stiff peaks. Set aside.

Hold the bowl with the gelatin over the bain-marie for a few seconds until the gelatin completely dissolves. Alternatively, heat the gelatin in a microwave for a few seconds. Stir the dissolved gelatin into the fruit purée and allow the mixture to cool completely.

Fold half of the fruit purée into the egg white mixture and fold the remaining half into the whipped crème fraîche. Transfer the crème fraîche mixture into the bowl with the egg whites, and carefully fold until combined. If the mixture does not look homogenous, use a whisk to give it a couple of turns, but do not overmix. Transfer the mousse into the piping bag or an airtight container. Refrigerate until ready to assemble the tiramisù.

To make the soaking liquid for the sponge cake, place the jam and the water in a small saucepan. Over low heat, stir until the jam dissolves. Remove from the heat and stir in the liqueur. Set aside.

Using the cookie cutter, cut out 8 rounds from the sponge cake.

Spoon the mascarpone mousse into the piping bag, if using. **>**

To assemble the tiramisù, cut a hole in the bottom of the piping bag and pipe each highball glass one-third full with frutti di bosco mousse. If a piping bag is not available, use an ice cream scoop. (At the restaurant, to make sure each tiramisù looks identical, we place each glass on a kitchen scale and add exactly 1½ ounces of mousse to it, so if you have a scale you can do this.) Be careful not to smudge the sides of the glasses with the mousse.

Place a sponge cake round inside each highball glass, crust side down, and gently push it down so that it presses against the mousse. Next, spoon 1 tablespoon of the soaking liquid over the cake and leave it to sit for 10–15 minutes for the cake to absorb the liquid.

Finally, pipe or spoon in the mascarpone mousse until it reaches the top of the glasses. Cover each tiramisù with plastic wrap and chill for several hours or overnight.

When ready to serve, decorate each tiramisù with a generous assortment of the reserved berries. Sprinkle the fruit with a teaspoon or two of crushed amaretti cookies and, if desired, finish with sifted confectioners' sugar on top.

Sponge Cake (makes one 9- x 13-inch cake)

The trick to keeping this sponge cake light and airy is first to incorporate the melted butter into a small portion of the batter then fold the smaller portion back into the rest of the batter.

4 large eggs, separated, at room temperature
¾ cup granulated sugar
1 tablespoon vanilla extract
¼ teaspoon kosher salt
¼ teaspoon cream of tartar
½ cup plus 2 tablespoons unbleached all-purpose flour
½ stick unsalted butter, melted and cooled

Equipment
A 9- x 13-inch rimmed sheet tray

Preheat the oven to 350°F.

Spray the sheet tray with nonstick spray, line with parchment paper, then spray the parchment paper.

Place the egg yolks and half of the sugar (6 tablespoons) in the bowl of a stand mixer fitted with a wire whisk. Beat the yolks and sugar on medium-high speed until the mixture is pale and thick, about 5–7 minutes, occasionally scraping down the sides. Once thick, add the vanilla extract. Continue beating for another minute until well combined. Transfer the mixture to another large bowl and set aside.

Wash and dry the mixing bowl and wire whisk attachment. Add the egg whites, salt, and cream of tartar to the clean bowl. Using the wire whisk, beat the egg whites on medium speed until foamy. Gradually add the remaining sugar one tablespoon at a time. Continue beating the egg whites until they hold stiff (but not dry) peaks.

Using a rubber spatula, fold one-quarter of the egg white mixture into the yolk mixture. Next add one-third of the remaining egg white mixture to the yolk mixture. Follow this by sifting one-third of the flour over the combined whites and yolks; gently fold everything together. Now add half of the remaining egg white mixture to the bowl with the yolks and sift in half of the remaining flour. Fold together. Repeat with the remaining egg whites and remaining flour until all of the egg white and egg yolk mixtures and flour are combined.

Transfer one-quarter of this batter to a small bowl. Add the melted butter and fold to combine thoroughly. Next, add this mixture to the remaining batter and gently fold everything together.

Pour the batter into the prepared pan and use an offset spatula to spread it evenly and smooth the top. (Do not tap the pan on the counter or you will lose the air that you have so carefully incorporated.)

Bake the cake for 20–25 minutes or until the surface is light golden brown and the cake is firm to the touch. Remove from the oven and let cool to room temperature before turning out.

The cake can be made a day in advance, enclosed in plastic wrap, and stored at room temperature—or stored in the freezer for up to 2 weeks.

Mascarpone Mousse (makes 3 cups)

8 ounces mascarpone cheese
¾ cup heavy cream
2 tablespoons granulated sugar

Using a stand mixer with a wire whisk attachment or a handheld electric mixer, combine the mascarpone, heavy cream, and sugar and beat on medium speed until the mixture holds medium to stiff peaks, about 2 minutes. Be careful not to over-whip the mixture or it will quickly turn to butter. Use immediately; or you can store it in an airtight container, refrigerated, for up to 1 day.

CRANBERRY-PUMPKIN BUDINO WITH APPLE VINEGAR CARAMEL AND SPICED PECANS

SERVES 8

As much as I love the bounty of berries and stone fruit in the summertime, I am equally excited when sweater weather rolls in and fall ingredients are around the corner. This dessert incorporates my favorite fall fruits: cranberries, pumpkin, and apples. Essentially an English sticky pudding with bold American flavors, it gets its Italian name (meaning "pudding") from the extra-virgin olive oil in the batter, which ensures a creamy, moist interior.

¾ cup unbleached all-purpose flour
½ teaspoon ground cinnamon
¼ teaspoon ground ginger
¼ teaspoon ground nutmeg
¼ teaspoon baking soda
¼ teaspoon kosher salt
1 large egg
½ cup plus 3 tablespoons dark brown sugar, kept separately
¼ cup plus 1 tablespoon granulated sugar, kept separately
½ cup plus 2 tablespoons excellent-quality, fruity, extra-virgin Italian olive oil
½ cup plus 2 tablespoons canned pumpkin purée
1½ teaspoons apple cider vinegar
3 tablespoons unsalted butter, at room temperature
1 teaspoon vanilla extract
2½ cups cranberries, fresh or frozen
1½ cups heavy cream

1 quantity Apple Vinegar Caramel Sauce (see recipe below, page 255)
1 quantity Spiced Pecans (see recipe below, page 255), broken into small pieces

Equipment
8 (4-ounce) ceramic ramekins
A disposable piping bag (optional)

Preheat the oven to 350°F.

Lightly spray the ramekins with nonstick spray. In a small bowl sift together the flour, cinnamon, ginger, nutmeg, baking soda, and salt. Set aside.

Whisk the egg in a large bowl. Add the ½ cup brown sugar and ¼ cup granulated sugar to the egg and whisk until smooth. Next add the olive oil, pumpkin purée, and apple cider vinegar and whisk again to combine. Add the sifted dry ingredients and whisk until the ingredients are just barely incorporated and the batter is smooth. Do not overmix. Set aside.

In another small bowl, stir together the remaining 3 tablespoons of brown sugar, the butter, and the vanilla extract until thoroughly combined. Divide the brown sugar mixture equally into the ramekins, about 2 teaspoons in each. Spoon an equal number of the cranberries into each ramekin over the sugar mixture. Press the cranberries down to compact the sugar and butter mixture. You should have 3 or 4 cranberries left over for each ramekin; these can sit on top of the others (they will lie inside the budino).

Cut a hole in the bottom of the piping bag and use it to distribute the pumpkin batter into the prepared ramekins; alternatively you can use an ice cream scoop. The ramekins should be three-quarters full.

Place the ramekins in a roasting pan. Pour enough hot tap water into the pan to come halfway up the sides of the ramekins. Tear off a piece of foil large enough to fit over the roasting pan and coat one side with nonstick spray. Place this side over the pan and crimp the edges to form a seal.

Carefully place the roasting pan in the oven and bake the puddings for 50–60 minutes or until a wooden skewer comes out clean from the center of each ramekin. Remove the roasting pan from the oven and discard the foil. After 10 minutes or so, gently remove the ramekins from the water bath and place on a rack to cool. Let them sit for 30–45 minutes, then serve warm.

Alternatively, let the ramekins cool completely and wrap each one with plastic wrap. The puddings can be re-warmed the following day (uncovered) in a 300°F oven for 5 minutes (or one at a time, uncovered, in a microwave for 50–60 seconds at 50 percent power).

While the puddings are baking, whisk the heavy cream with the remaining 1 tablespoon of granulated sugar. Whisk until the cream forms medium-stiff peaks. Refrigerate in an airtight container until ready to serve.

To plate, slide a paring knife between a pudding and the ramekin and ease the knife around the edge to loosen it. Gently turn the ramekin over and shake to release the pudding onto a plate, or bowl. Repeat with the rest of the puddings. Spoon a generous amount (about 2 tablespoons) of apple vinegar caramel sauce on top of the cranberries. Place a quenelle, or dollop, of the sweetened whipped cream next to each pudding and sprinkle the broken spiced pecans on top. Serve immediately.

Apple Vinegar Caramel Sauce (makes 1¾ cups)

1 cup granulated sugar
½ cup water
½ cup apple juice or nonalcoholic apple cider
6 tablespoons heavy cream
2 tablespoons apple cider vinegar
1 tablespoon applejack
¼ teaspoon salt
2 tablespoons unsalted butter, cold and diced

Place the sugar and water in a small saucepan over medium-low heat. Cook, stirring with a wooden spoon, making sure the mixture doesn't boil until the sugar has completely dissolved. Turn up the heat, and bring the syrup to a boil, then cook without stirring until it turns an amber caramel color, about 8–10 minutes. Swirl the pan, if necessary, to ensure that the caramel colors evenly. If sugar crystals form on the side of the pan, use a brush dipped in cold water to wash them back into the syrup.

Once the caramel is the desired color, remove the saucepan from the heat. Slowly add the cider or apple juice and the heavy cream; be careful—it will bubble up vigorously. Return the pan to the heat and stir to completely dissolve the caramel. Turn off the heat and whisk in the vinegar, applejack, and salt. Finally slowly whisk in the butter, one piece at a time, waiting for each to dissolve before adding the next.

The sauce can be served immediately or stored, refrigerated, for 1–2 weeks in an airtight container. Simply re-warm the sauce in a saucepan over low heat or in the microwave. If the sauce has separated, stir it to redistribute the ingredients. Even if slightly separated, the sauce will be equally delicious.

Spiced Pecans (makes 1½ cups)

1 large egg white, at room temperature
1 tablespoon granulated sugar
1 tablespoon dark brown sugar
¼ teaspoon ground cinnamon
¼ teaspoon ground ginger
¼ teaspoon ground nutmeg
¼ teaspoon kosher salt
1¼ cups pecan halves

Preheat the oven to 325°F. Line a sheet tray with a nonstick silicone mat or with parchment paper.

Place the egg white in a medium-size bowl. Whisk until it is frothy throughout but before peaks start to form. Add the granulated sugar, brown sugar, cinnamon, ginger, nutmeg, and salt. Whisk the

ingredients together to combine—the mixture will have the consistency of thick buttermilk.

Add the pecans to the egg white mixture and toss to combine. Make sure each pecan piece is thoroughly coated. Spread the pecans out onto the prepared sheet tray. Drizzle any remaining egg white mixture over the pecans. Bake until the nuts are toasted and aromatic, about 15–18 minutes. Remove from the oven and let cool. Taste a nut for seasoning. If you prefer, sprinkle them with another pinch of salt while they are still warm. After the nuts are cool, break them up into smaller pieces and place in an airtight container. The spiced pecans can be stored in a cool, dry place for 1–2 weeks.

Lipton black
BEVS
ARNIE PALMER 3
MEXICAN COKE 4
GINGER BEER
STILL/SPARKLING
Brooklyn
chocolate
must be
Happy
ANY
birth
PIE
CRACK
CAND
GRASS

CHRISTINA TOSI

lthough Christina Tosi, the owner and founder of Momofuku Milk Bar, says she eats at least one chocolate chip cookie a day, you won't find one at any of her five New York City bakeries or at her Toronto outpost; nor has she dispatched one from her industrious production kitchen in Williamsburg, Brooklyn. And she similarly hasn't devised a recipe for them in her *Momofuku Milk Bar* cookbook (2011). This recipient of the James Beard Rising Star Chef award (2012) and finalist for the James Beard Outstanding Pastry Chef award (2014 and 2015) claims that she is not brave enough to compete with your great aunt or mother, whom you know to make the very best chocolate chip cookies and, for that matter, apple pie, brownies, and red velvet cake. The truth is that Tosi doesn't lack courage. On the contrary, her shrewd business acumen inspired her to offer something altogether unique. She riffs off classic American desserts, creating sublime confections that avoid rivaling your family's cherished recipes but still speak to those same iconic treats.

So hordes visit Milk Bar for Tosi's luscious, cocoa-rich Red Velvet Ice Cream; her Brownie Pie, with its gooey fudge center and crushed homemade graham cracker base; and her Apple Pie layer cake, a towering structure comprising six components, from liquid cheesecake to an apple cider soak. And they visit it especially for Tosi's greatest invention, Crack Pie: a sinfully decadent buttery, salty sweet pie filling encased in an oat cookie crust.

"I did not have my first raw tomato until I was 18," recalls Tosi. Growing up (in Virgina) with busy parents— an accountant mother and agricultural economist father—Tosi was raised on macaroni and cheese, fish sticks, pizza, and hot dogs. An extremely picky eater, she would drink milk only when it accompanied sugary cereal. This breakfast staple became the inspiration for her legendary Cereal Milk concoction.

By the time she went to college, where she majored in math and Italian, Tosi had caught the baking bug. After graduation, she headed to New York City to attend the pastry program at the French Culinary Institute. Later, she slaved in the pastry section of Bouley six days a week, spending the seventh day as an editorial assistant at *Saveur* magazine. Eventually she landed in wd~50, working for Wylie Dufresne, one of the two most influential figures in her career—the other being David Chang, founder of the Momofuku empire. Tosi found Dufresne's knack of pairing unusual flavors and textures

in a single, technically complex dish both liberating and inspiring. When she had run her course there, she took on a girl Friday-esque role in the Momofuku offices. Each morning Tosi would arrive for her desk job armed with her baking project from the night before. David Chang grew so enamored of these domestic creations, he eventually assigned her to prepare a dessert for the menu at Ssäm Bar.

The strawberry shortcake she supplied marked the beginning of Tosi's tenure as Momofuku's pastry maven. Soon she was making soft-serve ice cream for Chang's Noodle Bar, popularizing her signature technique of steeping the milk base with eclectic flavors. Later she instituted a dessert program at Ko. That same year, 2008, the first Milk Bar was born. Tosi's menu of whimsical treats is a perfect exercise in contradiction—filled with lowbrow ingredients such as pretzels, cornflakes, marshmallows, and potato chips, yet executed with rigorous attention to detail and painstaking technique. What else to expect of the singularly focused, hardheaded businesswoman who, on the sidewalk outside two of her stores, hosts a weekly "cakewalk" (a take on musical chairs with cake as the prize)?

What do you think is the most underrated and underused ingredient in the pastry world?
Milk powder as a flavor enhancer. We joke that it's like MSG for bakers!

What's your most guilty gastronomic pleasure, sweet and savory?
Sweet: half-melted cookies and cream ice cream or a scoop of freshly mixed chocolate chip cookie dough
Savory: warm, gooey cheese sticks (or anything with gooey cheese).

What are the most important criteria for creating a delicious pie?
Texture, temperature, flavor, balance, point of view. I must say that these criteria ring true for any dessert from a multi-component, plated dessert to a slice of pie to a cookie.

What's the secret to the perfect chewy in the middle, crisp on the outside cookies?
A little less flour than usual and a little bit of glucose syrup!

Is there a dessert or a dish that you wished you had created?
THE CRONUT!!!

BIRTHDAY CAKE TRUFFLES

**MAKES ABOUT A
DOZEN 1-OUNCE BALLS**

My favorite offering at Milk Bar is our cake truffles, spawned entirely from leftover bits and pieces of cake and layering scraps! We once served slices of cake cut to order, but after hemming and hawing with our endearing staff of counter employees over the correct way to slice and serve a multilayered cake, we got smart. We decided to make cake truffles. Now, instead of committing to a whole slice of cake, customers can get a bite, or two or three.

You can choose to follow the recipe, or get crazy using leftovers to concoct your own combinations. Don't limit yourself to birthday cake; you can use any cake scrap and any leftover fillings, crumbs, or crunches from your kitchen.

1 cup Birthday Cake Sand (see recipe below, page 260)
3 cups Birthday Cake (see recipe below)
2–4 tablespoons Vanilla Milk (see recipe below, page 260)
3 ounces white chocolate, melted

Put the birthday cake sand into a medium sized bowl and set aside.

Combine the birthday cake and 2 tablespoons vanilla milk in a separate medium sized bowl and toss with your hands until moist enough to knead into a ball. If it is not moist enough to do so, add up to 2 tablespoons more vanilla milk and knead it in.

Using a small ice cream scoop, portion out 12 even balls, each half the size of a Ping-Pong ball. Roll each one between the palms of your hands to shape and smooth it into a round sphere. With latex gloves on, put 2 tablespoons of the white chocolate in the palm of your hand and roll each ball between your palms, coating it in a thin layer of melted chocolate; add more chocolate to your hand as needed.

Working quickly, add 3 or 4 chocolate-covered balls at a time to the bowl of birthday cake sand. Immediately toss them with the crumbs to coat, before the chocolate shell sets and no longer acts as a glue (if this happens, just coat the ball in another thin layer of melted chocolate). Arrange the coated cake truffles on a sheet pan and refrigerate for at least 5 minutes to fully set the chocolate shells before eating or storing. The truffles will keep for up to 1 week in the fridge, in an airtight container.

Birthday Cake (makes 1 quarter sheet pan cake)
4 tablespoons (½ stick) unsalted butter, at room temperature
⅓ cup vegetable shortening
1¼ cups granulated sugar
3 tablespoons tightly packed light brown sugar
3 eggs
½ cup buttermilk
⅓ cup grapeseed oil
2 teaspoons clear vanilla extract
2 cups cake flour
1½ teaspoons baking powder
¾ teaspoon kosher salt
⅓ cup rainbow sprinkles
Pam-spray, as needed

Preheat the oven to 350°F. Combine the butter, shortening, and sugars in the bowl of a stand mixer fitted with the paddle attachment and cream together on medium-high for 2–3 minutes. Scrape down the sides of the bowl, add the eggs, and mix on medium-high for 2–3 minutes. Scrape down the sides of the bowl once more.

On low speed, stream in the buttermilk, oil, and vanilla. Increase the mixer speed to medium-high and paddle for 4–6 minutes, until the mixture is practically white, twice the size of your original fluffy butter-and-sugar mixture, and completely homogenous. Don't rush the process. You're basically forcing too much liquid into an already fatty mixture that doesn't want to make room for that liquid. There should be no streaks of fat or liquid. Stop the mixer and scrape down the sides of the bowl. ➤

On very low speed, add the cake flour, baking powder, salt, and ¼ cup of the rainbow sprinkles. Mix for 45–60 seconds, just until your batter comes together. Scrape down the sides of the bowl.

Pam-spray a quarter sheet pan and line it with parchment, or just line the pan with a nonstick silicone baking mat. Transfer the cake batter into the prepared pan and using a spatula, spread the batter in an even layer. Sprinkle the remaining rainbow sprinkles (about 2 tablespoons) evenly on top of the batter.

Bake the cake for 30–35 minutes. The cake will rise and puff, doubling in size, but will remain slightly buttery and dense. At 30 minutes, gently poke the edge of the cake with your finger: the cake should bounce back slightly and the center should no longer be jiggly. Leave the cake in the oven for an extra 3–5 minutes if it doesn't pass these tests.

Take the cake out of the oven and cool on a wire rack or, in a pinch, in the fridge or freezer (don't worry, it's not cheating). The cooled cake can be stored in the fridge, wrapped in plastic wrap, for up to 5 days.

Vanilla Milk (makes ¼ cup)
¼ cup milk
1 teaspoon clear vanilla extract

Whisk together the milk and vanilla in a small bowl.

Birthday Cake Sand (makes about 1 rounded cup) *¼ cup granulated sugar*
1 tablespoon tightly packed light brown sugar
⅔ cup cake flour
¼ teaspoon baking powder
¼ teaspoon kosher salt
1 tablespoon rainbow sprinkles
1 tablespoon grapeseed oil
1 teaspoon clear vanilla extract

Preheat the oven to 300°F. Combine the sugars, flour, baking powder, salt, and sprinkles in the bowl of a stand mixer fitted with the paddle attachment and mix on low speed until well combined.

Add the oil and vanilla and paddle again to distribute. The wet ingredients will act as glue to help the dry ingredients form small sandy clusters; continue paddling until that happens.

Spread the clusters on a parchment or nonstick silicone mat-lined sheet pan. Bake for 20 minutes, breaking them up occasionally. The crumbs should still be slightly moist to the touch; they will dry and harden as they cool.

Let the crumbs cool completely before using. Grind down in a food processor, if necessary. If the crumbs are not small and sandy enough they will not glue to the white chocolate coating in the birthday cake truffle recipe! Stored in an airtight container, the sand will keep fresh for 1 week at room temperature or 1 month in the fridge or freezer.

CEREAL MILK PANNA COTTA

SERVES 4

I first made cereal milk panna cotta in 2007 as a very fancy plated dessert for the opening of Momofuku Ko. I have found for a perfect panna cotta, you need two ingredients: milk and gelatin. We add salt and brown sugar to our cereal-infused milk to elevate its overall flavor but the real trick for perfect panna cotta is to make sure you have just the right amount of gelatin. You want to use as little as possible, so that the second the dessert hits your mouth, it transforms into a silky river of flavored cream. I love to garnish cereal milk panna cotta with sliced bananas and berries, to play off the breakfast "vibe." Some cornflake crunch added to the top is never a bad idea either.

1½ cups cornflakes
2 cups whole milk
1 cup heavy cream
2½ tablespoons tightly packed light
 brown sugar
¼ teaspoon kosher salt
½ teaspoon powdered gelatin

Heat the oven to 300°F. Spread the cornflakes on a parchment-lined sheet pan. Bake for 15 minutes, until lightly toasted. Cool completely.

Transfer the cooled cornflakes to a large pitcher. Pour the milk and heavy cream into the pitcher and stir vigorously. Let steep for 20 minutes at room temperature.

Strain the mixture through a fine-mesh sieve, collecting the milk in a medium bowl. The milk will drain off quickly at first, then become thicker and starchy toward the end of the straining process. Using the back of a ladle (or your hand), wring the milk out of the cornflakes, but do not force the mushy cornflakes through the sieve. (We compost the cornflake remains or take them home to our dogs!)

Whisk the brown sugar and salt into the milk until fully dissolved. Transfer ½ cup of the cereal milk mixture to a small saucepan. Sprinkle the gelatin evenly onto the surface of the ½ cup cereal milk in the saucepan to "bloom" it, allowing the granules to soften entirely, 3–5 minutes. On low heat, warm the cereal milk and bloomed gelatin, whisking to dissolve the gelatin entirely. Whisk this warm mixture back into the larger bowl of cereal milk.

Put 4 small glasses on a flat, transportable surface. Pour the cereal milk mixture into the glasses, filling them equally. Transfer to the refrigerator to set for at least 3 hours, or overnight. Serve cold.

BLUEBERRY BAGEL BOMBS

MAKES 8 BOMBS

Living in New York for more than ten years makes me an official New Yorker—I'm quite sure. And being a New Yorker means paying homage to the classic New York-style bagel. I love sweet, compound cream cheese spreads between my bagel halves, so I decided to make bite size pre-stuffed bagels for the Milk Bar menu. This one's a blueberry cream cheese bagel bomb explosion!

1 quantity Mother Dough, proofed (see recipe below)
1 quantity Blueberry Cream Cheese Plugs (see recipe below, page 263)
1 egg
¼ cup granulated sugar (or turbinado sugar)

Preheat the oven to 325°F. Punch down and flatten the dough on a smooth, dry countertop. Use a dough cutter or sharp knife to divide the dough into 8 equal pieces. Use your fingers to gently stretch each piece of dough out into a mini pizza between 2 inches and 3 inches wide.

Put a cream cheese plug in the center of each dough circle. Bring up the edges of each round and pinch to seal so that the cream cheese plug is completely contained, then gently roll the ball between the palms of your hands to ensure the bomb has a nice, round, dinner roll-y shape. Arrange the bombs 2 inches apart on a parchment or nonstick silicone mat-lined baking sheet.

Whisk the egg and water together and brush a generous coat of egg wash all over the buns (but not their bases). Sprinkle an even coating of sugar all over the bagel bombs— every possible inch, except for the bottoms, should be coated.

Bake the bagel bombs for 20–30 minutes. While in the oven, the bombs will become a deep golden brown and a few may have cream cheese explosions. Continue baking until you see this happen! Not to worry—serve them as is or use your fingers to tuck the cream cheese back inside the bagel bomb. Bagel bombs are best served warm out of the oven—or flashed in the oven later to warm before serving. If you can't finish them all right away, once they are cool, wrap them well in plastic and store them in the fridge for up to 3 days.

Mother Dough
1¾–2 cups all-purpose flour
1½ teaspoons kosher salt
¾ teaspoon active dry yeast
¾ cup water, at room temperature
1 teaspoon grapeseed oil

Combine 1¾ cup flour with the salt and yeast in the bowl of your stand mixer—and stir by hand, using the dough hook like a spoon. Continue stirring, by hand, as you add the water, mixing for 1 minute, until the mixture has come together into a shaggy mass.

Engage the bowl and hook and have the machine mix the dough on the lowest speed for 3 minutes, or until the ball of dough is smoother and more cohesive. Then knead for 4 more minutes on the lowest speed. The dough should look like a wet ball and should bounce back softly when prodded. If your dough is too wet, and not forming a ball shape whatsoever (the humidity level in everyone's kitchen is a little different!), add the additional ¼ cup flour.

Brush a large bowl with oil and dump the dough into it. Cover with plastic wrap and let the dough proof at room temperature for 45 minutes.

Blueberry Cream Cheese Plugs

7 ounces cream cheese
1 cup fresh blueberries
1 tablespoon granulated sugar
1 teaspoon kosher salt

Put the cream cheese in the bowl of a stand mixer fitted with the paddle attachment and cream it on medium speed until softened. Scrape down the sides of the bowl. Add the blueberries, sugar, and salt and paddle briefly to incorporate.

Scoop the cream cheese mixture onto a quarter sheet pan in 8 even lumps. Freeze until rock hard, 1–3 hours. Once the plugs are frozen solid, they are ready to be used, or they can be stored in an airtight container in the freezer for up to 1 month.

PEACHES AND CREAM COOKIES

**MAKES ABOUT
A DOZEN COOKIES**

When I first started exploring what might make a great dessert at the Momofuku restaurants, I was just taking shots in the dark. No dessert had ever existed on the menus before, so there was literally NO starting place. Momofuku means lucky peach in Japanese, so I decided to play off of the "peach" in flavor form. My favorite classic American "dessert" is peaches and cream, so I decided to make a cookie that was a love letter, as such.

16 tablespoons (2 sticks) unsalted
    butter, at room temperature
¾ cup granulated sugar
⅔ cup tightly packed light brown
    sugar
¼ cup liquid glucose or 2
    tablespoons corn syrup (see note)
2 eggs
2 cups all-purpose flour
½ teaspoon baking powder
¼ teaspoon baking soda
1½ teaspoons kosher salt
1 quantity Milk Crumb (see recipe
    below)
¾ cup dried peaches, cut into
    eighths

Combine the butter, sugars, and glucose (or corn syrup) in the bowl of a stand mixer fitted with the paddle attachment and cream on medium-high for 2–3 minutes. Scrape down the sides of the bowl, add the eggs, and beat for 7–8 minutes.

Reduce the mixer speed to low and add the flour, baking powder, baking soda, and salt. Mix just until the dough comes together, no longer than 1 minute. (Do not walk away from the machine during this step, or you will risk overmixing the dough.) Scrape down the sides of the bowl with a spatula. Still on low speed, add the milk crumbs and mix until they're incorporated, no more than 30 seconds. Chase the milk crumbs with the dried peaches, mixing them in for 30 seconds.

Using a 2¾-ounce ice cream scoop (or a ⅓-cup measure), portion out the dough onto a parchment-lined sheet pan. Pat the tops of the cookie dough domes flat. Wrap the sheet pan tightly in plastic wrap and refrigerate for at least 1 hour, or up to 1 week. Do not bake your cookies from room temperature—they will not bake properly.

When ready to bake, preheat the oven to 350°F.

Arrange the chilled dough a minimum of 4 inches apart on parchment or nonstick silicone mat lined sheet pans. Bake for 18 minutes. The cookies will puff, crackle, and spread. After 18 minutes, they should be very faintly browned on the edges yet still bright yellow in the center; give them an extra minute or so if that's not the case.

Cool the cookies completely on the sheet pans before transferring to a plate or to an airtight container for storage. At room temperature, the cookies will keep fresh for 5 days; in the freezer, they will keep for 1 month.

Note
The glucose (or corn syrup) in this recipe helps give the cookie spread, while maintaining a crispy exterior and fudgy center, the qualities of a perfect cookie, if you ask me.

Milk Crumb

Milk crumbs are sweet, sandy clusters, meant to evoke the idealized flavors of milk and cream in a textural form.

¼ cup nonfat milk powder, plus 2
    tablespoons nonfat milk powder,
    kept separately
2 tablespoons all-purpose flour
1 tablespoon cornstarch
1 tablespoon granulated sugar
¼ teaspoon kosher salt
2 tablespoons butter, melted
1½ ounces white chocolate, melted

Heat the oven to 250°F. Combine ¼ cup milk powder with the flour, cornstarch, sugar, and salt in a small bowl. Toss with your hands to mix. Add the melted butter and toss, using a spatula, until the mixture starts to come together and form small clusters.

Spread the clusters on a parchment- or nonstick silicone mat-lined sheet pan and bake for 15 minutes. The crumbs should be sandy at that point, and your kitchen should smell like buttery heaven. Cool the crumbs completely. Crumble any milk crumb clusters that are larger than ½ inch in diameter, and put the crumbs in a medium bowl. Add the additional 2 tablespoons milk powder and toss together until it is evenly distributed throughout the mixture.

Pour the white chocolate over the crumbs and toss until your clusters are enrobed. Then continue tossing them every 5 minutes until the white chocolate hardens and the clusters are no longer sticky. The crumbs will keep in an airtight container in the fridge or freezer for up to 1 month.

JENNIFER YEE

Jennifer Yee presides over the bakery and the dining room desserts at Lafayette, a cavernous 160-seat NoHo (north of Houston Street) brasserie. Rarely does a pastry chef have such opportunity to take center stage.

Yee's calling card is the display case at the front of the restaurant, showcasing her intricate tarts, cookies, jewel-toned macarons, éclairs, and petits gateaux. The roots of Yee's creations are firmly entrenched in classic French patisserie, but she invests them with a deft measure of innovation. By modulating the flavors, textures, and even the mechanics of how a dessert is composed, she creates her own unique modern versions. Her Lemon Meringue Éclair is a study in playfulness. With its sharp lemon cream filling and burnished pouffe of creamy meringue, it's an elegant French pastry masquerading as the flamboyant all-American pie.

In the dining room, her plates are characterized by precision. "I don't need 90-degree angles, but I do want to present a very clean plate." Her simple approach, however, is not without dramatic effect. A dome of yogurt mousse embedded with a disc of angel food cake and sprayed with white chocolate, then accompanied by iced shards of coconut granita is presented to the diner. The all-white dessert is promptly "bloodied" by a server who spoons over it a ruby compote of red currants steeped in red wine.

Born and bred in San Francisco, Yee showed an early affinity for baking but initially trained for a career in interior architecture, which her parents felt was more stable. After a year at a design firm, though, the lure of pastry was too strong. She took on a job as a dessert plater in a local restaurant in order to fund culinary school.

With an English boyfriend (Andrew, now her husband), she enrolled, in 2002, in the nine-month patisserie program at the Cordon Bleu school in London. Six months in, she was hired at the Gordon Ramsay at the Connaught restaurant, where she soon was given charge of the afternoon tea service. Then in 2004, when Yauatcha, a stylish dim sum house and tearoom opened in London's bustling Soho, Yee was part of the inaugural crew. There she was introduced to large-scale production, with more than 400 perfectly executed cakes and tarts to finish every day, assisted by her team of ten.

Returning to the United States in 2006, Yee joined Gilt, in New York City; she has since remained on the East Coast. When Gilt's executive chef, Chris Lee, re-launched Charlie Palmer's flagship Aureole in 2009, he asked Yee to be his executive pastry chef. "There are so many things you have to prove as a first-time pastry chef," she says. "Do you go down the safe route, or do you go out on a limb? I did a mixture of the two." The result? Avant-garde combinations such as chilled melon soup with dehydrated black olives. Next came a year at SHO Shaun Hergatt.

Since Lafayette opened in 2013, Yee has been its pastry chef. Her commitment to hard work is clear. Only Sundays she keeps for herself and her husband, to cook him a traditional English roast dinner or visit a flea market. She aspires to have two days off a week, but is sanguine about her lot. "I hope that this is the place that I can stay for a while. You go through the motions of learning from different chefs and working at different places, but you know when it's time to settle down."

What is your favorite unexpected flavor combination, that, in theory, shouldn't work, but, in reality, is delicious?
Aside from the standard cheesecake, there are so many beautiful cheeses that can make a great component in a dessert. The salty, crumbly "queso fresco" is incredible with strawberries.

What is your favorite holiday to make desserts/pastries for, and why?
I'm a spring baby, so I always love the pastel freshness of Easter. Winter is over and fruit is really coming into play. And who doesn't love making chocolate bunnies?!

What is the most important lesson that you've learned in your career, that you pass on to the chefs that work for you?
"Sharing is caring." Share and pass down with your team as much knowledge as you can. In the end, this builds internal trust and a strong team and support system.

Is there one rule of conduct in your kitchen that, above all others, has to be abided by/that you enforce most strictly?
Respect your peers. Keep clean!!

What's your favorite thing to do on your day off?
What else? EAT!! Oh, and I'm a flea market junkie ... drives my husband crazy.

JASMINE TEA AND APRICOT MOUSSE CAKE

MAKES ONE 10–INCH CAKE; SERVES 12–14

We call this cake "Yoshi" at the bakery because its pale green glaze and dots of apricot jelly mimic the colors of the popular video game character. The star of the cake is the rich and silky mousse, infused with fragrant jasmine tea leaves. Be sure to use the highest quality loose-leaf tea to get the best flavor. We make individual portions of this cake at the bakery, but I've provided the recipe for a large version, which is ideal for a small party.

For the apricot compote
12 ounces frozen apricot halves or pieces, defrosted (or sliced frozen peaches)
3 tablespoons granulated sugar
2 (140 bloom) gelatin leaves (see suppliers, page 286)

For the shortbread base
1 stick butter, cold
1¾ ounces granulated sugar
¼ teaspoon salt
3 ounces all-purpose flour
1 ounce rice flour or cornstarch

For the jasmine tea mousse
2 (140 bloom) gelatin leaves
1½ cups plus 2 cups heavy cream, kept separately
¾–1 cup loose jasmine tea leaves
14½ ounces white chocolate

For the white chocolate ganache glaze
¾ cup heavy cream
7 ounces white chocolate, chopped
2 drops green gel food coloring

Equipment
A kitchen scale (see suppliers, page 286)
A cake ring 10 inches in diameter and 2 inches deep and another ring 8 inches in diameter and 1 or 2 inches deep
A candy thermometer
A hand blender
A handheld mixer
A cake board or platter about 11–12 inches in diameter
2 silicone mats (optional)
A microwave (optional)
A blowtorch (optional)

Make this cake the day before you plan to serve it.

First set the smaller cake ring on a silicone mat or parchment paper placed on a sheet tray and put in the freezer to chill.

Combine the apricots and sugar in a medium saucepan and simmer, stirring frequently, until a thick, jamlike consistency is achieved, about 10–15 minutes; do not allow the apricots to get too dark. (Add a small amount of water, up to ¾ cup, if needed.)

Meanwhile, soak the gelatin leaves in ice water until they are completely softened, with no brittle parts, about 5–10 minutes. Drain the gelatin and squeeze out the excess water. Remove the apricot compote from the heat, add the softened gelatin, and stir until dissolved.

Pour all but 3 tablespoons of this compote into the prechilled ring on the tray, spreading it out evenly. Immediately return it to the freezer to solidify, about 3 hours. Reserve the remaining compote in a small container in the fridge for decorating.

Make the shortbread base. Preheat the oven to 375°F. In the bowl of a stand mixer fitted with the paddle attachment, cream the butter, sugar, and salt together until smooth but not aerated. Add the flours all at once, and mix on low speed until just combined.

Place the larger cake ring on a sheet tray lined with parchment paper or a silicone mat. Press the dough into the bottom of the ring and prick it all over with a fork to prevent too much shrinkage. Bake until golden around the edges and dry in the center, about 10–15 minutes. Allow to cool completely, then place the tray with the ring into the freezer to chill for about 30 minutes.

Make the jasmine tea mousse. Soak the gelatin leaves in ice water, until they are completely softened. Drain and squeeze out the excess water. Set aside.

Place the 1½ cups of heavy cream in a saucepan and heat until small bubbles form around the edges. Remove from the heat and whisk in the tea leaves. Cover and leave to infuse for 6–8 minutes. Strain into a large bowl; discard the leaves.

Melt the white chocolate in a glass or plastic liquid measuring cup in the microwave on a medium setting. (Alternatively, place in a bowl and set over a pan of simmering water, stirring until melted.) Add the softened gelatin to the chocolate and stir until dissolved.

Bring about 1 cup and 2 tablespoons of the tea-infused cream to a boil in a small saucepan (you can discard the remainder or use it elsewhere), then pour it over the chocolate and gelatin mixture. Using a hand blender or a whisk, blend together until the mixture is smooth and lump-free. Leave to cool to about 104°F.

Meanwhile, whip the remaining 2 cups of heavy cream to soft peaks using a handheld mixer. Once the chocolate and cream mixture has cooled, carefully fold in the whipped cream in 3 additions using a rubber spatula. Be careful not to overmix this mousse.

Remove the tray with the shortbread base from the freezer. Pour half of the jasmine tea mousse over the shortbread and immediately return to the freezer for 10 minutes.

Next, remove the disc of apricot compote from the freezer and unmold from its ring. Place this directly on top of the semi-frozen jasmine tea mousse. Pour the remaining mousse mixture over the compote, and return to the freezer to harden completely, about 4 hours.

Once frozen, remove the ring of shortbread and frozen mousse from the tray and set it over an upside-down bowl that is smaller in diameter than the ring. Use a blowtorch, or a towel soaked in very hot water and squeezed dry, to warm the sides of the ring and gently ease the ring away from the cake. Transfer the cake to a cooling rack set over a tray. Put back in the freezer for 10 minutes to re-chill the sides of the mousse.

Meanwhile, make the white chocolate ganache glaze. In a small saucepan, bring the cream for the glaze to a boil. Place the white chocolate in a bowl and pour the hot cream over the chocolate. Using a hand blender or a whisk, blend together to create a smooth ganache. Drop in the coloring as you blend until a pale green glaze is achieved. Use the glaze while still slightly warm and still fluid, around 90°F.

Remove the cake from the freezer and immediately pour almost all of the chocolate ganache glaze over the top. Quickly and gently glide an offset spatula across the top of cake to remove the excess glaze. Tap the tray on the counter to help the excess glaze fall through the cooling rack into the tray beneath. Check to see that the entire cake is covered. If there are some spots unglazed, dab them with the reserved glaze, using a spatula.

Immediately transfer the glazed and still-frozen cake to the cake board or platter. Allow to defrost in the fridge overnight. Decorate it with dots of the reserved apricot compote. (If the compote is too thick, purée it in a blender or food processor with a little water.)

MILK CHOCOLATE POTS DE CRÈME WITH CHAI TEA FOAM AND CACAO NIB CRUMB

SERVES 6–8

This has become one of our customers' favorite desserts at Lafayette. It's simple and homey, yet so delicious, with a play on textures. A dinner party winner for sure!

For the chai tea foam
½ cup heavy cream
½ cup whole milk
1 tablespoon sugar
3 high-quality chai tea bags
1 (140 bloom) gelatin leaf (see suppliers, page 286)

For the chocolate custard
2 ounces dark chocolate, 70% cacao, roughly chopped
10 ounces milk chocolate, 40% cacao, roughly chopped
2¼ cups heavy cream
1 cup whole milk
7–8 cups egg yolk (about 11 egg yolks)
½ teaspoon salt

For the cacao nib crumb
3½ ounces all-purpose flour
2 (rounded) tablespoons raw cacao nibs
4 ounces granulated sugar
A pinch of salt
⅛ teaspoon baking soda
7 tablespoons cold butter, cubed
1½ tablespoons milk

To decorate
Chocolate Lace Tuile (optional; see recipe below, page 272)

Equipment
A kitchen scale (see suppliers, page 286)
A instant-read thermometer
A 1-pint whipped cream syphon and 2 chargers (see suppliers, page 286)
A hand blender (optional)

Make the chai tea foam the day before you plan to serve the pots de crème.

Soak the gelatin leaf in a bowl of ice-cold water until softened, about 10 minutes. Put the cream, milk, and sugar in a small saucepan and place over medium-high heat until small bubbles appear around the edges. Remove the scalded mixture from the heat, stir in the tea bags, and cover the pan. Allow to infuse for 5 minutes, then remove the tea bags. Squeeze the softened gelatin to remove excess water and add to the warm liquid. Stir until the gelatin has dissolved completely, then cover the mixture and chill in the fridge overnight.

To make the chocolate custard, start by combining the dark and milk chocolate in a deep bowl. Set aside.

In a medium saucepan, bring the cream and milk to a boil. Meanwhile whisk together the yolks and salt in a medium bowl. Pour about ¼ cup of the hot liquid onto the yolks and whisk quickly to combine. Repeat this twice more in ¼-cup additions, whisking well between each addition. Now pour this warm egg-yolk-and-dairy mixture into the pan with the remaining cream

mixture. Stirring all the time with a rubber spatula, cook the custard over very low heat until it thickens and reaches 170°–175°F on an instant-read thermometer. This will cook the egg yolks. Immediately remove from the heat and strain the hot custard over the chopped chocolate.

Using a hand blender (or just a whisk), blend the mixture to emulsify the custard with the chocolate, being careful not to create air bubbles. Set the bowl of chocolate custard over another bowl half-filled with ice, and stir with a rubber spatula until the mixture has cooled and thickened substantially but is still pourable. Transfer to a large pitcher.

Pour the chocolate custard evenly into 8 ramekins or small glasses (each serving will be about ⅝ cup). For larger portions, divide into 6 glasses. Allow to set in the fridge, about 1–2 hours. Test by tilting a ramekin or glass; the custard should not move.

Meanwhile, make the cacao nib crumb. Preheat the oven to 350°F.

In the bowl of a stand mixer fitted with the paddle attachment, mix all the ingredients except the milk on low-medium speed until the butter has dispersed evenly and the mixture looks sandy. Add the milk and mix until just combined.

Transfer this dough to a sheet tray lined with parchment paper or a nonstick silicone mat and pat out >

into a very thin layer using an offset spatula or fingers dampened with water to stop them from sticking to the dough. Bake until evenly golden throughout, about 10–20 minutes, depending on the thickness. Leave on the tray to cool completely.

Once it has cooled, break the cookie into pieces and pulse in a food processor to create a rough-textured crumb. The crumb can be made beforehand and stored in an airtight container until ready to use.

When ready to serve (or a few hours before serving, but no more) put the chai mixture into the canister of a 1-pint whipped cream syphon. Close and charge with 2 whipped cream chargers. Shake vigorously and keep in the fridge until ready to use.

Remove the pots de crème from the fridge. Spoon about a tablespoon of the cacao nib crumb over one side of the custard in each serving. Gently pump a mound of foam on top of the crumb, and decorate with a piece of lace tuile, if using. Serve immediately.

Chocolate Lace Tuile

½ stick unsalted butter
2 ounces unsweetened chocolate
1¾ fluid ounces corn syrup
3½ fluid ounces water
6½ ounces sugar
¼ teaspoon powdered apple pectin
  (available at health food stores or
  specialist bakery supply stores)
½ ounce cocoa powder

Equipment
2 silicone mats

In a small saucepan set on very low heat, gently melt together the butter, chocolate, and corn syrup, whisking frequently. Whisk the water into the chocolate mixture and bring to a boil.

Meanwhile, in a bowl, whisk together the dry ingredients. Once the mixture in the pan is boiling, sprinkle in the dry mixture, whisking all the time. Bring back to a boil then transfer to a bowl. Place plastic wrap directly on the surface of the tuile batter to prevent a skin from forming and refrigerate until cold. (The batter can be kept for up to 1 month in the refrigerator, or even frozen; defrost before using.)

When ready to bake (no more than 1 day ahead of serving), preheat the oven to 350°F.

Using an offset spatula, spread some of the cold batter onto a tray lined with a silicone mat in a thin, but still opaque layer—if you can see the pattern of the mat through the batter, you have spread it too thinly. Place another silicone mat directly on top and bake for about 10–12 minutes. Allow to cool completely before releasing the tuile from the tray.

To release the tuile, first carefully peel off the top silicone mat. If the tuile feels soft or gummy, it needs a couple of extra minutes more of cooking; if it is crisp, it is ready. To release from the bottom mat, place

a sheet of parchment paper the same dimensions as the mat on top of the tuile, then gently flip over the bottom mat with the tuile still attached. Now carefully peel off the silicone mat so that the tuile is left on the parchment paper.

Carefully transfer pieces of the tuile into an airtight container (it will be very brittle and delicate), layering them between sheets of parchment paper.

Repeat with the rest of the batter until the desired number of tuiles pieces are made.

BUTTERSCOTCH COFFEE ÉCLAIRS

MAKES 2 DOZEN

We take great pride in our éclairs at Lafayette, and this butterscotch version is a favorite. We sell out almost every day, much to the chagrin of my husband (it's his favorite as well) because there are rarely any left to bring home! The combination of the sweet-bitter-salty butterscotch and the aromatic coffee really does make the perfect afternoon break.

For the butterscotch pudding

5½ ounces dark brown sugar
½ teaspoon kosher salt
2 tablespoons water
2 cups heavy cream
1 cup whole milk
¾ cup egg yolk (about 6 egg yolks)
1 whole egg
1¼ ounces cornstarch
3 tablespoons butter, cubed
1 teaspoon dark rum

For the éclair batter, or pâte à choux

¾ cup water
¾ cup milk, preferably skim or 2%
1 stick unsalted butter, cut into
   ½-inch pieces
1½ teaspoons granulated sugar
¾ teaspoon salt
7½ ounces all-purpose flour
6 large eggs

For the coffee glaze

10 ounces fondant icing (also known
   as pouring fondant [not rolled
   fondant]; see Suppliers, page 286)
1 teaspoon warm water
1 teaspoon coffee extract

To decorate

ground espresso or other coffee
   (optional)

Equipment

A kitchen scale (see suppliers, page
   286)
2 disposable pastry bags and a
   large open star decorating tip (at
   Lafayette, we use Ateco French
   Star #879)
An instant-read thermometer
2 half-sheet trays
2 silicone mats, or parchment paper
A spray bottle (optional)

Make the butterscotch pudding filling. Put the brown sugar, salt, and water into a medium saucepan and place over medium heat. Cook, stirring constantly with a wooden spoon to prevent the mixture from scorching, until it is smoky and reduces down to a sticky caramel paste, about 8 minutes, lowering the heat as necessary. Remove from the heat when the caramel is ready.

Heat the cream and milk in another small saucepan just until small bubbles form around the edges, then immediately remove from the heat. Very slowly, stream in the hot cream mixture into the hot caramel, at the same time stirring with a long-handled spoon. Be careful: the mixture will bubble up rapidly. Return to a boil, stirring until smooth, then remove from the heat.

In a medium bowl, whisk together the egg yolks, egg, and cornstarch until thoroughly blended. Pour about a cup of the hot, creamy caramel liquid into the egg mixture and whisk vigorously to prevent the eggs from curdling. Once combined, whisk in another cup of liquid. Repeat until the caramel liquid is completely incorporated into the egg and cornstarch mixture.

Pour the mixture into a clean saucepan and cook on medium heat, whisking constantly, until it thickens slightly, about 3 minutes. Remove from the heat and whisk in the butter and rum. Transfer to a medium bowl and place a sheet of plastic wrap directly on the surface of the pudding to prevent a skin from forming. Refrigerate until cooled completely, about 4 hours or, preferably, overnight.

To make the choux batter, place the water, milk, butter, sugar, and salt in a medium saucepan and bring to a boil. Turn off the heat and immediately dump all the flour into the pot at once. With a wooden spoon, stir until the mixture is evenly combined and homogenous. Now turn the heat back on to medium and continue to cook the mixture, stirring, until a thin film of dough sticks to the bottom of the pan, about 2–3 minutes.

Transfer the hot choux batter into the bowl of a stand mixer fitted with the paddle attachment. Mix on medium-low speed for about 2 minutes to allow the batter to cool down a little. Crack open the eggs and drop them, one by one, into the moving batter, scraping down the sides of the bowl between each addition. Keep mixing until the eggs are completely incorporated and the batter has a silky, pastelike consistency.

Place a piece of plastic wrap directly across the entire surface of the batter and refrigerate for about an hour. Chilling the batter firms it up making it easier to pipe.

Preheat the oven to 400°F.

Place the cold choux batter in a pastry bag fitted with the decorating tip. Pipe 5-inch-long tubes of batter, about 2 to 3 inches apart, on the half sheet trays. Lightly mist the piped éclairs using a water sprayer (or brush on water sparingly); this keeps the batter moist and prevents too much cracking in the oven. Place the trays into the oven, spacing them out evenly throughout the middle shelves, and bake until the éclairs are a rich golden brown all over, about 30–40 minutes, depending on your oven.

When the éclairs have started to brown, rotate the trays once for even coloring. Don't be tempted to open the oven door before then, as this would allow the steam in the oven to escape, which might deflate them.

Once the éclair shells are baked, turn off the heat and leave them to cool completely in the oven with the door open. This helps the interiors to dry out, making room for more filling.

When ready to assemble the éclairs, punch 3 small holes along the length of the bottom of each éclair using scissor points or a small star pastry tip. Remove the butterscotch pudding from the fridge, stir until smooth, then transfer to a disposable pastry bag and snip a small opening in the end. Pipe the pudding into each of the three holes in the éclair shells until it starts to ooze out through them a little. The filled éclairs should feel heavy for their size.

To complete the éclairs, place the ingredients for the coffee glaze in a large bowl and mix until thoroughly combined. Place the bowl over a pot of lightly simmering water, making sure that the bottom of the bowl doesn't touch the water. Stir constantly until the mixture reaches 95°F on an instant-read thermometer. Remove from the heat and use immediately.

Dip the top third of each filled éclair into the coffee glaze; sweep off any excess glaze lightly with your index finger. Place on a tray, glazed side up, and immediately sprinkle with ground espresso or coffee, if desired. Allow the glaze to set before serving, about 10–20 minutes. (The glaze is best used at 95°F; if it cools too much while dipping the éclairs, replace the bowl over the simmering water to bring it up to the correct temperature.)

Serve the éclairs immediately, or refrigerate until ready to eat.

RASPBERRY PISTACHIO MACARON TARTLETS

MAKES ABOUT 1 DOZEN

These beautiful tartlets are worth the extra time and effort needed to make them. Pairing the crisp macaron with the slightly dense ganache and bright, explosive raspberries really makes for a delicious experience. The macaron recipe provided yields more than 1 dozen to allow for mistakes and breakage.

For the pistachio macaron shells

1¼ cups egg whites (from about 10 large eggs)
10 ounces granulated sugar
5 drops green gel food coloring
13¼ ounces confectioners' sugar
8 ounces blanched almond flour
3 ounces pistachio flour

For the white chocolate ganache filling

10 ounces white chocolate
⅜ cup heavy cream
1 teaspoon corn syrup

For the whipped cream

½ cup heavy cream
½ teaspoon confectioners' sugar
¼ teaspoon vanilla extract

To assemble

3 (½-pint) containers of fresh raspberries (you will need about 9 or 10 berries per tartlet)
2–3 tablespoons raspberry jam
2–3 tablespoons toasted pistachio halves

Equipment

A kitchen scale (see suppliers, page 286)
3 disposable piping bags, along with a medium round tip and a small star tip
4 half sheet trays
4 silicone mats (or parchment paper)
A handheld blender (optional)
A microwave (optional)

Begin by making the macaron shells. Preheat the oven to 325°F. Fit the bowl of a stand mixer with the metal whisk attachment, making sure that both whisk and bowl are completely clean, with no traces of oil. Add the egg whites to the bowl and whisk on medium speed until foamy. With the machine running, add about one-fifth of the granulated sugar. Allow the whites to gain a bit of volume, then add a little more sugar; repeat in this way until all the sugar has been added. Now turn the speed to high and whisk for about 5 more minutes or until the meringue is thick and shiny and holds firm peaks. Add the green coloring, reduce the speed to low, and mix until the color is evenly combined.

Sift together the remaining ingredients for the macarons and place in a large bowl. Add about one-quarter of the meringue to this mixture and mix well with a rubber spatula; there's no need to be too delicate at this point, as we need to make sure the batter is smooth.

Next add the remaining meringue and incorporate gently in a folding motion, turning the bowl as you stir; do not beat the mixture. The finished batter should be shiny and slightly slack and it should fall from the spatula in a thick ribbon. You can also test that the batter is ready by drawing the spatula through it. If the line made by the spatula disappears within about 5 seconds, it is ready. If not, it's too stiff and needs more folding. Do not over-stir the batter, however, or the consistency may get too loose and the macarons won't hold their shape on the tray.

Transfer the batter to a pastry bag with a medium round tip, and pipe mounds about 2 inches in diameter onto half sheet trays lined with silicone mats or parchment paper. Pipe them at least 3 inches apart to allow for the batter to spread. Gently pat down any peaks with a wet fingertip. Once you've completed a whole tray gently tap it against the table or the heel of your hand to settle the batter—the macarons should spread out to between 2¾–3 inches in diameter. Allow the macarons to dry out at room temperature for about 30 minutes.

Place 2 of the trays in the oven and lower the temperature to 300°F (you can leave the other out at room temperature). Bake for about 18–20 minutes, or until the tops appear dry, switching the trays over after 8–9 minutes. If the shells begin to look mottled once out of the oven, bake for a little longer, in 2–3 minute increments, until they are dry.

Bake the remaining macarons. Leave the cooked macarons to cool ➤

completely on the trays then very carefully peel them off the silicone mats or parchment paper. One by one, turn them over, hold in the palm of one hand so the flat side is up, then use the thumb of your other hand to gently press in a 2-inch-diameter indentation in the center to hold the white chocolate ganache. Keep the indented macarons on the trays until ready to fill.

For the white chocolate ganache, melt the chocolate in a glass or plastic measuring cup in the microwave on a medium setting. (Alternatively, place in a heatproof bowl, set over a pan of simmering water, and stir until melted.) In a small saucepan, bring the cream and corn syrup to a boil over medium-high heat, then pour this over the warm melted chocolate. Using a handheld blender or a whisk, blend this mixture until smooth.

Using a spoon, gently pour the ganache into the indented macarons, stopping when it reaches the edge of the indentation, then arrange them on trays, ganache-side up.

Chill the filled macarons in the refrigerator or freezer until the ganache is completely set. The macarons can be frozen in an airtight container, separated with wax paper, for up to 1 month. (Allow them to defrost in the refrigerator for a few hours before assembling the tartlets.)

When ready to assemble, prepare the whipped cream. Place all the ingredients in a bowl and whisk, using a handheld mixer, or a stand mixer with a whisk attachment, until stiff peaks form. Place the cream in a piping bag with a small star tip.

Place the raspberry jam in a small piping bag and cut a small opening at the end. Fill each raspberry with some jam. Arrange the filled raspberries in small mounds on top of the tartlets, covering the ganache completely. With the whipped cream, pipe small rosettes randomly between the raspberries. Decorate with a few pistachio halves placed on the cream rosettes.

Keep the tartlets in the refrigerator until ready to serve. They are best eaten the same day they are assembled.

INDEX

SUPPLIERS

acetate sheets www.bakedeco.com

anise extract www.thespicehouse.com

apple pectin powder www. vitaminshoppe.com

apricot purée www.northernbrewer.com

Arbequina olive oil from Spain www. tienda.com

Ateco French Star No. 879 decorating tip www.amazon.com

Cacao Barry Hazelnut/Almond Praline Paste www.lepicerie.com

candied lemon strips www.chefshop.com

candied pistachios www.santenuts.com

chestnut paste, sweetened www. lepicerie.com

chestnut purée, unsweetened www. lepicerie.com

chinois www.williams-sonoma.com

chocolate www.valrhona-chocolate.com

citric acid, powdered (aka sour salt) www.thespicehouse.com

clear vanilla extract www.wilton.com

coconut purée www.perfectpuree.com

crystallized hazelnuts www. vermontcountrystore.com

curing salt www.williams-sonoma.com

dextrose www.modernistpantry.com

Flexipan Molds www.jbprince.com

fondant icing www.amazon.com

gelatin leaves www.modernistpantry. com

glucose powder www.modernistpantry. com

half-sheet pan frame/extender www. jbprince.com

hazelnut praliné paste (Valrhona) www. amazon.com

kimchi; daikon kimchi www.hmart.com

kitchen scale www.bedbathandbeyond. com

lemon verbena leaves, dried www. herbco.com

licorice paste www.alibaba.com

licorice root sticks www.nuts.com

liquid glucose www.amazon.com

maple chips www.woodinc.com

melon purée www.gourmetfoodworld. com

Mexican (stoneground) chocolate www. ranchogordo.com

micro peonies shop. www. gourmetsweetbotanicals.com

mishmish N.33 www. shop.laboiteny.com

orange blossom water www. kingarthurflour.com

pectin NH www.lepicerie.com

pouring fondant www.amazon.com

silicone molds in tray www.jbprince.com

smoke gun www.williams-sonoma.com

soy salt www.mtckitchen.com

spiral slicer machine www.williams-sonoma.com

sultan pastry tip www.jbprince.com

Tanoreen spices 7523 3rd Ave, Brooklyn, NY 11209

tea, loose www.harney.com

Valrhona Praline à l'Ancienne en.valrhona.com

whipped cream syphon www.amazon. com

ACKNOWLEDGMENTS

First and foremost, thank you to the 25 women without whom this book would not exist. Not only did these inspiring chefs take the time out of their already-overfilled schedules to meet with me, provide recipes, and sit for their portraits, they then also patiently fielded my many queries. For their commitment to this project, I thank them profusely; for their fine efforts, I congratulate them!

As for my wonderful publisher, Jon Croft, it has been a joy to author this book for you. I am immensely grateful for your faith in me and your sanguine solutions to any setback I encountered.

An especially prodigious thank-you to Meg Avent, who first thought of me as a likely author for this book, and then continued to support and guide me with an expert hand throughout the making of this book.

To my delightful project editors, Alice Gibbs and Emily Holmes, thank you very much for your acute attention to detail. For keeping me organized and on track and for your kindness even when you were chastising me (rightfully so) for my tardiness!

For her beautiful photography that so perfectly brings this book to life and captures the essence of all the personalities within its pages, thank you to the lovely Alice Gao.

To Eleanor van Zandt—copywriter extraordinaire—thank you for not exposing my horrific abuse of the standard rules of punctuation! But seriously, your efforts were very much appreciated.

Kim Musgrove, how lucky I was to find myself in the company of such a first rate designer! Thank you for imagining such a stunning book.

A special callout to my ever-cheerful kitchen assistant Camille Shoemaker for her invaluable help in testing and re-testing and, occasionally, re-testing the re-tested recipes!

To Peter and Zain, my two most favorite distractions during this project, we must do this again soon!

Finally, a note of immeasurable gratitude and love to family near, and far.

Nadia Arumugam is an Association of Food Journalists award-winning food writer, editor, and cookbook author. A food columnist for Forbes.com and *Slate*, she has had her writing and recipes appear in numerous publications and websites including *Fine Cooking*, *Saveur*, *Condé Nast Traveller*, *Epicurious*, and TheAtlantic.com. Nadia is also the author of the cookbooks *Chop, Sizzle & Stir* and *1000 Sauces, Dips and Dressings*. She's received masters degrees in English literature, journalism and international relations from Oxford University, New York University, and the London School of Economics. Nadia was born in Malaysia, raised in London, and now lives in New York City with her husband, Peter, and son, Zain.

Publisher Jon Croft
Commissioning Editor Meg Avent
Designer Kim Musgrove
Projects Editor Alice Gibbs and Emily Holmes
Photographer Alice Gao
Editor Eleanor van Zandt
Recipe Tester Nadia Arumugam
Proofreader and Indexer Zoe Ross